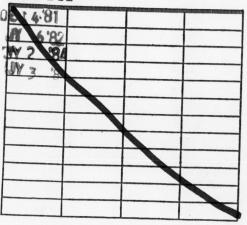

Schmidhauser
The Supreme Court as final arbiter in Federal-State relations

# The Supreme Court as Final Arbiter in Federal-State Relations, 1789-1957

# THE SUPREME COURT AS FINAL ARBITER IN FEDERAL-STATE RELATIONS

## 1789-1957

By JOHN R. SCHMIDHAUSER

GREENWOOD PRESS, PUBLISHERS
WESTPORT, CONNECTICUT

**Library of Congress Cataloging in Publication Data**

Schmidhauser, John Richard.
The Supreme Court as final arbiter in Federal -State relations, 1789-1957.

Reprint of the ed. published by University of North Carolina Press, Chapel Hill.
Bibliography: p.
1. United States. Supreme Court. 2. Federal government--United States. I. Title.
[KF8748.S275 1973] 347'.73'26 73-7676
ISBN 0-8371-6945-3



Originally published in 1958 by The University of North Carolina Press, Chapel Hill

Reprinted with the permission of The University of North Carolina Press

First Greenwood Reprinting 1973

Library of Congress Catalogue Card Number 73-7676

ISBN 0-8371-6945-3

Printed in the United States of America

*To* Thelma and the Boys

# *Preface*

The purpose of this study is twofold. The first objective is the investigation of the origin of the Supreme Court's power in federal-state relations. The second and major consideration is the analysis of the manner in which the Supreme Court exercised that power.

One underlying assumption governs the organization of the research and the presentation of the material. The Supreme Court, in spite of certain institutional traditions that have endured through many generations of individual justices, is essentially a transitory body. The transitions in Court membership do, it is true, ordinarily occur at a far lower rate than those which take place in the politically responsible branches of the national government. Yet despite the time lag, certain patterns of social, economic and political attitudes, often corresponding to those of distinct eras in American history, have rather consistently appeared in the stream of Supreme Court decisions.

The association of these congeries of ideas and attitudes with the names of individual chief justices is admittedly arbitrary. The tenures of some chief justices tended to overlap new ideological eras in judicial decision-making. The heyday of the Jacksonian Democrats ended in 1861 even though Roger B. Taney lingered on until 1864. The economically-conservative majority of the early Hughes Court conceded defeat in 1937, but the Chief Justice, himself a transitional figure, remained at the helm until 1941. But despite the ideological overlapping, the tenures of the chief justices, occasionally in necessary combinations, serve as fairly accurate indicators of the evolutionary and generally undramatic transition of ideas and attitudes within the Court itself.

The frequently used phrase "to arbitrate" is often utilized as a substitute for the more technically correct phrase "to adjudicate" because it connotes more appropriately the essentially political aspect of the Supreme Court's role in federal-state relations.

The editors of the *Wayne Law Review* very graciously permitted the reproduction in Chapter I of material which appeared in somewhat different form in my article on "States' Rights and the Origin of the Supreme Court's Power in Federal-State Relations" (4 *Wayne Law Review* 101 [Spring, 1958]).

Several acknowledgments are in order. To Professors James Hart and George W. Spicer of the University of Virginia, I am indebted for helpful criticism, advice, and at crucial junctures, firm prodding and encouragement. To my fellow graduate students Chester Bain, John Chamberlayne and Robert Steamer, I am grateful for stimulating exchanges and contagious enthusiasm. Mrs. Moore of Charlottesville, Virginia, and Mrs. Richard Christensen of Iowa City, Iowa, provided expert typing assistance on the original and final drafts of the study. Mr. Merle Arp of Iowa City, Iowa, checked the case citations and footnoting and assembled the index. Any errors of analysis or judgment are, of course, my own.

I am indebted to the State University of Iowa for partial aid for publication of this study and to the Ford Foundation for a grant under its program for assisting American university presses in the publication of works in the humanities and the social sciences.

John R. Schmidhauser
*State University of Iowa*

*Contents*

The Supreme Court as Final Arbiter in
Federal-State Relations, 1789-1957

# CHAPTER I

## *The Origin of the Supreme Court's Power as Arbiter in Federal-State Relations*

Any federal system requires an institution to determine conflicts of authority between the nation and the states comprising it. In the four most important modern federal states, Australia, Canada, West Germany, and the United States, such authority has been lodged in a judicial body. The highest judicial institution of the last, the Supreme Court of the United States, in many respects served as a prototype for application of the judicial arbiter principle in the federal systems of Australia, Canada, and West Germany. Within the United States itself, the influence of Supreme Court decisions upon the American federal system is generally recognized as determinative. An examination of the manner in which the Supreme Court fulfilled its responsibilities as arbiter of American federalism is the primary purpose of this study. Such an examination may contribute to greater understanding of the characteristics of American federalism and may also provide data for a broader study of comparative judicial institutions.

How well suited is the Supreme Court of the United States for its role as umpire in federal-state relations? For an understanding of the Court's present potentialities and limitations, analysis of its past performance is in order. Such analysis embraces investigation and interpretation of one hundred and sixty years of judicial arbitership. The task of interpretation, of necessity, raises the question of criteria. By what standards may the performance of the Supreme Court be measured? Past expectations perhaps modified by present necessities can throw light on this problem. The study of origins provides a logical starting point. What role did the framers of the Federal Constitution and the members of the ratifying conventions envisage for the Supreme Court?

Interestingly enough, one school of constitutional interpretation persistently denies the legitimacy of the Supreme Court's power to render definitive decisions in conflicts between the federal government and the states or between individuals and states which denied them rights guaranteed by the federal constitution. The continued vitality of this old constitutional argument was strikingly illustrated on March 12, 1956, when Senator Walter George introduced a manifesto signed by nineteen senators and seventy-seven representatives from the Southern states. The manifesto referred to the Supreme Court's decision in *Brown* v. *Board of Education*[1] as "judicial usurpation," a substitution of "naked power for established law" and an "unwarranted exercise of power . . . contrary to the Constitution."[2]

Although the supporters of this manifesto made no attempt to formulate serious theoretical or historical arguments to buttress their charge of judicial usurpation, they may properly be considered the intellectual heirs of the constitutional argument of John C. Calhoun. For in advocating the repeal of the 25th section of the Judiciary Act of 1789, Calhoun unequivocally denied that the framers of the Constitution had chosen the Supreme Court as federal umpire.[3]

The challenges of judicial usurpation of the power to arbitrate in federal-state relations, whether made by a Calhoun or by one of his modern protagonists such as Byrnes or Talmadge, are susceptible to historical examination. The record of history unequivocally demolishes these challenges.

### THE COLONIAL AND CONFEDERATION PERIODS

The conception of a powerful judicial body maintaining a division of powers in a federal system did not appear miraculously to the justices of the Supreme Court after the adoption of the Constitution. It was clearly understood and partially applied during the period when America was a colony of Great Britain and under the Articles of Confederation.

The British Empire maintained the fiction that it was a unitary system until after the American Revolution, but the Empire's relationships with the thirteen colonies had, in reality, become essentially federal. The government of the whole Empire, that of Great Britain, had been forced by the pressure of European wars and great distances to leave most problems of domestic legislation and administration to the governments of the "parts" of the Empire, notably the American colonial governments. Naturally enough, the development of local autonomy in the colonies led to conflicts of authority between the mother country

1. 349 U.S. 294 (1954).
2. *Congressional Record,* 84th Congress, Second Session, Vol. 102, No. 43, p. 3948.
3. Richard Crallé (ed.), "Discourse on the Constitution and Government of the United States," *Works of John C. Calhoun,* I, 238.

and the colonies as well as among the colonies themselves. It was a quasi-judicial institution of the British Empire, the Committee on Trade and Plantations of the British Privy Council, which resolved such conflicts.[4]

After the American colonies broke with Great Britain, a new problem arose, that of balancing the powers of the states and the new central government in North America. A temporary solution was found in the creation of a confederate system. The Articles of Confederation established a very limited form of judicial arbitration in two narrow fields, the settlement of disputes between the states and the settlement of disputes between the Confederation Congress and the states concerning cases of capture on the high seas.

The first category of disputes was to be settled in accordance with the ninth of the Articles of Confederation. This provided that "the united states in Congress assembled shall also be the last resort on appeal in all disputes and differences now subsisting or that hereafter may arise between two or more states concerning boundary, jurisdiction or any other cause whatever. . . ." The parties to a dispute could be directed by Congress "to appoint by joint consent, commissioners or judges to constitute a court for hearing and determining the matter in question." Or if the disputing parties could not agree, Congress could itself make the appointments. The Article further provided that "the judgment and sentence of the court . . . shall be final and conclusive. . . ." A serious land dispute was peacefully resolved under this article in 1782.[5] Yet such a court of arbitration lacked permanence. Consequently, it was probably the second judicial institution created under the Confederation which was more influential in the evolution of the judicial arbiter concept in American federalism. The Court of Appeals in Cases of Capture was a permanent judicial body which heard 118 cases before the Articles of Confederation were replaced by the new federal Constitution. A member of this Court, Judge John Lowell, made the experiences of this judicial body available to the Constitutional framers in 1787 and to the Senate in 1789, sketching a plan for a federal judiciary in a letter to some of the framers and later, in 1789, giving his counsel and advice to the Senate Judiciary Committee.[6]

4. The Committee later became the Board of Trade; Oliver M. Dickerson, *American Colonial Government, 1695-1765*, pp. 225ff.; Andrew McLaughlin, "The Background of American Federalism," 12 *American Political Science Review* 215ff.

5. Merrill Jensen, *The New Nation: A History of the United States during the Confederation, 1781-1789*, pp. 335-37.

6. John Franklin Jameson, "The Predecessor of the Supreme Court," *Essays in the*

During the waning years of the Confederation itself, serious attention was given to various proposals to establish a more powerful central judiciary capable of putting an end to state encroachments on or defiance of the authority of the Confederation government. Although these proposals never were adopted by the Confederation, they do provide unmistakable evidence that political leaders of this era were fully aware of the potentialities of a judicial arbiter in confederate or federal governmental systems. A Confederation Congress committee report submitted in 1786 by Charles Pinckney contained, in essence, a complete arrangement for the creation of a federal court capable of umpiring federal-state disputes. Pinckney's committee suggested that the Confederation Congress be authorized:

> . . . to institute a federal judicial court for trying and punishing all officers appointed by congress for all crimes, offenses, and misbehavior in their offices, and to which court an appeal shall be allowed from the judicial courts of the several states in all causes wherein any question shall arise on the meaning and construction of treaties entered into by the United States with any foreign power, or on any law of nations, or wherein any question shall arise respecting any regulations that may hereafter be made by congress relative to trade and commerce, or the collection of federal revenues pursuant to powers that shall be vested in that body, or wherein questions of importance may arise, and the United States shall be a party. . . .[7]

Similar ideas for strengthening the Confederation government through creation of some sort of federal judicial arbiter were formulated or were discussed by Rufus King,[8] James Madison,[9] and Nathan Dane.[10] Just prior to the Philadelphia Convention of 1787, however, a significantly different argument was discussed widely. Instead of viewing a federal judicial arbiter as primarily a defender of the central government, a broadly circulated pamphlet proposed that

> In order to prevent an oppressive exercise of powers deposited with Congress, a jurisdiction should be established to interpose and determine between the individual States and the Federal body upon all disputed points,

---

*Constitutional History of the United States in the Formative Period, 1775-1789,* pp. 3-44.

7. Quoted in George Bancroft, *History of the Formation of the Constitution,* II, 376-77.

8. Letter to Jonathan Jackson, September 3, 1786; as quoted by Charles Warren, *The Supreme Court in United States History,* I, 5. Hereinafter cited as *History.*

9. Letter to George Washington, April 16, 1787; as quoted by Hampton L. Carson, *The History of the Supreme Court,* p. 88; Madison deemed this of secondary importance to a congressional negative of state laws, however.

10. As quoted by Charles Warren, *The Making of the Constitution,* p. 319. Hereinafter cited as *Making.*

and being stiled The Equalizing Court, should be constituted and conducted in the following manner. . . .

This proposal was reprinted in the leading newspapers, and appeared in the *Pennsylvania Gazette* in Philadelphia on June 6, 1787, during the early days of the Convention.[11] Thus, while supporters of the idea of a strong national government had begun to favor the judicial arbiter as a means of restraining the states, those who feared the encroachments of a strong national government had begun to look upon a strong judicial system as a protector of individual and states' rights. Recognition of this development makes more understandable the absence of states' rights or anti-Federalist opposition to most of the proposals made in the Convention which strengthened the federal judiciary.

### THE PHILADELPHIA CONVENTION

One of the major reasons for holding the Philadelphia Convention had been the necessity to find a remedy for the evils arising from state legislation which hurt or interfered with the interest of other states, infringed treaties made by the Confederation Congress, oppressed individuals, or invaded the sphere of authority of the Confederation government. The Convention delegates were faced with the task of finding suitable means of restraining such state legislation or action. Despite the fact that the idea of a judicial arbiter was understood and widely discussed before the opening of the Convention, the creation of a high federal court to solve this problem was by no means a foregone conclusion. Years after the close of the Convention, James Madison referred to the situation in the following manner—"the obvious necessity of a control on the laws of the State so far as they might violate the Constitution and laws of the United States left no option, but as to mode. . . ," noting as the three possible choices "a veto [executive] on the passage of the State laws, a Congressional repeal of them, a judicial annulment of them."[12]

Analysis of the record of the Philadelphia Convention underscores the fact that the granting of power to the federal Supreme Court to arbitrate finally in federal-state relations came about through a complex series of developments. Basically, they represented a compromise between the strong nationalists who originally wanted a veto over the states vested in the new national legislature or executive and the states' righters who either opposed such supervision of the states or

11. As quoted by Warren, *Making*, p. 169.

12. Letter to Nicholas P. Trist, 1831; as quoted by Warren, *Making*, p. 318.

preferred that this power be vested in what they considered a weaker and more impartial agency, notably the supreme federal court suggested in the original Paterson Plan.

Among the more important of these developments were (a) the repudiation of coercion of the states by force and the adoption of coercion of individuals by law, (b) the readiness of every major bloc in the Convention to set up a federal judiciary, (c) the demands of one powerful group for a system of inferior federal tribunals, (d) the defeat of the congressional negative proposals and the substitution by Luther Martin of a supremacy clause, and (e) the tendency to look upon a federal judiciary as a protector of individual and states' rights which was reflected in the proposals for a Council of Revision. Very often these developments seemed totally unrelated, but their cumulative effect was the granting of final interpretive powers in federal-state relations to a supreme federal tribunal.

Prominent among the resolutions for union was a provision for congressional veto of state laws presented by Edmund Randolph at the opening session of the Convention. It provided "That the national legislature ought to be empowered . . . to negative all laws, passed by the several States, contravening, in the opinion of the national legislature, the articles of union." Later, on May 31, the Convention, in committee of the whole house, amended it by addition of the phrase "or any treaties subsisting under the authority of the Union." The entire resolution was agreed to by the committee without debate or dissent.[13] However, when this resolution was reported from the Committee to the Convention on July 17, it met with violent opposition. Gouverneur Morris thought such power "likely to be terrible to the States"; Luther Martin considered it improper; and Sherman believed that since the state courts would hold invalid any laws contravening the authority of the Union, such a veto would be unnecessary. Madison and Charles Pinckney did not share Sherman's confidence in the state courts, however, and held that the congressional negative was necessary as, in the words of Madison, "the most mild and certain means of preserving the harmony of the system." In spite of Madison's appeal, the Convention defeated the proposal for a congressional negative on state laws by a vote of seven to three.[14]

Even before the rejection of the congressional negative by the Convention on July 17, there was clearcut evidence that the advocates

13. Max Farrand (ed.), *Records of the Federal Convention,* I, 54. Hereinafter cited as *Records.*

14. *Ibid.,* II, 27-28.

of a strong central government were prepared to limit the congressional negative by providing for final appeal to a national judiciary. As early as July 10, Randolph had sent Madison a list of concessions to be used "as an accommodating proposition to small states" which then were bitterly opposed to the principle of representation based upon population.[15] In terms of the judicial arbiter concept, the fourth and fifth of Randolph's proposals were particularly significant because they clearly anticipated the Supreme Court's modern role as both a federal umpire and as a defender of individual rights against state infringement. His suggestions provided:

IV. That, although every negative given to the law of a particular state shall prevent its operation, any state may appeal to the national judiciary against a negative, and that such negative if adjudged to be contrary to the powers granted by the articles of the Union, shall be void.

V. That any individual, conceiving himself injured or oppressed by the partiality or injustice of a law of any particular state, may resort to the national judiciary, who may adjudge such a law to be void, if found contrary to the principles of equity and justice.[16]

Randolph was prepared to offer these conciliatory proposals to the Convention on July 16, but did not do so because of the victory of the small states, on that day, in securing equal voting rights in the Senate.[17]

Throughout the course of the Philadelphia Convention the major discussions of the federal judicial arbiter were generally related to the nationalists' attempts to gain approval for the congressional negative of state laws. However, other discussions in the Convention also contributed to the evolution of the supreme federal tribunal. The proposals for a Council of Revision composed of the chief executive and judges of the highest national court, while eventually defeated, stimulated discussion of the power of judicial review.[18] Rejection by the Convention of the proposals to coerce the states by force contained in both the Randolph and Paterson plans were followed by adoption of the principle of direct coercion of individuals by the national government itself. This solution reflected the recognition by Convention leaders of the need to discover a peaceful mode of limiting state interference with national authority.[19] The initiative in finding such a

15. *Ibid.*, III, 55.

16. Published in Jonathan Elliot, *Debates of the State Ratifying Conventions*, V, 579-80. Hereinafter cited as *Debates*.

17. Farrand, *Records*, II, 17-18.

18. *Ibid.*, I, 93-94, 96-97, 138-40; and in Volume II, 73, 76, 298-99.

19. *Ibid.*, II, 21, 34, 54, 165, 245, 256, 320, 339-40.

solution was now taken by the leaders of the small-state bloc in the Convention, many of whom were of states' rights persuasion.

Using as their starting point a clause from the Paterson Plan guaranteeing the supremacy of the national government within the sphere of its legitimate authority, states' rights supporters attempted to placate the nationalists who were bitterly disappointed by the defeat of the congressional negative proposal on July 17. Luther Martin submitted what he undoubtedly considered a mild substitute for such a negative.[20] His original proposal stated:

> . . . that the Legislative acts of the United States made by virtue and in pursuance of the Articles of Union, and all treaties made and ratified under the authority of the United States shall be the supreme law of the respective States, as far as those acts or treaties shall relate to the said states, or their citizens and inhabitants—and that the Judiciaries of the several States shall be bound thereby in their decision, anything in the respective laws of the individual States to the contrary notwithstanding.[21]

Later, the nationalists in the Convention changed this relatively mild resolution in several important respects. These amendments were made in the closing days of the Convention in August and September. On August 5, 1787, the Convention's committee on detail had compressed Martin's resolution and made two significant changes—federal laws were declared supreme over state constitutions as well as state laws, and the duty to uphold the supreme law was imposed on "the Judges in the several States" instead of on "the Judiciaries of the respective states." On August 23, John Rutledge proposed the following important addition: "This Constitution and the laws of the United States made in pursuance thereof . . . shall be the supreme law of the several states." Thus the Constitution was made judicially enforceable law. The Convention adopted this proposal without debate.[22] Finally, on September 12, the committee on style completed the final draft of the Constitution. Luther Martin's resolution had become a part of Article VI. From the point of view of federal-state relations this was the crucial provision in the fundamental document. Section 3 of that article read:

> This Constitution, and the laws of the United States which shall be made in pursuance thereof; and all treaties made, or which shall be made, under the authority of the United States, shall be the supreme law of the land;

20. See Martin's "Reply to the Landholder," Farrand, *Records*, III, 286-87.
21. Farrand, *Records*, II, 28-29.
22. *Ibid.*, p. 389.

and the judges in every state shall be bound thereby, anything in the Constitution or laws of any state to the contrary notwithstanding.

Defeat of the plan for a congressional negative left the Convention with two institutional alternatives for the enforcement of national supremacy. The first was an ultra-nationalistic suggestion put forth by Alexander Hamilton in his plan for union. Section 10 of the plan provided that "all laws of the particular States contrary to the Constitution or laws of the United States to be utterly void; and the better to prevent such laws being passed, the Governour or president of each state shall be appointed by the General Government and shall have a negative upon the laws about to be passed in the state of which he is Governour or President." Hamilton's alternative was not even seriously considered by the Convention. The second was the judicial arbiter which had been an integral part of the original Paterson Plan. Section 5 had provided "that a federal judiciary be established to consist of a supreme tribunal the Judges of which to be appointed by the Executive. . . ." Section 2 of the same plan proposed that violations of acts of the federal Congress be tried in the first instance in "the superior Common law Judiciary" of the state concerned, "subject . . . for the correction of all errors, both in law and fact. . . , to an appeal to the Judiciary of the United States."[23]

Actually, every major plan for union—Randolph's, Hamilton's, and Paterson's—had provided for a national judicial system.[24] The essential difference between the nationalistic plans of Randolph and Hamilton and the states' rights plan of Paterson is that the latter failed to provide a system of inferior federal courts. The nationalists did not actually oppose the adoption of a judicial arbiter, but merely felt, as James Wilson later indicated, that a judicial check on the states would not be sufficient to maintain a strong central government. On August 10, Charles Pinckney grudgingly admitted that the federal judges "will even be the Umpires between the United States and individual states as well as between one State and another." However, a few days later, on August 23, he tenaciously sought to reinstate the congressional negative, but was defeated by a six to five vote. In urging support for Pinckney's motion, Wilson recognized impliedly that in the absence of a congressional negative, the national judiciary would seek to maintain the supremacy of the national government. This he felt was not enough because "the firmness of Judges is not of itself sufficient. Some-

23. *Ibid.*, I, 243-44, 293.
24. *Ibid.*, pp. 21, 243-44, 292.

thing further is requisite—It will be better to prevent the passage of an improper law, than to declare it void when passed."[25]

A letter exchange between Thomas Jefferson and James Madison concerning the relative merits of the congressional negative and the judicial arbiter illustrates clearly the contrasting positions of the states' righters and the nationalists.[26] Although he did not attend the Convention, Jefferson was representative of those who, while they feared establishment of a national government in which all authority would be centralized, realized quite clearly that some degree of centralized control was necessary to bring stability to the then chaotic thirteen states. In his reply to Madison's inquiry concerning a congressional negative on state laws, Jefferson presented a viewpoint which might be taken as indicative of the attitude of other advocates of a strictly limited central government. He wrote:

The negative proposed to be given them on all the acts of the several Legislatures is now for the first time suggested to my mind. Prima Facie I do not like it. It fails in an essential character, that the hole and the patch should be commensurate; but this proposes to mend a small hole by covering the whole garment. . . . Would not an appeal from the state judicatures to a federal court in all cases where the act of Confederation controlled the question, be as effectual a remedy, and exactly commensurate to the defect?

On the other hand, the advocates of a strong central government, while favoring the granting of broad judicial powers, had realized that judicial nullification of state laws was possible only when federal questions arose in bona fide cases before the new Supreme Court. Madison's letter to Jefferson after the close of the Convention indicated the lack of assurance he shared with other advocates of strong government. He wrote:

It may be said that the Judicial authority under our new system will keep the states within their proper limits and supply the place of a negative on their laws. The answer is that it is more convenient to prevent the passage of a law than to declare it void, after it is passed; that this will be particularly the case, where the law aggrieves individuals who may be unable to support an appeal against a state to the Supreme Judiciary, that a state which would violate the legislative rights of the Union would not be very ready to obey a Judicial decree in support of them, and that a recurrence to force, which in the event of disobedience would be necessary, is an evil which the new Constitution meant to exclude as far as possible.

25. *Ibid.*, II, 248, 390-91.

26. Jefferson to Madison, June 20, 1787, and Madison to Jefferson, October 24, 1787, as quoted by Warren, *Making*, pp. 168-69, 324.

A Constitutional negative on the laws of the states seems equally necessary to secure individuals against encroachments on their rights. The mutability of the laws of the States is found to be a serious evil.

After the final defeat of the congressional negative in the Convention on August 23, the nationalists determined to make the best of an unhappy situation by strengthening the federal arbiter by means of grants of broad constitutional jurisdiction and through institution of a complete system of inferior federal courts. The extension of the Supreme Court's jurisdiction to all cases, state and federal, arising under the Constitution was made without states' rights argument. But the attempt at creation of a system of inferior federal courts aroused such fierce opposition that the nationalists were compelled to accept a compromise by which the establishment of such courts was left to the discretion of the new Congress.[27]

Nationalist bitterness at the substitution of a judicial arbiter for their cherished congressional negative persisted to the end of the Convention. For example, on September 12, James Madison supported a motion by Mason which provided that the clause relating to export duties be amended to allow the states to lay such duties for "the sole purpose of defraying the charges of inspecting, packing, storing and indemnifying the losses in keeping the commodities in the care of public offices before exportation." Gorham and Langdon had asked: "How was redress to be obtained in case duties should be laid beyond the purpose expressed?" Madison coldly replied that "there will be the same security as in other cases—The jurisdiction of the Supreme Court must be the source of redress. So far only had provision been made by the plan against injurious acts of the States. His own opinion was, that this was insufficient,—A negative on the State laws alone could meet all the shapes which these could assume. But this had been overruled."[28]

The Philadelphia Convention record indicates unmistakably that the new Supreme Court had been clearly designated the final judicial arbiter in federal-state relations and that it was primarily the states' righters in the Convention who had brought this to pass. The nationalists had not opposed the creation of the judicial arbiter but had felt strongly that a national judiciary would not, by itself, be strong enough to cope with state encroachments on national authority.

27. Warren, *Making*, pp. 326, 334-38.
28. Farrand, *Records*, II, 588-89.

### THE STATE RATIFYING CONVENTIONS

In spite of their misgivings, the advocates of strong central government did not let lack of confidence in a federal judiciary weaken their efforts to secure ratification of the Constitution. Two of the contributions to the *Federalist* by Madison and Hamilton were devoted to an examination of the proposed judicial arbiter, its purposes and its impartial character.[29] Within the state ratifying conventions, the nationalists frequently found themselves the staunchest defenders of the same judicial arbiter for which they had indicated only lukewarm enthusiasm during the Philadelphia Convention, for serious states' rights objections were raised to certain provisions of the judicial clauses in the new Constitution, notably those concerning the possible establishment of a system of inferior federal courts and extending federal jurisdiction to suits between a state and individuals. In five of the state ratifying conventions—Connecticut, Pennsylvania, Virginia, North Carolina, and South Carolina—the new Supreme Court's function of resolving state and federal conflicts was discussed clearly and ultimately was accepted.[30] In virtually all of the ratifying conventions some jurisdictional grants to the new federal court system were subjected to severe criticism. Out-and-out opponents of the Constitution, such as Robert Yates of New York, recognized the scope of the Supreme Court's power and made the judicial grants a major point for attack on the proposed new system of government. As "Brutus,'" Yates went so far as to charge erroneously that

> the opinions of the Supreme Court . . . will have the force of law; because there is no power provided in the Constitution that can correct their errors or control their jurisdiction. From this court there is no appeal.[31]

But in the end, the nationalists managed to secure early ratification in all of the most important states.

These facts stand out as a result of this analysis of the Philadelphia Convention and the state ratifying conventions. Both the nationalists and the states' righters were in substantial agreement on the need for a supreme judicial arbiter in federal-state relations. By 1789 it was clearly understood that the Supreme Court of the United States was to fulfill that role. Naturally enough, the nationalists tended to emphasize the aspect of judicial arbitership concerned with the protection of

29. Henry Cabot Lodge (ed.), *The Federalist*, Nos. 39 and 80, pp. 238, 494-95.

30. Elliot, *Debates*, II, 196, 408-9, 439-40, 445-46, 468-69, 478, 480-81; III, 532; IV, 155, 257-58.

31. Quoted in Horace A. Davis, "Annulment of Legislation by the Supreme Court," 7 *American Political Science Review* 577.

national supremacy against state encroachments. However, both nationalists and states' righters explicitly recognized that the Supreme Court's role was that of an *impartial* arbiter. Thus it was also anticipated that federal laws violative of states rights were to be declared unconstitutional. The prevailing contemporary conception of the new Supreme Court's role is best illustrated by Oliver Ellsworth's description in the Connecticut Ratifying Convention of January, 1788:

This Constitution defines the extent of the powers of the general government. If the general legislature should at any time overleap their limits, the judicial department is a constitutional check. If the United States go beyond their powers, if they made a law which the Constitution does not authorize, it is void; and the judicial power, the national judges, who, to secure their impartiality, are to be made independent, will declare it to be void. On the other hand, if the states go beyond their limits, if they make a law which is a usurpation upon the general government, the law is void; and upright, independent judges will declare it so.[32]

### THE FIRST JUDICIARY ACT

While the constitutional framers had drawn the broad outlines of the judicial power, they had left to congressional discretion the composition of the federal courts, the extent of the appellate jurisdiction of the Supreme Court, the existence or non-existence of any inferior federal courts, and the extent of their jurisdiction. Consequently, the manner in which the first Congress dealt with these problems in the judiciary act of September 24, 1789, set the pattern for subsequent development of the federal judicial system. This act was especially important because without broad grants of appellate jurisdiction to the Supreme Court by Congress, the entire plan for a judicial arbiter would have fallen into abeyance for lack of implementation.

The first Judiciary Act was largely the product of the Senate Judiciary Committee, and within the committee, Oliver Ellsworth and William Paterson took leading roles in drafting the bill. In the early stages of this drafting Ellsworth sought to establish a complete network of inferior federal courts and to extend their jurisdiction to the limits set by the Constitution. However, to secure the concurrence of Richard Henry Lee, Ellsworth apparently had to accept a more limited inferior federal court system. This setback was mitigated by inclusion of a provision which allowed a defendant sued in a state court in a case involving a federal question to remove the case to a federal circuit court or to appeal to the Supreme Court by writ of error after trial

32. Elliot, *Debates,* II, 196.

"in the highest court of law or equity in a State in which a decision in the suit could be had."[33]

When debate on the draft bill began in the Senate in committee of the whole, on June 22, the issue centered around the question of whether there should be any district courts at all or whether the functions of executing federal laws should be left in the first instance to the state courts. Ellsworth had been opposed to giving the state courts such power on the grounds discussed in a letter[34] he wrote later on the subject. He felt that

> to annex to State Courts jurisdiction which they had not before, as of admiralty cases, and perhaps, of offenses against the United States, would be constituting the Judges of them, *pro tanto,* Federal Judges, and of course they would continue such during good behavior, and on fixed salaries, which in many cases, would illy comport with their present tenure of office. Besides, if the state courts, as such, could take cognizance of those offences, it might not be safe for the General Government to put the trial and punishment of them entirely out of its own hands.

Debate over the various proposals in the bill raged for three months in the Senate and the House. The crucial issues were whether there should be any inferior federal courts, and, if there were to be any such courts, whether the Constitution required that they be vested with the full jurisdiction which the Constitution permitted. In its final form the bill was a compromise. The nationalists were forced to abandon their contention that the federal courts be granted the broadest jurisdiction possible under the Constitution, while the states' righters were unable to confine federal cases to state courts, subject only to final appeal to the new federal Supreme Court. Section 25, which became the very cornerstone of federal judicial supremacy, established the appellate jurisdiction of the Supreme Court over state courts where such courts decided against a claimed federal right. Significantly, the states' righters in Congress actually advocated this crucial grant of jurisdiction in 1789.[35]

### CONCLUSION

In sum, the modern states' rights charges of federal "judicial usurpation" of power to arbitrate in federal-state relations may be viewed as a particularly persistent bit of political mythology. Examination of the Philadelphia Convention, the state ratifying conventions,

33. Charles Warren, "New Light on the History of the Federal Judiciary Act of 1789," 37 *Harvard Law Review* 60-62.

34. To Law, August 4, 1789, Warren, *ibid.*, p. 66.

35. *Ibid.*, pp. 102-5.

and the legislative history of the first Judiciary Act indicates unmistakably that the framers clearly intended that the Supreme Court be given responsibility for umpiring the federal system, that the federal judicial arbiter was understood and accepted by the more important of the state ratifying conventions, and that appellate jurisdiction necessary for the fulfillment of its responsibilities was granted the Supreme Court by the first Congress.

Ironically, it was the states' righters of that era—the anti-Federalists—who were largely responsible for the acceptance of the judicial arbiter in the Philadelphia Convention. Similarly, they strongly supported its implementation in the first Congress. Later their basic assumption, gloomily shared by many nationalists, that the federal judicial arbiter would be a rather mild check on state authority proved to be false. And later, the confidence of the states' righters in the impartiality of the Supreme Court was shaken, particularly during the tenure of Chief Justice John Marshall. But during the formative period, 1786-89, both the states' righters and the nationalists, the former with confidence, the latter with grave misgivings, had accepted the new Supreme Court as the arbiter in federal-state relations.

# CHAPTER II

## *The Formative Decade of the Supreme Court*

### EARLY ACTIVITY OF THE CIRCUIT COURTS

IN 1790, THE POWERS of the new Supreme Court of the United States were broad and untested; its jurisdiction overlapped areas in which older, entrenched institutions, the state courts, had hitherto reigned supreme. The effectiveness of the new judicial institution as final arbiter in federal-state relations was still a matter of conjecture. The nearly universal confidence in the impartiality of the new court remained unshaken in spite of President Washington's determination to appoint none but staunch nationalists or Federalists to the Supreme Court.[1]

The initial contacts between the long-established state court systems and the new federal courts were made by the members of the federal circuit courts. These included the members of the Supreme Court when they were on circuit duty. Since the Supreme Court itself did not make any decisions until the April term of 1792, the decisions of the circuit courts were of crucial importance in this early period. Sketchy historical accounts of these court actions indicate that a federal circuit court in Connecticut held void a state law on the ground that it infringed the treaty of peace with Great Britain and that circuit courts in Rhode Island, Georgia, and South Carolina utilized the contract clause to hold unconstitutional state laws which impaired the obligation of contracts.[2]

Supreme Court Historian Charles Warren contended that these early federal circuit court invalidations of state laws were made without serious states' rights opposition,[3] but there is evidence to the contrary. As early as 1791, the legislature of North Carolina voted approval of a state court which had refused to comply with a writ of

1. Warren, *History,* I, 31-32.
2. *Ibid.,* pp. 65-67.
3. *Ibid.,* p. 69.

certiorari issued it by a federal circuit court.[4] However, states' rights disapproval of some of these early federal circuit court decisions emerges historically as a relatively minor preliminary skirmish when compared to the impact of the first major Supreme Court decision affecting federal-state relations—*Chisholm* v. *Georgia*.[5]

### THE SUABILITY OF "SOVEREIGN" STATES

Article III, section 2, of the new Constitution provided that the judicial power of the United States extends to controversies "between a state and citizens of another state." In a number of state ratifying conventions, this clause had occasioned strong opposition from states' righters who contended that a sovereign state cannot be sued without its consent. Leading nationalists such as James Madison, John Marshall, and Alexander Hamilton publically denied that the clause would be interpreted in that manner.[6] In the *Chisholm* case, however, the Supreme Court chose to consider a suit brought by two citizens of South Carolina against the state of Georgia.

The prospect of numerous suits arising under diverse citizenship jurisdiction was not simply a problem in political theory. It had serious economic implications for Georgia and a good many other states as well. For a veritable horde of British creditors were seeking payment for debts incurred before the Revolutionary War.[7] Consequently, it is not surprising that a Georgia House of Representatives protest resolution set the problem in these terms:

> . . . if acquiesced in by this state [the Chisholm suit] would not only involve the same in numberless lawsuits for papers issued from the Treasury thereof to supply the armies of the United States, and perplex the people of Georgia with perpetual taxes . . . but would effectually destroy the retained sovereignty of the states. . . .[8]

Georgia refused to appear before the Supreme Court, contending that the Court did not possess jurisdiction in a suit brought against a sovereign state without its consent. This argument was turned down by the Court in a four to one decision. The decision was robbed of some of its impact because the members of the Court followed the

4. James Iredell to Chief Justice John Jay, January 17, 1792, Griffith J. McRee (ed.), *Life and Correspondence of James Iredell*, pp. 337-38.

5. 2 Dallas 419 (1793).

6. Albert Beveridge, *The Life of John Marshall*, I, 449, 454; Paul L. Ford (ed.), *The Federalist*, p. 545.

7. Charles A. Beard, *Economic Origins of Jeffersonian Democracy*, pp. 1-12.

8. Herman V. Ames, *State Documents on Federal Relations*, I, 7. Hereinafter cited as *Documents*.

practice of writing separate opinions. Nevertheless, a consistent thread running through the opinions of those in the majority was the denial that the states were sovereign. This conclusion was reached by Justices Blair, Wilson, and Chief Justice Jay on historical grounds and by Justice Cushing on the basis of a literal interpretation of the Constitution. Justice Iredell, alone, argued that the states had individually inherited sovereignty from Great Britain.

In many respects the consequences of the *Chisholm* case were far more important than the legal decision itself. Swift on the heels of the announcement of the decision came a flurry of political and journalistic denunciations. Objections were raised by those who viewed the ruling as evidence of nationalist repudiation of an interpretation made to secure ratification of the Constitution, by those who feared for the solvency of states which were beset by creditors, and by those who were genuinely concerned about the possible destruction of state sovereignty.[9] Within two days a proposed constitutional amendment was introduced in the Senate. Within a year it was submitted to the states and by January, 1798, it became the eleventh amendment to the Constitution.

This amendment, providing that "The judicial power of the United States shall not be construed to extend to any suit in law or equity, commenced or prosecuted against one of the United States by citizens of another State, or by citizens or subjects of any foreign State," obviously limited the jurisdiction of the federal courts in this area. But the position of the Court's majority in the *Chisholm* case regarding state sovereignty was not challenged. From the vantage-point of hindsight it appears that a precedent was unwittingly set whereby a Supreme Court decision against a state could be set aside only by successful invocation of the arduous amending process. This pyrrhic victory for states' rights was soon followed by a number of judicial decisions and political actions which put states' righters definitely on the defensive.

## FEDERAL SUPREMACY AND THE TREATY POWER

The controversial treaty of peace made with Great Britain at the conclusion of the Revolutionary War became a source of federal and state conflict very soon after the new court system began to function. A wartime sequestration law of the state of Georgia was held invalid because it thwarted the purposes of the peace treaty. The initial decision was made by Justice Iredell in circuit court in 1791. This lower

9. Warren, *History*, I, 96-98.

court decision was upheld by the Supreme Court in *Georgia* v. *Brailsford*.[10] But, because of the intricate legal procedures utilized and the method of presenting the final decision,[11] the important principle of this case, i.e., that the Treaty of Peace was, like the Constitution, superior to state laws that conflicted with it, was obscured. This was not true, however, of the second important decision involving the treaty power.

Like the *Georgia* case, *Ware* v. *Hylton*[12] concerned the constitutionality of a state sequestrating law, in this instance a statute of Virginia. This state law, which was uncontrovertibly valid at the time of its adoption, would have rendered impossible American fulfillment of its treaty obligations with Great Britain. The supremacy clause of the Constitution was invoked by a unanimous (four member) Court to hold the state law unconstitutional. From the standpoint of constitutional precedent, the decision firmly established the doctrine that a valid federal treaty is superior to any state laws or constitutional provisions which may conflict with it. Politically it contributed to the growing states' rights discontent and to a growing suspicion that the Supreme Court was "partial" to nationalistic claims.

### JURISDICTIONAL QUESTIONS

Even under the Articles of Confederation assertions of jurisdictional authority by the Confederation Court of Appeals in Cases of Capture occasionally met with strong state opposition, especially from New Hampshire and Pennsylvania. The former continued this opposition when the Supreme Court sustained a federal circuit court decision asserting authority to carry into effect the decrees of the old Confederation Court.[13] The New Hampshire legislature presented a remonstrance to Congress denouncing the ruling as a "violation of state independence and an unwarrantable encroachment in the courts of the United States."[14] Although states' rights sentiments could ordinarily be associated with the Jeffersonian Republicans in this era, New Hampshire's legislature was then a Federalist stronghold, indicating the fact reiterated many times historically that the major political parties were often willing to profess concern over states' rights on the basis of political expediency rather than constitutional scruples.

Two additional assumptions of jurisdictional power were made by

10. 3 Dallas 1 (1794).
11. The case was tried by a special jury.
12. 3 Dallas 199 (1796).
13. *Penhallow* v. *Doane's Administrators*, 3 Dallas 54 (1795).
14. Ames, *Documents*, I, 11-15.

the Supreme Court without provoking any manifestations of states' rights opposition. In 1797 the Court exercised the important power granted it by the 25th section of the Judiciary Act of 1789, taking four cases on writs of error from the High Court of Appeals of Maryland.[15] And two years later the federal Supreme Court for the first time considered a suit brought by one state against another.[16]

One jurisdictional approach precipitated a veritable storm of states' rights opposition—that concerning a federal criminal common law jurisdiction. Jeffersonian leaders were convinced that establishment of such jurisdiction would lead to complete submergence of the rights of states and individuals and to unlimited consolidation of judicial power in the court system of the nation. Members of the federal judiciary, with the exception of Justice Samuel Chase, steadfastly maintained that the national judicial power embraced such jurisdiction.[17] The resulting public controversy over application of this doctrine contributed to the worsening political position of the Supreme Court.

Outside the realm of decision making, the rejection by the nationalist dominated Senate of President Washington's nominee to the Chief Justiceship also served to underscore the ever deepening involvement of the Court in partisan politics. The Federalists had rejected John Rutledge ostensibly on grounds of mental illness but actually because of his public opposition to the Jay Treaty. This rejection set the stage for rising charges of judicial partiality, for the Jeffersonian Republicans began to recognize clearly that there was an intimate relationship between judicial selection and political and constitutional attitudes.[18]

### STATE INTERPOSITION

Although the members of the federal judiciary were frequently criticized by Republican leaders and the Republican press after 1793, it was not until the advent of the Alien and Sedition Acts that the opposition party leaders formulated a constitutional theory that challenged

15. *Clerke v. Harwood,* 3 Dallas 342 (1797). Three additional cases are mentioned by Charles Warren, "The First Decade of the Supreme Court," 7 *University of Chicago Law Review* 650 (June, 1940).

16. *New York* v. *Connecticut,* 4 Dallas 1 (1799).

17. Francis Wharton, *State Trials,* pp. 49-56; *United States* v. *Worrall,* 2 Dallas 384 (1798).

18. Charles Grove Haines, *The Role of the Supreme Court in American Government and Politics, 1789-1835,* p. 146. All the appointees to the Supreme Court during the period 1790-1800 were Federalists. These included John Jay, John Rutledge, William Cushing, James Wilson, John Blair, James Iredell, Thomas Johnson, William Paterson, Samuel Chase, Oliver Ellsworth, Bushrod Washington, and Alfred Moore.

the supremacy of the judicial branch of the national government in determining the limits of federal and state powers. When the Federalists passed a stringent naturalization law, an Alien Act, an Alien Enemies Act, and a Sedition Act, the Republicans became fully convinced that the new legislation was designed to destroy opposition to the administration in power, and eventually provide a legal façade for the institution of a monarchical form of government.[19] These convictions became strengthened when Federalist authorities systematically instituted proceedings against the leaders of the Republican press.[20]

Convinced that judicial partisanship would make impossible a Supreme Court decision holding the Alien and Sedition Acts void, the Republican leaders, Madison and Jefferson, collaborated in drawing up a set of resolutions which were introduced in the legislatures of Kentucky and Virginia. Although the resolutions were drafted primarily to influence voters in the coming presidential campaign, their chief importance lies in the constitutional theory embodied in them.

This theory posed a direct challenge to the exercise by the Supreme Court of power to arbitrate finally in disputes between the states and the federal government. The Virginia Resolutions, which were drawn up by Madison and presented by John Taylor of Caroline, were worded as follows:

> In case of a deliberate, palpable, and dangerous exercise of other powers not granted by the said compact, the states, who are parties thereto, have the right and are in duty bound to interpose for arresting the progress of the evil, and for maintaining within their respective limits the authorities, rights and liberties appertaining to them.[21]

The Kentucky Resolutions were drafted by Jefferson and presented by Breckinridge. The challenge to the exclusive power of the federal judiciary in federal-state relations was a more direct and unequivocal one:

> . . . the government created by this compact was not made the exclusive and final judge of the extent of the powers delegated to itself; since that would have made its discretion, and not the Constitution the measure of its powers; but . . . as in all other cases of compact among parties having no common

19. Homer Hockett, *The Constitutional History of the United States*, I, 287-89. Hereinafter cited as *History*.

20. Frank Malory Anderson, "The Enforcement of the Alien and Sedition Laws," *Annual Report of the American Historical Association*, p. 120 (1912). Hereinafter cited as *AHA*.

21. Brant, *James Madison, Father of the Constitution, 1787-1800*, III, 460-61.

judge, each party has an equal right to judge for itself, as well of infractions as of the mode and measure of redress.[22]

Copies of the Virginia and Kentucky Resolutions were sent to the "Co-States." Most of the states replied, but none adopted resolutions at this time approving the doctrine set forth in the Virginia and Kentucky documents. All rejected the contention that a state legislature could declare an act of the national government unconstitutional; Rhode Island, New Hampshire, and Vermont held that this power was vested exclusively in the federal judiciary.[23]

In a report to the Virginia legislature in 1800, Madison described declarations concerning the constitutionality of congressional legislation by citizens or state legislatures as "expressions of opinion unaccompanied with any other effect that what they might produce on opinion by exciting reflection."[24] However, the mischief was done. The compact theory was later adopted and altered to suit the purposes of the Federalists of New England in the War of 1812 period, the nullificationists of South Carolina in 1832, the secessionists of 1861, and the interpositionists of 1956.

## CONCLUSION

Because John Marshall was able to bring to the Supreme Court the delicate combination of judicial audacity and political timing which enabled him to establish that institution as the supreme checking and balancing factor in the American constitutional system, the accomplishments of the justices in the first decade of the federal judiciary have often been considered insignificant. However, an examination of the record of the judiciary in the period from 1790 to 1800 reveals an imposing record of decisive action as arbiter in federal-state relations.

Throughout this period the accent was upon assertion of federal authority, on some occasions in a manner neither judicially defensible, as in the attempt at engrafting upon the Constitution a federal common law criminal jurisdiction,[25] nor politically wise, as in the *Chisholm*

22. As quoted by Hockett, *History,* I, 290.

23. Ames, *Documents,* I, 16-26.

24. Corwin, "National Power and State Interposition," *Selected Essays in Constitutional Law,* III, 1181.

25. This judgment is based upon the conception that adoption of the Constitution represented the establishment of a national legal system which was, in effect, a closed one. Thus no jurisdictional power could be asserted unless based upon or implied from the Constitution. Professor Crosskey's challenging work, *Politics and the Constitution,* maintained that federal common law criminal jurisdiction was considered an integral part of the broad grant of judicial power. (See Volume I, pp. 563-674.) There exists, however, a great deal of contradictory evidence supporting the Jeffersonian view that colonial common law criminal jurisdiction depended upon the individual states.

decision. In both the circuit courts and the Supreme Court, the federal judges and justices established, often in the face of strong states' rights opposition, the power of the judicial branch of the national government to nullify state laws and state constitutional provisions which conflicted with the federal Constitution or with valid treaties. In addition, they exercised the power granted in the 25th section of the Judiciary Act of 1789 to reverse state court decisions which infringed upon federal rights, and assumed jurisdiction, which had been granted in Article III, section 2, of the federal Constitution, in a controversy between two states. Thus in the decade before the appointment of John Marshall as Chief Justice, the federal judiciary asserted its right to arbitrate in federal-state relations, and, subject only to reversal through the cumbersome amending process, established its authority in this sphere as final and conclusive.

The pre-Marshall Supreme Court also managed to fill the debit side of the ledger. By 1799 most of the issues upon which the Federalists and Republicans were sharply divided had been presented in cases to the justices in circuit courts or in the Supreme Court itself. The decisions of the federal judges and justices on problems relating to state sovereignty, federal common law criminal jurisdiction, and the constitutionality of the Alien and Sedition laws generally had been adverse to the views of the advocates of states' rights. By the end of the first decade of the Court, states' righters were generally convinced that the members of the federal judiciary were partisans of nationalism bent upon acquiring and consolidating national power at the expense of the states or individuals.

The widespread confidence in the impartiality of a judicial arbiter of federalism that had prevailed during the period of the making and ratification of the Constitution was largely dissipated by 1800. Subsequent decisions of the Supreme Court which curtailed state authority were to be frequently greeted by the cry of judicial partiality, or in more serious situations, the interpositionists' charge of judicial usurpation.

# CHAPTER III

## *The Marshall Court, 1801-1835*

### NATIONAL POLITICS AND THE SUPREME COURT

ANY ATTEMPT to evaluate the early 19th century role of the Supreme Court as arbiter in federal-state relations without consideration of the influence of national politics would be wholly unrealistic. The very fact that Thomas Jefferson was to be President had given the nationalists a thrill of horror. And after their bitter and crafty attempt at resolving the tie in the electoral college vote in favor of Jefferson's running mate, Aaron Burr, the defeated nationalists were aware that after the new office holders took their seats, the national executive and legislature would be in the hands of the party of states' rights. It is not surprising that the nationalists then turned to their last alternative, fully convinced, in the candid words of President John Adams, that, "In the future administration of our country, the firmest security we can have against the effects of visionary schemes of fluctuating theories will be a solid Judiciary. . . ."[1]

In order to make the federal judiciary "solid," the nationalists in the "lame-duck" session of Congress in 1800-01 hastily drew up an act containing a number of important alterations in the existing judicial system. The tragedy of the whole situation was that while many of the reforms included in the bill, such as the creation of new districts, circuits and judgeships and the relief of the Supreme Court justices from the arduous circuit riding duty, were long overdue from the standpoint of judicial efficiency,[2] the political timing of the legislation aroused fierce opposition. In addition the inclusion of a provision for reduction of the Supreme Court's membership after the next vacancy was correctly viewed as an attempt to deny the incoming President the opportunity to make an appointment to the Court. And finally

1. Warren, *History*, I, 172.

2. Max Farrand, "The Judiciary Act of 1801," 5 *American Historical Review* 682-85.

the hasty filling of the new judicial posts with Federalist politicians (sometimes defeated ones) was scarcely calculated to arouse Republican enthusiasm for the measure. In short, the desperate political maneuvers of the nationalists after their defeat in the election of 1800 projected the national judiciary more directly into the arena of partisan politics.

The Jeffersonian Republican reactions were swift and often decisive. Soon after they took office the Republicans repealed the Judiciary Act of 1801. Although there were occasional references to states' rights in the congressional debates relating to repeal, it is significant that once the Republicans achieved executive and legislative control, emphasis upon states' rights diminished appreciably.[3]

The contention has been made recently that "Jefferson's election was rightfully looked upon as an endorsement of the states-rights interpretation of the 'federal compact,'"[4] yet Jefferson himself gave no indication by action or utterance that he believed that the election victory was a popular mandate for establishment of the doctrine of state interposition as a determinative constitutional principle. On the contrary, in his inaugural address, he stated that one of the guiding principles of his administration was "the preservation of the general government in its whole constitutional vigor."[5] In fact, the doctrine of state interposition ceased to have a great deal of importance for a number of years after the election of Jefferson. If the Jeffersonian Republicans had really wished to enhance the position of the states, they would have attempted to repeal the Judiciary Act of 1789 rather than that of 1801. For it was the former rather than the latter act which had implemented the Supreme Court's powers in federal-state relations.

The repeal of the Judiciary Act of 1801 can be viewed, therefore, as simply one manifestation of the struggle being waged by the Jeffersonian Republicans to extend the fruits of their election victory throughout the national government and to thwart Federalist attempts to defeat their executive and legislative actions. Other major items included an attempt by Federalist judges to prosecute for libel the editor of a Republican newspaper, a refusal of a Connecticut (federal) circuit court to recognize as valid a Presidential order, the *mandamus*

3. William S. Carpenter, "Repeal of the Judiciary Act of 1801," 9 *American Political Science Review* 527.

4. Charles Grove Haines, *The Role of the Supreme Court in American Government and Politics, 1789-1835*, p. 185. Hereinafter cited as *Role*.

5. Henry Adams, *History of the United States during the First Administration of Thomas Jefferson*, I, 203.

case, *Marbury* v. *Madison,* the disagreement over the right of the Supreme Court to declare acts of Congress unconstitutional, and the attempt to impeach Justice Chase.[6]

While the controversies between the Federalist Supreme Court and the Republican executive and legislative branches of the national government multiplied, the newly appointed Chief Justice, John Marshall, quietly assumed leadership of the Supreme Court. During almost half of his career of thirty-five years on the Supreme Court, Marshall followed the practice of delivering the major constitutional opinions for the whole Court. His predecessor, Oliver Ellsworth, had done this occasionally, but Marshall's consistent adherence to this practice for over a decade created an impression of unity which the pre-Marshall Supreme Court had conspicuously lacked. Even when the Jeffersonian Republicans comprised a five to two majority, the old practice of writing seriatim opinions was not revived. Marshall's monopoly on major opinion-writing was broken, however, when, in 1812, the members of the Court began taking turns writing majority opinions.[7]

### BROAD CONSTRUCTION AND NATIONAL SUPREMACY

The major emphasis in decision-making on the Marshall Court, even after the advent of a non-Federalist majority,[8] was upon the assertion and maintenance of national power. One of the most important constitutional questions affecting the future development of American federalism concerned the interpretation of the necessary and proper clause.

The issue had originally been raised by members of President Washington's cabinet when a proposal was made for the creation of a national bank. Thomas Jefferson, then Secretary of State, had immediately recognized the implications that Treasury Secretary Hamilton's broad constructionist interpretation held for the states. The elastic expansion permitted the national government under this doctrine, when considered together with the constitutional imperative laid

6. Warren, *History,* I, 194-95, 198-218, 269-82.

7. 7 Cranch, *passim* (1812). When Jefferson took office in 1801, the entire membership of the Supreme Court was Federalist—Chief Justice Marshall, and Justices William Cushing, William Paterson, Samuel Chase, Bushrod Washington, and Alfred Moore.

8. With the exception of President Adams' appointment of John Marshall as chief justice in 1801, all of the appointees to the Supreme Court during the period 1801-35 were nominal Jeffersonian Republicans or Jacksonian Democrats. They included William Johnson, Brockholst Livingston, Thomas Todd, Gabriel Duval, Joseph Story, Smith Thompson, Robert Trimble, John McLean, Henry Baldwin, and James Wayne. Story's judicial record well illustrates the fact that there is no necessary relationship between one's party affiliation and constitutional beliefs.

down in the supremacy clause, could only bring the gradual contraction of state authority and steady growth of central governmental power. Ultimately, believed Jefferson, this would lead to the destruction of the federal system. As a consequence he insisted that the word "necessary" meant "indispensable."

Hamilton had argued that the clause must be given an interpretation which emphasized Congress' convenient selection of any means reasonably related to a constitutionally legitimate purpose and not expressly prohibited by the Constitution itself.[9]

The contribution of the Marshall Court, and John Marshall himself, to the establishment of the broad constructionist interpretation was obviously not noteworthy because of its originality. Its significance lay in the political courage and consistent application by the Court in irrevocably asserting and reasserting the doctrine in the face of mounting states' rights opposition.

The initial application of the doctrine was in a relatively obscure decision concerned with the unexciting subject of the national government's priority in situations where debtors to the government became bankrupt.[10] However, even this cautious assertion of the doctrine was followed up, within a year, by a constitutional amendment introduced by Representative Clopton of Virginia which defined "necessary and proper" to include "only such laws as shall have a rational connection with and immediate relation to the powers enumerated."[11] Clopton's challenge to the broad constructionist interpretation was relatively mild when compared to the attacks made a few years later.

One basic reason for mounting opposition to this interpretation was the widening economic distress created by the financial depression of 1819-22. This economic disaster was, with partial justification, viewed by the public as caused by the new Second Bank of the United States.[12] But the opponents of this Bank generally chose to attack it on constitutional rather than social or economic grounds. Consequently, the whole question of the constitutionality of the Bank, which President Madison had considered closed,[13] was reopened and with it, of necessity, the issue of strict versus broad construction of the

9. *Writings of Thomas Jefferson* (Ford edition), V, 285; *Works of Alexander Hamilton* (Lodge edition), III, 192.

10. *United States* v. *Fisher,* 2 Cranch 358 (1805).

11. *Annals,* 9th Congress, Second Session (December 11, 1806), pp. 131-38; cited in Haines, *Role,* p. 268.

12. Samuel Rezneck, "The Depression of 1819-1822, a Social History," 39 *American Historical Review* 28-29.

13. Haines, *Role,* p. 352, note 61.

necessary and proper clause. The Supreme Court considered these issues in *McCulloch* v. *Maryland*.[14]

The Maryland legislature had levied a tax intended to destroy the branch of the National Bank operating in Baltimore. Maryland's counsel, in defending the levy, argued that the power to tax was held concurrently by the nation and the states, that the necessary and proper clause limited Congress' selection of the means to carry out its enumerated powers to those absolutely necessary to the fulfillment of its delegated authority, and that the Second United States Bank represented an unconstitutional assumption of national power.

John Marshall's very elaborate opinion touched deliberately upon many more questions than those raised by Maryland's counsel. First, with the recent attack upon the Supreme Court's grant of appellate jurisdiction obviously in mind,[15] the Chief Justice reaffirmed that the Supreme Court had been selected to resolve conflicts of authority between the nation and the states. Second, he denied the allegation made by the lawyers for Maryland that the Constitution was a compact created by sovereign and independent states, restating the Federalist argument that constitutional ratification was made by the people, represented in conventions which for convenience were set up in each state.

Thirdly, Marshall reiterated the principle of national supremacy, pointing out that "the government of the Union, though limited in its powers, is supreme within its sphere of action." He then turned his attention to the fourth and crucial question—that concerning the validity of the congressional creation of the Second National Bank. The felicity of Marshall's prose did not conceal the fact that the reasoning was basically Hamilton's. Yet Marshall's statement was part and parcel of a definitive interpretation of the Constitution by an institution capable of rendering such interpretations. Thus Hamilton's opinion on the Bank was given the imprimatur of the highest judicial authority of the United States in a period when both the broad constructionist philosophy and the federal judicial arbiter were under growing states' rights attack. Only when measured in terms of political courage and astute timing can Marshall's particular contribution to American federalism be fully understood. It is for this reason that Marshall's classic statement of the doctrine, which follows, is a commonplace in every government textbook, while copies of Hamilton's

14. 4 Wheaton 316 (1819).
15. *Martin* v. *Hunter's Lessee*, 1 Wheaton 304 (1816).

original letter only occasionally are seen outside the confines of musty archives.

> We admit, and all must admit, that the powers of the government are limited, and that its limits are not to be transcended. But we think the sound construction of the constitution must allow to the national legislature that discretion, with respect to the means by which the powers it confers are to be carried into execution, which will enable that body to perform the high duties assigned to it, in the manner most beneficial to the people. Let the end be legitimate, let it be within the scope of the constitution, and all means which are appropriate, which are plainly adapted to that end, which are not prohibited, but consistent with the letter and spirit of the constitution, are constitutional.

In short the necessary and proper clause was construed as an addition rather than a limitation on congressional power and in the utilization of that additional power, Congress could, with certain limitations, choose any means reasonably related to the purposes set forth in the Constitution.

Marshall's fifth major assertion in the *McCulloch* case was that of the corollary doctrine of implied limitations. As he put it,

> . . . the states have no power, by taxation or otherwise, to retard, impede, burden, or in any manner control, the operation of the constitutional laws enacted by congress to carry into execution the powers vested in the general government. This is, we think, the unavoidable consequence of that supremacy which the constitution has declared.

Under this doctrine, the Maryland tax on the operations of the Second Bank of the United States was held unconstitutional and void.[16]

Indicative of the turbulent opposition to national authority characteristic of the Marshall era was the fact that within a relatively brief span of years two additional cases, *Osborn* v. *Bank of the United States* and *Weston* v. *Charleston*,[17] involving the same basic issues as the *McCulloch* case, came before the Supreme Court. They were decided on essentially the same grounds as the *McCulloch* decision, although several technical questions were raised in the *Osborn* case which had not been determined previously.[18]

16. The opinion did not nullify a state tax on the real property of the Bank.

17. 9 Wheaton 738 (1824); 2 Peters 449 (1829).

18. Four additional technical points were decided. First, the fact that a case involved several questions which were not connected with the interpretation of a federal law did not prevent the assumption of jurisdiction by a federal court. Second, the process of a federal circuit court restraining state officers did not violate the Eleventh Amendment because this amendment applied to suits to which a state is a party on the record. (Actually, Marshall himself did not adhere to this doctrine; see *Governor of*

The applications of the broad constructionist doctrine of implied powers in the *McCulloch* and *Osborn* cases were primarily defensive of federal authority. In the same category can be placed *Brown* v. *Maryland*, and *Martin* v. *Mott*.[19] The *Brown* case, like the *McCulloch* case, involved the constitutionality of a Maryland tax, in this instance a license tax, on importers of foreign commodities. The constitutional issues were whether such a levy interfered with Congress' power to regulate foreign commerce and whether the tax was a duty on imports prohibited by Article I, section 10, of the Constitution. In holding the tax void, Chief Justice Marshall made it clear that he considered congressional power over foreign commerce to be exclusive. The Maryland levy was held invalid on two grounds. Under the "original package" doctrine, imported commodities were held immune from state taxing authority while retained in the importer's warehouse in their original forms or packages. A state tax on goods in this status was, in Marshall's eyes, "too plainly a duty on imports to escape the prohibition in the Constitution." The tax also was deemed a penalty "inflicted on the importer, for selling the article. . . ." This, held Marshall, was "in opposition" to an act of Congress of March, 1799, authorizing importation.

The case of *Martin v. Mott*[20] settled decisively in favor of national authority a question that had troubled the national executive for a number of years. During the War of 1812, General Dearborn, acting under the authority of the President of the United States, had attempted to requisition the militia of the New England states for coastal defense. Governor Strong of Massachusetts had refused to obey his order. The Massachusetts Governor based his refusal on an advisory opinion of the judges of the Supreme Court of Massachusetts. The state judges had held that though the militia may be employed in the service of the United States to execute the laws of the Union, to suppress insurrections, and to repel invasions, the power to determine

*Georgia* v. *Madrazo*, 1 Peters 110 [1828]; it was abandoned completely in *Pennoyer* v. *McConnaughy*, 140 U.S. 1 [1891]; Willoughby, *Constitutional Law*, III, 1399.) Third, a federal injunction may be granted to enjoin state officers from executing an unconstitutional state statute where the complainants show a proper interest. And fourth, if state officers do execute such an unconstitutional state statute and seize funds which might be lost to the owner if transferred, a federal injunction may be issued to prevent such a transfer. (Daniel H. Chamberlain, "Osborn v. the Bank of the United States," 1 *Harvard Law Review* 225 [December, 1887].)

19. 12 Wheaton 419 (1827); 12 Wheaton 19 (1827).

20. 12 Wheaton 19 (1827).

whether any of these exigencies existed was vested not in the President, but in the governors of the states.[21]

The Supreme Court, in an opinion by Justice Story, upheld the authority of the President. The repudiation of the Massachusetts doctrine of state discretion in determining the existence of military exigencies was based on the constitutional grants to Congress of power "to provide for calling forth the militia, to execute the laws of the Union, suppress insurrections, and repel invasions," and "to provide for organizing, arming and disciplining the militia, and for governing such part of them as may be employed in the service of the United States,"[22] and an act of Congress of 1795 which provided "that whenever the United States shall be invaded, or be in imminent danger of invasion from any foreign nation or Indian tribe, it shall be lawful for the President of the United States to call forth such number of the militia of the state or states most convenient to the place of danger or scene of action, as he may judge necessary to repel such invasion. . . ." Any interference, ruled Story, with the President's discretionary power would "tend to jeopardize the public interests."

One of the most serious conflicts of federal-state authority developed as a result of certain actions taken by Georgia which deliberately violated a treaty between the United States and the Cherokee Nation. This treaty had placed the Indians under the protection of the United States. The situation was complicated by the existence of an agreement made between the national government and Georgia in 1802 in which the national government had promised to remove all Indians from within the territory of the state as soon as practicable. By the 1820's many Georgians became impatient, but the National Government refused to use force to drive out the Indians, who then consisted of Creeks as well as Cherokees. By treaty, President John Quincy Adams' agents had persuaded the Creeks in Georgia to move west. However, before the agreement went into effect, Governor Troup of Georgia sent surveyors into Creek territory in defiance of the Secretary of War's letter forbidding the action. When President Adams threatened to use force against Georgia, Troup called out the state militia. When Adams called upon Congress to support him, he was humiliated to find it unwilling to do so. Adams then complied with Georgia's wishes and sent agents to induce the Creeks to surrender their lands.[23]

21. Allen Johnson, *Readings in American Constitutional History, 1776-1876*, pp. 261-68. Hereinafter cited as *Readings*.

22. Article I, section 8, clauses 15 and 16.

23. Ulrich B. Phillips, "Georgia and State Rights," *AHA* (1901), II, 46-51.

In a letter to Georgia's Congressmen written in February, 1827, Governor Troup discussed Georgia's victory and gave the following challenge to the Supreme Court's exercise of final determinative authority in federal-state relations:

> I consider all questions of mere sovereignty as a matter for negotiation between the states and the United States, until the proper tribunal shall be assigned by the Constitution itself for the adjustment of them. . . . The states cannot consent to refer to the Supreme Court, as of right and obligation, questions of sovereignty between them and the United States, because that Court, being of exclusive appointment by the Government of the United States, will make the United States judge in its own cause. . . .[24]

The governmental leaders of Georgia acted upon this doctrine in the case of Corn Tassel, a Cherokee who had been convicted of murder and sentenced to death by a Georgia court. When this court decision was taken to the federal Supreme Court on writ of error, Georgia refused to honor the writ and, before the Supreme Court could take further action, hung Corn Tassel. An injunction against the state was continued by the Cherokee Nation but ultimately was denied by the Supreme Court on the ground that the action concerned a political question.[25]

In order to prevent Cherokee defendants from carrying their cases to the Supreme Court, Georgia courts allowed their cases to drag for as long a time as possible. However, the case of Worcester, a minister convicted under a Georgia statute forbidding unauthorized white men in Cherokee country, provided an opportunity to test the validity of Georgia's Indian laws. The minister had been appointed postmaster at New Echota, capital of the Cherokee Nation, by President John Q. Adams. Later, after Worcester's arrest, Governor Gilmer of Georgia requested his removal, and Adams' successor, President Jackson, readily complied. The minister and a number of other missionaries were tried in a Georgia court for illegal residence and sentenced to four years hard labor in the state penitentiary. The Governor offered to pardon them if they left the state. Only Worcester and Elizur Butler refused, taking the state court decision to the Supreme Court.

*Worcester* v. *Georgia*[26] was argued only by the counsel for the Cherokees, the Georgia Governor and legislature having again angrily denied that the Supreme Court had the authority to issue the writ of error to a court of a sovereign state. Marshall, after an unusually long

24. *Ibid.*, pp. 52-65.
25. *Cherokee Nation* v. *Georgia*, 5 Peters 2 (1831).
26. 6 Peters 515 (1832).

historical argument, declared that according to the treaty of Hopewell, "the Cherokees are under the protection of the United States." Through the operation of treaties and acts of Congress, the state of Georgia was barred from enforcing its laws in the territory of the Cherokee Nation. "The whole intercourse," continued Marshall, "between the United States and this nation is by our Constitution and laws vested in the government of the United States." The Georgia legislative acts which interfered "forcibly with the relations established between the United States and the Cherokee Nation" were declared repugnant to the Constitution, and hence Worcester's state court conviction was "reversed and annulled." A special mandate to the state court was sent ordering the release of Worcester and Butler.

Georgia disregarded the Court's mandate, and in 1834 the state legislature authorized the distribution of Cherokee lands to Georgians by the land-lottery system. President Jackson also sent agents to persuade the Cherokees to move west. However, that Jackson refused to carry out the Supreme Court's decision is yet to be proven historically. Ever since the publication in 1864 of Horace Greeley's *The American Conflict,* a number of historians have given credence to the report that President Jackson intimated, if he did not expressly state, that since Marshall had made his decision he (Marshall) would have to enforce it.[27] Yet, Supreme Court Historian Charles Warren has pointed out that Jackson was never actually called upon to enforce the Court's mandate. In 1832, Jackson's political opponents accused him of refusing to aid the Court, but such charges were premature, for when the Supreme Court adjourned in March, 1832, it had not actually issued the mandate. No action could have been taken until the 1833 term. Only after the Court should have issued the mandate and it should have been disobeyed could the Court direct a United States marshal to summon a *posse comitatus* to execute its mandate. Presumably, if the marshal had been successfully resisted, the chief executive would have been called upon to set in motion the armed forces of the federal government.[28] But before any of these steps could be taken, President Jackson indicated in his powerful rejection of South Carolina's Nullification Ordinance of November, 1832, that he would use the military forces of the whole nation to execute the laws of the Union.

President Jackson's action in the face of South Carolina's nullification threat was undoubtedly a factor in settling the Georgia issue.

27. Phillips, *AHA,* II, 82-85; Haines, *Role,* p. 603.
28. Warren, *History,* I, 757-66.

At President Jackson's request, Congress enacted the Force Bill. This act, among other things, enlarged the jurisdiction of the federal circuit courts, providing for removal to such courts of any suit commenced in a state court against a federal officer or against persons for acts done under the federal revenue laws. Provision was also made for *habeas corpus* in cases of prisoners in state jails held for acts done or committed in pursuance of a federal law. Within a few months of Jackson's show of force against South Carolina, Governor Lumpkin of Georgia pardoned Worcester and Butler, thus avoiding a real test of strength with the national government.[29]

The whole series of conflicts with Georgia left the Marshall Court in something less than a successful position. Georgia had, in effect, defied the Supreme Court and when put in a position where the national executive might have intervened, managed to avoid an open conflict without any discoverable loss of prestige. Had the state of Georgia continued to defy the Court, the controversy might have taken a different turn. For in the *Peters* case, which had been decided nearly three decades earlier, the logical consequence of state defiance of the Supreme Court had been clearly indicated by President Madison.

The decision referred to, that of *United States* v. *Judge Peters,*[30] had been handed down in 1809 under circumstances very critical for the preservation of federal supremacy and the federal judicial arbitership. The danger lay in the growth of two totally unconnected movements toward extreme states' rights positions. One, native to the state of Pennsylvania, had its roots in the objections of that state to the jurisdiction of the old Court of Appeals in Cases of Capture created under the Article of Confederation[31] and in the long-standing attitude of members of the state judicial system toward the federal judicial arbiter. The Pennsylvania Judiciary had, to a great extent, accepted the theoretical assumptions of the Kentucky and Virginia Resolutions of 1798.[32] The second, originating in New England, reflected deep Federalist resentment over the Jeffersonian Embargo Acts and the Louisiana Purchase.[33] It was in this critical period that the sovereignty-

29. The missionaries had shown a conciliating attitude and had, by January, 1833, abandoned attempts to prosecute their case further before the Supreme Court; Phillips, *AHA,* II, 83.

30. 5 Cranch 115 (1809).

31. Richard Peters, *The Whole Proceedings in the Case of Olmstead and Others versus Rittenhouse,* as discussed in Haines, *Role.*

32. Warren, *History,* I, 367-74; *Respublica* v. *Cobbett,* 3 Dallas 473 (1798); *Miller* v. *Nicholls,* 4 Yeates, 251 (1805).

33. For example, as early as January 29, 1804, Pickering wrote to Cabot: "I do not believe in the practicality of a long continued Union. A Northern Confederacy would

conscious legislature of Pennsylvania sought to assert its version of the constitutional doctrine of state sentinelship maintained by states' righters.

The legal issue was joined over a long dormant prize claim case originally brought before the Confederation Court of Appeals in Cases of Capture by one Gideon Olmstead. In this early controversy the state of Pennsylvania had refused to honor the decision favoring Olmstead made by the Confederation Court. However, after years of waiting Olmstead resurrected his claim in 1803 when he filed suit in a federal district court. By a recent Supreme Court decision in *Penhallow* v. *Doane,* federal district courts were held to have authority to execute the decrees of the old Confederation Court of Appeals in Cases of Capture. In January, 1803, District Judge Peters upheld Olmstead's claims and, under the *Penhallow* doctrine, decreed that the prize money be paid to Olmstead.

The Pennsylvania legislature immediately passed a law defying the district court's ruling as a usurpation of jurisdiction. The statute directed the Governor "to protect the just rights of the state from any process issued out of any Federal Court." Finally, after five years, this direct challenge to the federal judiciary was reviewed by the Supreme Court. In 1808, Olmstead, now eighty-two years old, applied to the highest national tribunal for issuance of a *mandamus* to Judge Peters to compel him to enforce obedience to his district court decision of 1803. Such a *mandamus* was issued directing Peters to exercise the sentence pronounced or show cause for not so doing. Judge Peters answered that "from prudential, more than other motives, I deemed it best to avoid embroiling the government of the United States and that of Pennsylvania (if the latter government should choose to do so), on a question which has rested on my single opinion."[34]

In considering the return of Judge Peters to the *mandamus* in *United States* v. *Judge Peters,* Chief Justice John Marshall pointed out that,

> If the legislatures of the several states may, at will, annul the judgments of the courts of the United States, and destroy the rights acquired under those judgments, the constitution itself becomes a solemn mockery; and the nation is deprived of the means of enforcing its laws by the instrumentality of its own tribunals. So fatal a result must be deprecated by all; and the people of Pennsylvania, not less than the citizens of every other

---

unite congenial characters. . . ." Henry Adams, *Documents Relating to New England Federalism,* p. 340, *passim*. See also Warren, *History,* I, 321-24.

34. 5 Cranch 115 (1809).

state, must feel a deep interest in resisting principles so destructive of the Union, and in averting consequences so fatal to themselves.

Marshall held that "the ultimate right to determine the jurisdiction of the courts of the Union" necessarily resides in "the supreme judicial tribunal of the nation," not the state legislatures. After briefly reviewing and upholding the lower federal court decision, Marshall "with extreme regret" awarded a peremptory *mandamus*.

Governor Snyder of Pennsylvania immediately sent a message to the state legislature informing the representatives that he intended to call out the militia to prevent enforcement of the decree. On March 24, Judge Peters issued process against the holders of the contested prize money, Mrs. Sergeant and Mrs. Waters, executrices of the deceased state treasurer, David Rittenhouse. When a United States marshal attempted to serve process, he met with the resistance of a body of state militia commanded by General Bright. He then summoned a *posse comitatus* of two thousand men. For a time bloodshed seemed imminent. On April 3, the Pennsylvania legislature adopted resolutions denying that the Supreme Court had the power "to decide on State rights." But by April 6th, the Pennsylvania authorities began to weaken.[35] For Governor Snyder wrote to the President of the United States, James Madison, expressing the hope that the latter would "justly discriminate between opposition to the Constitution and laws of the United States and that of resisting the decree of a Judge founded . . . on a usurpation of power." The newly-elected President, although a staunch Republican, replied as follows: "The Executive is not only unauthorized to prevent the execution of a decree sanctioned by the Supreme Court of the United States, but is expressly enjoined, by statute, to carry into effect any such decree, where opposition may be made to it."[36]

The Pennsylvania legislature ordered removal of the state militia from the Rittenhouse residence and began consideration of a bill to appropriate enough money to restore the contested prize fund. Mrs. Sergeant, now under arrest for refusal to obey the federal court order, applied for a writ of *habeas corpus* to Chief Justice Tilghman of the Pennsylvania Supreme Court. He dismissed her petition, holding that she was properly in federal custody. By April 26, the state made the payment required by the federal court. A final humiliation for the state came when General Bright was tried and convicted before Justice Bushrod Washington in federal circuit court. For forcibly resisting a

35. Johnson, *Readings*, pp. 254, 260-62.
36. Warren, *History*, I, 382-87.

federal marshal, Bright and his associates were sentenced to fine and imprisonment. However, President Madison pardoned them on the ground that "they had acted under a mistaken sense of duty."

At the very height of the controversy, the Pennsylvania legislature had stated, in resolutions which were submitted to the legislatures of the other states, its own version of the doctrine of state sentinelship. It acknowledged the supremacy of "the General Government," but while it submitted to the latter's authority when such authority was:

> . . . exercised within Constitutional limits, they [the state legislature] trust they will not be considered as acting hostile to the General Government, when, as guardians of the State rights, they cannot permit an infringement of those rights, by an unconstitutional exercise of power in the United States Courts. . . . To suffer the United States' courts to decide on state rights will, from a bias in favor of power, necessarily destroy the Federal part of our government.

The Pennsylvania resolutions were answered by resolutions of disapproval by the legislatures of Tennessee, Kentucky, New Jersey, Maryland, Ohio, Georgia, North Carolina, Virginia, New Hampshire, and Vermont. In reply to the Pennsylvania proposal that the "sister states" support it in endeavoring to get a constitutional amendment establishing an "impartial tribunal to determine disputes between the General and State Governments," the Virginia legislature resolved that

> . . . a tribunal is already provided by the Constitution of the United States; to wit: the Supreme Court, more eminently qualified from their habits and duties, from the mode of their selection, and from the tenure of their offices, to decide the disputes aforesaid in an enlightened and impartial manner, than any other tribunal that could be erected.[37]

Interestingly enough, it was the state of Virginia which, in a few years, directed the most concentrated and logically organized attacks upon the Supreme Court's exercise of power as judicial umpire in the federal system. For while Pennsylvania's attacks had been intensive, they had not been directed against the statutory provision which provided the key to the Supreme Court's power in federal-state relations—the 25th section of the Judiciary Act of 1789. In *Fairfax's Devisee* v. *Hunter's Lessee* and later in *Cohens* v. *Virginia*,[38] Virginia challenged directly the Supreme Court's jurisdictional authority under this vitally important section.

The rich timber and tobacco lands comprising the northern neck of

37. *Ibid.*, pp. 260-61, 287; Johnson, *Readings*, p. 254.
38. 7 Cranch 603 (1813); 6 Wheaton 264 (1821).

Virginia had belonged to Lord Fairfax, who died in England in 1781. The State of Virginia had confiscated the land in 1777 and had sold portions of it. Fairfax's nephew, Denny Martin, also a British alien, sought to protect his right to the land which he had inherited from Lord Fairfax by invoking the treaty of peace made with Great Britain in 1794. In the initial Supreme Court action, *Fairfax's Devisee* v. *Hunter's Lessee,* Martin's claim, based upon the supremacy clause, was upheld in a three to one decision.[39] This decision had reversed a Virginia Court of Appeals ruling. However, when the Supreme Court sent its reversal to Virginia, the state Court of Appeals refused to honor it, holding that Congress' grant of appellate jurisdiction to the Supreme Court under the 25th section of the Judiciary Act of 1789 was unconstitutional. This conclusion was based upon a conception of the Constitution best stated by Judge Cabell of the Virginia court. According to his interpretation,

> . . . neither [Federal or state] government . . . can act *compulsively,* on the other or on any of its organs in their political or official capacities. . . . The Constitution of the United States contemplates the independence of both governments, and regards the *residuary* sovereignty of the states, as not less inviolable, than the delegated sovereignty of the United States. It must have been foreseen that controversies would sometimes arise as to the boundaries of the two jurisdictions. *Yet the Constitution has provided no umpire*. . . . to give the general government or any of its departments a direct and controlling operation upon the state departments, as such, would be to change at once the whole character of our system.[40]

In *Martin* v. *Hunter's Lessee,*[41] the Supreme Court, in an opinion by Justice Story, met this challenge to federal judicial power. Interpreting the Constitution's preamble in a manner that was destined to be utilized approvingly by Webster and fiercely challenged by Calhoun in subsequent decades, Justice Story started with the premise that "the constitution of the United States was ordained and established, not by the states in their sovereign capacities, but emphatically, as the preamble of the constitution declares, by 'the people of the United States.'" Thus the sections of the Constitution defining the jurisdiction of the federal courts are "the voice of the whole American people, solemnly declared, in establishing one great department of the government which was, in many respects, national, and in all, supreme. It is a part of the

39. Chief Justice Marshall disqualified himself apparently because of his financial interest in the outcome of the case.

40. *Hunter* v. *Martin,* 4 Mumford 8-9 (1814).

41. 1 Wheaton 304 (1816).

same instrument which was to act not merely upon individuals, but upon states; and to deprive them altogether of some powers or sovereignty, and to restrain and regulate them in the exercise of others." In order to accomplish this, the jurisdiction of federal courts was extended to all cases arising under the Constitution, laws and treaties of the United States. It was the case, not the court, that determined jurisdiction. On these grounds the state court challenge to the constitutionality of the crucial 25th section was rejected.

This decision provoked further states' rights attacks on the Supreme Court and in fact within six years Virginia raised the same constitutional question. In terms of its legal aspects the new decision, that of *Cohens* v. *Virginia*,[42] is identical with that of *Martin* v. *Hunter's Lessee*. However, the *Cohens* case not only reaffirmed Story's decision, but established an interpretation of the Eleventh Amendment vital to the maintenance of national supremacy. For Virginia's counsel had argued that a case in which a state was forced to appear as a defendant in error was a suit against a state forbidden by the Eleventh Amendment. Acceptance of this argument would have seriously curtailed the Court's power under the vital 25th section of the Judiciary Act of 1789. The Supreme Court rejected this reasoning and held that the amendment inhibits federal courts only in suits commenced by individuals against a state and not by a state against individuals, the situation at the beginning of the *Cohens* litigation.

In the context of the rising states' rights agitation characteristic of this era, the *Cohens* decision probably had far greater influence because of its non-legal, ideological and political aspects than as a vehicle of constitutional exegesis. For it was in this decision that Chief Justice Marshall answered decisively the challenges of Spencer Roane, of John Taylor of Caroline, and of the incipient sectionalist movements of Kentucky and Ohio. Just as the prolix writings of John Taylor of Caroline were to provide the theoretical starting point for Calhoun and for the secessionists of 1861, so did the *Cohens* and *McCulloch* decisions of John Marshall provide the basis for the theoretical arguments of such nationalists as Daniel Webster and, later, Abraham Lincoln. And, as Marshall's biographer Albert Beveridge has pointed out, the *Cohens* decision "gave strength and courage" to the hard-pressed nationalists in 1821.[43]

42. 6 Wheaton 264 (1821); the Supreme Court also had to defend its power as final arbiter against an erroneous construction by the New York judicial system. See *Gelston* v. *Hoyt*, 3 Wheaton 246 (1818).

43. William E. Dodd, "Chief Justice Marshall and Virginia, 1813-1821," 12 *American*

Not all of the Marshall Court decisions were merely defensive of national authority. A number were squarely in the expansionist category of *McCulloch* v. *Maryland.* In two cases concerned with Congress' power to acquire and govern territory, the broad constructionist interpretation of the necessary and proper clause was applied to insure Congress the widest discretion to control such territory.[44] These territorial cases did not touch directly upon contemporary problems of federal-state conflict. The case of *Gibbons* v. *Ogden* did, however.

Modern attempts at evaluating the Marshall Court's contributions to the constitutional law of the commerce clause may be placed in two broad categories—those which felt its interpretations were bold departures from the sort of narrow construction typified by President Monroe's rationale for his veto of a Cumberland Road Bill[45] and those which felt that the Marshall Court, through fear of states' rights opposition, actually handed down a narrower interpretation of the clause than the framers of the Constitution had intended.[46] The available evidence lends support to the second of these views but does not completely contradict the first.

The Marshall Court's cautious assertions of federal authority in interstate commerce become understandable when viewed in the light of the implications which an extremely broad interpretation of this power held for the already fearful slave states. John Marshall's studied unwillingness to openly assert the exclusiveness of federal power to regulate interstate commerce in the *Ogden* case and his unusual show of regard for the reserved powers of the states in the *Blackbird Creek* case seemed strangely out of keeping with his overriding insistence upon maintaining or aggressively asserting national authority. But the sensitivity of the slave states to any expansion of national authority over interstate commerce evidenced after an earlier circuit court decision provides a clue.

Laws had been passed in South Carolina and Virginia forbidding the entrance of free Negroes into the states and providing for their detention in custody until the ship in which they arrived should leave port. These statutes were based upon the belief prevailing in the South that the presence of northern free Negroes would stir up insurrections

*Historical Review* 782-83; Warren, "Legislative and Judicial Attacks on the Supreme Court," 47 *American Law Review* 5-26

44. *Seré and Laralde* v. *Pitot,* 6 Cranch 332 (1810); *American Insurance Co.* v. *Canter,* 1 Peters 511 (1828).

45. George W. Wickersham, "Federal Control of Interstate Commerce," 23 *Harvard Law Review* 243.

46. William W. Crosskey, *Politics and the Constitution,* I, 17-292.

among the slave population. In 1823 the South Carolina law was held invalid by a federal circuit court as in contravention of Congress' power to regulate interstate commerce, a power described by Justice Johnson as "paramount and exclusive."[47] Shortly thereafter the South Carolina legislature adopted resolutions denying that the Supreme Court had power to exercise jurisdiction in cases involving state legislation. South Carolinian courts actually refused to apply Justice Johnson's decision for over a quarter of a century.

Chief Justice Marshall's reaction to developments in South Carolina are instructive with regard to his position in the *Gibbons* case the following year. To Justice Story he wrote:

"Our brother Johnson, I perceive, has hung himself on a democratic snag, in a hedge composed entirely of thorny States Rights in South Carolina. . . . We have its twin brother [i.e., to the South Carolina law] in Virginia; a case has been brought before me in which I might have considered its constitutionality, had I chosen to do so; but it was not absolutely necessary, and as I am not fond of butting against a wall in sport, I escaped on the construction of the act."[48]

The case of *Gibbons* v. *Ogden*[49] was the first interpretation of the commerce clause made by the Supreme Court. At issue was the constitutionality of the steamboat monopoly law of the state of New York, a statute which by 1822 had aroused great resentment in other states and prompted retaliatory legislation in New Jersey, Connecticut, and Ohio.

The major argument of counsel for the New York monopoly was that commerce did not embrace navigation, but merely comprised traffic, i.e., the interchange of commodities. Marshall rejected this view and held that commerce not only embraced navigation, but comprehended "every species of commercial intercourse as well." This broad interpretation of the scope of the commerce power paved the way for the application of the commerce clause to the regulation of railroads and all the modern media of mass communication.

To regulate commerce, said Marshall, Congress may prescribe rules for its governance. This power to regulate commerce is, stated Marshall, ". . . complete in itself, may be exercised to its utmost extent, and acknowledges no limitations, other than are prescribed in the constitution."

47. *Elkinson* v. *Deliesseline,* Federal Cases No. 4366 (1823).

48. Charles Warren, "Legislative and Judicial Attacks," 47 *American Law Review* 20.

49. 9 Wheaton 1 (1824).

Marshall also distinguished between interstate and intrastate commerce, interpreting the phrase "among the several states" as embracing "commerce that concerns more states than one." The criteria he utilized to determine what portion of the internal commerce of a state might be regulated by Congress he described as follows:

> The genius and character of the whole government seem to be, that its action is to be applied to all the external concerns of the nation, and to those internal concerns which affect the states generally; but not to those which are completely within a particular state, which do not affect other states, and with which it is not necessary to interfere, for the purpose of executing some of the general powers of the government. The completely internal commerce of a state, then, may be considered as reserved for the state itself.

Although he intimated that Congress' power to regulate interstate commerce was an exclusive one, Marshall dismissed "that inquiry" because Congress had already acted to regulate navigation. "The sole question" was, "can a state regulate commerce with foreign nations and among the states, while Congress is regulating it?" The laws of Congress regulating commerce embraced vessels propelled by steam as well as by wind. Accordingly the New York steamboat monopoly law was declared repugnant to the Constitution as interfering with navigation which was regulated by Congress under its commerce power.

In a concurring opinion Justice Johnson maintained, as he had in the *Elkinson* case, that Congress' power over interstate commerce was exclusive, a position logically consistent with subsequent interpretations dealing with foreign commerce. The question whether congressional control of interstate commerce was exclusive or not was again raised in 1820. In *Wilson* v. *Blackbird Creek Marsh Company*[50] the question of exclusiveness was implicit. But here again the Marshall Court avoided giving a direct answer, taking the position that since Congress had passed no law regulating commerce on streams of this kind, the state could validly construct a dam obstructing navigation under its reserved power to provide for the welfare and health of the inhabitants of the area. This decision is of particular significance in an evaluation of the record of the Marshall Court as federal umpire because it represents a rare instance in which the Marshall Court clearly exhibited an awareness of the need to maintain the constitutional vigor of the states in the federal system. Largely because the states were

50. 2 Peters 245 (1829).

aggressively challenging various exercises of federal power, and probably in part because of judicial acceptance of the orthodox Federalist view that the chief danger to a federal system lay in the tendency of the "parts" to encroach upon the powers of the "whole," the Marshall Court generally gave its attention to safeguarding or enhancing federal power.

### THE CONTRACT CLAUSE AND THE STATES

Strictly speaking, the constitutional safeguards protecting individual rights against state action may be considered as subjects outside the traditional arena of federal-state relations. But since the federal Supreme Court is granted jurisdictional power to enforce such safeguards, and since the exercise of such power can determine the ability or inability of a state or states to regulate in the areas affected, the exercise of power by the Supreme Court to enforce individual rights against state action vitally affects the position of the states in the federal system. The contract clause decisions of the Marshall Court provide notable examples. For while they may be viewed in one light as simply safeguarding constitutionally determined, individual rights, they may also be viewed as seriously curtailing the powers of the states in the regulation of their internal economies. The exercise of such power by the Supreme Court thus could not fail seriously to affect the economic position of the states in relation to that of the national government.

The first Marshall Court contract clause decision was rendered in the case of *Fletcher* v. *Peck*.[51] The legislature of Georgia, in the winter session of 1794-95, sold to four companies of land speculators more than thirty-five million acres of fertile land for five hundred thousand dollars, less than one and one-half cents an acre. When the people of Georgia learned of the venality of their representatives, they elected new members to the legislature at the next election. Within a year the Yazoo land grants were declared void by the new legislature, but the Yazoo speculators had acted even more swiftly. They had disposed of most of their holdings to purportedly "innocent purchasers" throughout the United States.

When the constitutionality of the rescinding law came before the Supreme Court, Chief Justice John Marshall asserted that the Court could not inquire into the motives of the legislators. The lands in question had already been resold to "innocent" purchasers. Then Marshall intimated that even if Georgia had been a sovereign, independent state, its legislature, by repealing the granting law, had violated

51. 6 Cranch 87 (1810).

"principles of equity" or a higher law deduced from "the nature of society and of government."[52] However, the Georgia rescinding law was dealt with through application of the contract clause.

From the standpoint of the development of federal judicial power to invalidate state statutes which conflicted with the federal Constitution or national laws or treaties, Marshall's assumptions about application of the clause were of crucial importance. For by interpreting the contract clause to include grants made by state legislatures as well as private contracts, the Chief Justice broadened immensely the scope of federal judicial power. "If," asked Marshall, "under a fair construction of the constitution, grants are comprehended under the term contracts, is a grant from the state excluded from the operation of the [constitutional] provision?'" He did not answer positively, but chose instead to place the burden of proof upon opponents of extension of the constitutional prohibition to state grants. Thus he answered the previous question with another question: in effect, since the contract clause is a general prohibition, how can one imply that the framers intended to except violations of the prohibition by a state? On the basis of this reasoning, the Georgia rescinding law was held to be an impairment of the obligation of a contract, in this instance an executed grant, and as such was declared, in "the unanimous opinion of the court," null and void as a violation of "the general principles which are common to our free institutions," or of the "provisions of the constitution of the United States."

It is of some significance that Marshall's interpretation of the contract clause had been made without reference to the intentions of the constitutional framers, and necessarily so. As Professor Benjamin F. Wright has pointed out, "If the broad interpretation of the contract clause enunciated by Chief Justice Marshall depended for its historical justification on the opinions expressed by the men who wrote and adopted the Constitution in 1787-1788, that justification would be indeed weak." The framers had, with only two exceptions, apparently accepted a narrow definition of contract, limiting the application of the constitutional prohibition to private contracts rather than grants made by a state.[53] Marshall's broad interpretation of the scope of the clause immeasurably enhanced federal judicial authority over the states and laid the foundation for subsequent decisions which seriously weakened the autonomy of the states in domestic economic matters.

52. A decision in *Terrett* v. *Taylor*, 9 Cranch 43 (1815), handed down by Justice Story, also was based in part upon natural law.

53. Wright, *The Contract Clause of the Constitution*, pp. 3-16. Hereinafter cited as *Contract Clause*.

The case of *New Jersey* v. *Wilson*[54] provides a good example. Here again the validity of a state rescinding law was the issue, this time involving an act of the New Jersey colonial legislature granting certain lands to the Delaware Indian tribe and stipulating that the land thus granted could neither be sold nor taxed. In 1801 the Indians had requested and obtained permission from New Jersey to sell the land. The new owners, non-Indians, claimed that the tax exemption was attached to the tract in perpetuity. Counsel for New Jersey argued with historical plausibility that the tax exemption was never distinct from Indian possession because the exemption had been granted to prevent seizure of the land for taxes. However, Marshall maintained that the privilege of tax exemption was annexed to the land, not to the Indians. According to Marshall, tax exemption was "annexed to the land, because in the event of a sale, on which alone the question could become material, the value would be enhanced by it." Here it might be noted again that a companion provision of that for tax exemption in the original act was one forbidding the leasing or selling of the Indian lands! In *New Jersey* v. *Wilson* as in *Fletcher* v. *Peck* and the subsequent *Dartmouth College* case, the primary interest of the majority of the Marshall Court appears to have been the protection of the rights of private property and, very probably, the establishment of a doctrine of vested rights. In expanding the Supreme Court's authority under the contract clause in the *New Jersey* case, Chief Justice Marshall did not face the serious problem created by his decision: whether a state legislature may permanently bargain away its virtually indispensable power to tax by entering into a contract.

The *Dartmouth College* case further expanded federal judicial power under the contract clause. And, in the opinion of an eminent student of the period, its doctrine determined the relation between government and economic life throughout most of the nineteenth century.[55] For if economic regulation of any kind was undertaken in this period it was by the states and not the nation. Consequently, the decision, which held that the charter of a private eleemosynary institution could not be impaired by a state, set up a serious impediment to state regulatory authority at a critical juncture in American economic development.

Before 1827 the Marshall Court sustained only one state legislative act which had been challenged as impairing the obligation of a contract.

54. 7 Cranch 164 (1812).

55. *Dartmouth College* v. *Woodward,* 4 Wheaton 518 (1819). See Wright, *Contract Clause,* p. 39.

The occasion was the decision in *Gozler* v. *Georgetown*.[56] Here the Court suggested the doctrine that a municipal corporation cannot "abridge its legislative power" by entering into a permanently binding contract, but it did not discuss this at any length. Doctrines such as those in the *Peck* and *Dartmouth* decisions had weakened immensely the ability of the states to regulate publicly-chartered corporations. By the time the issues involved in *Ogden* v. *Saunders*[57] were considered in 1827, a majority of the members of the court were becoming increasingly concerned with the need to maintain for the states some degree of control in regard to the regulation of contracts.

Justice Johnson pleaded for a construction of the contract clause which left the regulation of contracts largely to the wisdom of the state governments. In his words: "It is the motive, the policy, the object, that must characterize the legislative act, to affect it with the imputation of violating the obligation of contracts." Justice Bushrod Washington argued for resolution of doubts concerning the validity of state contract regulations in favor of the state legislatures. In so arguing he laid down for the first time the important presumption of validity doctrine: "It is but a decent respect due to the wisdom, the integrity, and the patriotism of the legislative body, by which any law is passed, to presume in favor of its validity, until its violation of the constitution is proved beyond all reasonable doubt." Although the *Ogden* decision was closely divided, it proved to be a turning point in terms of contract clause decisions. For in all the contract clause cases decided by the Marshall Court subsequent to 1827, the Court upheld every state act under consideration.[58]

Some years earlier, in *Sturgis* v. *Crowninshield*,[59] the Marshall Court had invalidated under the contract clause a New York bankruptcy law which had been applied to a contract made before the enactment of the law. *Ogden* v. *Saunders*, conversely, involved the question whether a state insolvency law (again one of New York) could regulate contracts made or entered into after the enactment of the law. By a narrow margin, the Court established the doctrine that the state

56. 6 Wheaton 593 (1821).

57. 12 Wheaton 213 (1827).

58. *Mason* v. *Haile*, 12 Wheaton 370 (1827); *Satterlee* v. *Matthewson*, 2 Peters 380 (1829); *Jackson* v. *Lamphire*, 3 Peters 288 (1830); *Providence Bank* v. *Billings*, 4 Peters 514 (1830); *Hawkins* v. *Barney's Lessee*, 5 Peters 457 (1831); *Lessee of Livingston* v. *Moore*, 7 Peters 469 (1833); *Watson* v. *Mercer*, 8 Peters 88 (1834); *Mumma* v. *Potomac Co.*, 8 Peters 281 (1834); and *Beers* v. *Haughton*, 9 Peters 329 (1835); cited in Wright, *Contract Clause*, pp. 52-53.

59. 4 Wheaton 122 (1819); the *Ogden* case also raised the question whether a state insolvency law could discharge a contract of a citizen of another state.

laws existing at the time contracts are made shall be considered a part of the obligation of such contracts. This doctrine strengthened the position of the states in regard to the regulation of contracts, for it enabled the state legislatures to enact general reservations governing subsequent corporate charters.

### CONCLUSION

With the exception of a decision involving federal admiralty jurisdiction,[60] the later contract and commerce clause decisions of the Marshall Court represent the only ones which appreciably enhanced state power or circumscribed federal authority. Only in these cases did the Marshall Court give any appreciable attention to the problem of maintaining the vigor of the states in the federal system. Although this resulted in part from the fact that many of the cases involving federal-state conflicts arose from situations in which the states resisted or interfered with federal authority, to a great extent the trend of decisions in the Marshall era reflected the nationalistic assumptions which had originally been associated with the Federalist Party. In sum, the Marshall Court's heaviest emphasis was upon the maintenance or extension of national authority, whether this was in the form of strong assertions of federal judicial authority to arbitrate in federal-state relations, impressive defense of congressional authority against state interference, or definitive broad constructionist interpretations of the contract or implied powers clauses.

60. *The Thomas Jefferson,* 10 Wheaton 428 (1825), in which Justice Story ruled that federal admiralty jurisdiction did not extend beyond the ebb and flow of the tide.

## CHAPTER IV

# *The Taney Court, 1836-1864*

FROM THE PERIOD when vindictive contemporaries such as Charles Summer and Horace Greeley castigated it to more recent times when, in a superficial treatment, Charles A. Beard repeated the charges of the early critics of the Taney Court, popular opinion had consistently accepted the stereotyped conception of the Taney tribunal as the "States'-Rights" Court. Included in this stereotype is the underlying assumption that constitutional safeguards and particularly the principle of national supremacy were seriously weakened or left to wither from disuse during the period beginning with the Jackson Presidency and ending with the Civil War.[1]

Undeniably, the most significant contribution of the Marshall Court was its role in firmly maintaining the supremacy of the national government. In fulfilling this role, the Marshall Court gave most of its attention to asserting federal authority in areas untouched by its predecessor and to defending federal authority against state attacks. Little attention was given to commensurate safeguarding of state authority because, at least for Marshall and the more nationally-inclined of his colleagues, the overriding federal problem of their period was the protection of a weak national government from state interference. This point of view finds support as late as 1835, the year of Marshall's death, in the writings of one of the keenest observers of American political and social development, Alexis de Tocqueville. He went so far as to intimate that the federal government was declining in authority, stating, ". . . so far is the federal government from acquiring strength, and from threatening the sovereignty of the states, as it grows older, that I maintain it to be growing weaker and weaker. . . ."[2]

1. See Charles and Mary Beard, *The Rise of American Civilization,* I, 689. Perhaps the fairest early appraisal was that by George W. Biddle, *Constitutional History of the United States as Seen in the Development of American Law,* Part III, 123-99 (1889); in recent times the judicial biography of Taney by Carl Brent Swisher is, of course, a significant contribution toward redressing the balance in historical interpretation.

2. Alexis de Tocqueville, *Democracy in America,* I, 438-50.

Actually, the federal government was not on the decline, for not only had the Marshall Court strongly asserted federal authority in such far-reaching decisions as that of the *McCulloch* case, but President Jackson had successfully met the threat of nullification with the threat of national force. And aside from these judicial and political victories, the tariff dispute of 1832 had established that the national Congress could, in effect, determine, by favoring one section over another, the economic future of the states in the American national economy.[3] History has shown that De Tocqueville's prediction concerning the strength of the federal government was inaccurate. For by 1836, the year of Chief Justice Taney's appointment, the federal government was not only secure, but growing in strength. While the primary problem of the Marshall Court had been to protect a rather weak national government from state interference, the major problem of the Taney Court was to attempt to maintain a balance between federal and state authorities. This the Taney Court clearly recognized.

The Taney Court policy in facing this paramount problem was twofold. Whenever state authorities threatened or interfered with legitimate federal powers, this Court, like its predecessor, was firm in its application of the constitutional principle of national supremacy. But whenever the absence of clear-cut interference with federal authority or constitutional limitations permitted it, this Court tended to sustain the freedom of state legislative authority. The second attitude was not based upon suspicion or distrust of federal authority on the part of the Taney justices,[4] but simply upon the concept, originating with the framers, that the states have vital roles to play in the operation of a truly federal system.

### FEDERAL SUPREMACY

Regarding the first of the two interpretative policies referred to above, the Taney Court ably demonstrated that in the face of serious states' rights threats to national authority, it would steadfastly enforce federal supremacy.

The most significant example is its decision in *Ableman* v. *Booth*.[5] For here a situation arose in which the judicial system of the state of Wisconsin defiantly obstructed the judicial processes of the federal courts and refused to honor a writ of error sent it by the Supreme Court

3. Woodrow Wilson, *Constitutional Government in the United States*, p. 175.

4. Justice Daniel is a possible exception.

5. 21 Howard 506 (1858); in two additional decisions, federal judicial authority was upheld in the face of crippling interpretations. See *Gordon* v. *Longest*, 16 Peters 97 (1842); *McNutt* v. *Bland*, 2 Howard 9 (1844).

of the United States. The state court actions reflected the bitter anti-slavery sentiment in Wisconsin. Booth, the editor of an abolitionist newspaper, had been tried and convicted in a federal court for violation of the Fugitive Slave Law of 1850. First, a Wisconsin judge and later the Supreme Court of the state issued writs of *habeas corpus* to free Booth. When the Supreme Court of the United States issued a writ of error, the Wisconsin Supreme Court ordered its clerk to disregard it. Finally, the Attorney General of the United States, in 1857, presented a copy of the record of the highest Wisconsin tribunal to the Supreme Court of the United States. This copy was entered on the court's docket and was acted upon as if it had been properly returned by the clerk of the Wisconsin court.

In delivering the opinion of the federal Supreme Court, Chief Justice Taney analyzed carefully the relationship of Article III and the supremacy clause, emphasizing the framers' intention to create a judicial arbiter in federal-state relations, and clearly recognizing that this arbiter, the Supreme Court, was given the dual responsibility of maintaining both the supremacy of the national government within its legitimate sphere and the vitality of the states as components of the federal system. The Wisconsin judicial attempts at circumventing or thwarting the processes of the federal judiciary were held invalid under Articles III and VI of the Constitution.

It is interesting to note that this forceful decision roused the Wisconsin legislature to the point where it adopted resolutions condemning the decision as "without authority, void, and of no force." In language reminiscent of the Virginia and Kentucky Resolutions of 1798-99, Wisconsin legislators protested that the states could determine the constitutionality of federal acts and interpose to prevent enforcement of those which were deemed not constitutionally valid.[6] The slavery issue tended to drive Northern states with large abolitionist populations toward interposition and even nullification, while forcing, in the period before Lincoln's election, the Southern states to take positions considered constitutionally orthodox.[7]

Without minimizing the importance of its strong defense of federal judicial authority in *Ableman* v. *Booth,* the Taney Court's reputation in respect to the assertion of federal supremacy rests solidly, not on one

6. Ames, "Slavery and the Union, 1845-1861," *Documents,* VI, 63-65.

7. The charge that Taney was forced to take states' rights or slavery in the *Ableman* case and deliberately chose slavery seems unfair on two important grounds. First, most of the other Taney Court decisions which upheld federal authority had nothing to do with slavery. Secondly, Swisher reveals that Taney was personally opposed to slavery. See Swisher, *Roger B. Taney,* pp. 92-98.

isolated decision, but on an imposing aggregate handed down throughout its historical period of almost three decades. Illustrating this point are its strong defenses of congressional authority over United States property and territory in *United States* v. *Gratiot, Wilcox* v. *Jackson,* and *United States* v. *Chicago;* its assertion of the national government's paramount and exclusive authority over external relations in *Holmes* v. *Jennison;* its similar holding in regard to fugitive slave legislation in *Prigg* v. *Pennsylvania;* its defense of federal judicial authority in *Gordon* v. *Longest* and *McNutt* v. *Bland;* and its defense of congressional commerce authority in *Sinnot* v. *Davenport.*

In the first of these important cases—*United States* v. *Gratiot*[8]—the constitutional issue was raised whether the President (as authorized by an act of Congress of March 3, 1807) had the power under Article IV, section 3, of the Constitution to reserve from sale lead mines owned by the United States, and to enter into a contract leasing the mines to private individuals for a percentage of the lead mined and smelted.

Article IV, section 3, of the Constitution provides that "Congress shall have power . . . to dispose of and make all needful rules and regulations respecting the territory or other property, belonging to the United States." Thomas Hart Benton, counsel for the defendant, interpreted this clause narrowly, claiming that the power granted to Congress was only the power to dispose of territory, not to lease or even hold it. Further, he maintained, "the power to make rules and regulations applies to the power to dispose of the lands," and the preparation of such lands for sale, not for "letting or leasing." Benton also asserted that the states would never have ceded their western lands if they had anticipated the establishment of a "tenantry to the United States upon them."[9] This narrow interpretation was rejected by the Court, the property clause being treated as an affirmative grant of authority to Congress, not as a virtual limitation.

Just as the Taney Court's *Gratiot* decision construed broadly Congress' authority over United States territory and property and defended it against interference by individuals who invoked states' rights arguments, so did its decisions in *Wilcox* v. *Jackson* and *United States* v. *Chicago*[10] sustain federal authority over such territory and property against interference by the states.

The *Wilcox* case raised the constitutional question whether a state

8. 14 Peters 526 (1840).

9. The Court evidently chose to decide the case in the light of Benton's argument, for the state had not actually asserted any such claim, and the case was really between private individuals and the national government, not between the latter and a state.

10. 13 Peters 498 (1839); 7 Howard 185 (1849).

legislature could establish legal remedies for its citizens which would, in effect, defeat the purposes of congressional legislation dealing with the regulation and disposal of United States territory. The *Chicago* case dealt with an attempt by the city of Chicago to open to public use streets on federal territory, in this instance a military reservation. In both cases the Taney Court applied the broad constructionist interpretation of Congress' power to regulate federal territory and property and held the state interferences invalid under the supremacy clause.

In all probability the Taney Court's decision in *Holmes* v. *Jennison*[11] would be ranked today as one of the definitive interpretations in the constitutional law of foreign relations if a relatively minor jurisdictional problem had not robbed it of its impact. For in an opinion notable both for its literary qualities as well as its forcefulness, Chief Justice Taney unequivocally asserted that the authority of the federal government in foreign relations was not only paramount, but exclusive. Consequently, state action in this area, even when taken in the absence of national governmental action, was deemed invalid. However, Taney's staunch opinion has survived in relative obscurity because it was not embodied in a majority opinion of the Supreme Court. This result was reached because the Supreme Court divided four to four on the question whether it had jurisdiction or not.[12]

The slavery issue plagued the Taney Court to an extent even greater than the Marshall Court. One particularly trying problem arose out of federal attempts to enforce the Fugitive Slave Law of 1793. This act provided for the arrest of a fugitive slave and his removal from the state where he was captured upon receipt by his captor of a certificate from a federal or state judge or magistrate. To obtain this certificate, the captor was required to show "satisfactory proof" that the person arrested was a fugitive slave. In a number of Northern states, state judges had, because of their anti-slavery sentiments, refused to issue such certificates. In 1842 the Taney Court considered a challenge to this law presented by a statute of the state of Pennsylvania and by a magistrate of that state who refused to issue the necessary certificate. In *Prigg* v. *Pennsylvania*[13] it considered the

11. 14 Peters 540 (1840).

12. Taney had been supported by Justices Story, McLean, and Wayne. Justice Catron accepted Taney's doctrine of the exclusiveness of federal authority in external affairs, but felt that Jennison's order authorizing the transferral of Holmes to Canada was not an agreement. Therefore, he voted against Taney on the jurisdictional question. Justices Thompson, Baldwin, and Barbour took the position that the existence of "dormant" federal power in external affairs did not prevent state activity in this field.

13. 16 Peters 539 (1842).

question whether the state actions were consistent with Article IV, section 3, of the Constitution. This clause provides that

> No person held to service or labor in one state under the laws thereof, escaping into another, shall in consequence of any law or regulation therein, be discharged from such service or labor; but shall be delivered up, on claim of the party to whom such service or labor may be due.

Justice Story, in rendering the majority opinion, interpreted this provision in a manner assuring "citizens of the slave holding states the complete right and title of ownership in their slaves, as property, in every state in the Union into which they might escape from the state where they were held in servitude." Slaveowners possessed a "positive unqualified right" which no state law or regulation could in "any way qualify, regulate, control or restrain." A slaveowner had "the authority in every state of the Union, to seize and recapture his slave; wherever he can do it without any breach of the peace, or illegal violence." The authority to legislate regarding fugitive slaves was exclusively a federal one, both by "the nature of the problem" and the "terms" of the Constitution. Thus, ruled Story, the states could neither interfere in the matter nor be compelled to take action to aid slave owners, and the Pennsylvania law was unconstitutional. Since Article IV, section 3, neither referred to Congress specifically nor expressly prohibited action by the states, the doctrine adopted by a majority of the Taney Court that federal authority regarding rendition of fugitive slaves was exclusive represented an unduly broad interpretation.

### EXPANSION OF FEDERAL AUTHORITY

In some areas, such as that of federal judicial enforcement of constitutional limitations on the states, the Taney Court was less aggressive than the Marshall Court in regard to the expansion of federal authority. Yet in at least four decisions, the Taney Court actually extended federal authority further than had its predecessor.[14] All of these enhanced federal judicial power. For many years the jurisdictional ruling of Justice Story in the *Thomas Jefferson*,[15] to the effect that federal admiralty jurisdiction was limited to the ebb and flow of the tide, had been a source of uncertainty and inconvenience in the federal courts. By an act of 1845, Congress extended federal district court jurisdiction to certain cases arising on the Great Lakes and the

14. They are: *The Genesee Chief* v. *Fitzhugh; Swift* v. *Tyson; Louisville, Cincinnati, and Charleston R.R.* v. *Letson*, and *Rhode Island* v. *Massachusetts;* see also the *Dobbins* case and *Searight* v. *Stokes*.

15. 10 Wheaton 428 (1825).

navigable waters joining them. This act was challenged as an unconstitutional enlargement of federal admiralty jurisdiction in *The Genesee Chief* v. *Fitzhugh.*[16]

Chief Justice Taney countered this argument with an entirely new doctrine. The decision in the *Thomas Jefferson* did not correctly reflect the thinking of the framers of the Constitution, he argued. Story had followed English judicial precedents which, according to Taney, were now inapplicable. The intentions of the framers had been accurately preserved in the provisions of the first great Judiciary Act of Congress, that of 1789. Section 9 of the act indicated that admiralty jurisdiction depended "upon the navigable character of the water, and not the ebb and flow of the tide." State equality provided another ground for Taney's new doctrine. As he put it,

> . . . it would be contrary to the first principles on which the Union was formed to confine these rights to courts of admiralty jurisdiction to the states bordering on the Atlantic, and to the tide-water rivers connected with it, and to deny them to the citizens who border on the lakes and the great navigable streams which flow through the western states.

In sum, the decision in the *Thomas Jefferson* was overruled and federal admiralty jurisdiction extended to all "public navigable waters."

Another Marshall Court decision, *United States* v. *Deveaux,*[17] had held that a corporation was not a citizen. As a consequence, a corporation could not sue or be sued in the federal courts under diverse citizenship jurisdiction unless "the rights of the members [of the corporation could] be exercised in their corporate name." The *Deveaux* doctrine was unanimously overruled by the Taney Court in *Louisville, Cincinnati and Charleston R.R.* v. *Letson.*[18] Under the new ruling a corporation was presumed to have the same standing as a citizen of the state by which it was chartered in diversity of citizenship suits in the federal courts. This doctrine opened the way for a substantial increase in corporation cases before the federal courts.

In both the *Genesee Chief* and *Letson* decisions, the Taney Court actually overruled Marshall Court decisions in order to enlarge federal judicial authority. In another decision, the Taney Court further enhanced federal judicial power not by overruling a narrow interpretation of federal authority by the Marshall Court, but by simply by-

16. 12 Howard 443 (1851); reaffirmed in *Fretz* v. *Bull,* 12 Howard 466 (1851); *Steamboat New World* v. *King,* 16 Howard 469 (1853); *Jackson* v. *The Steamboat Magnolia,* 20 Howard 296 (1857).

17. 5 Cranch 61 (1809).

18. 2 Howard 497 (1844).

passing an earlier construction of section 34 of the Judiciary Act of 1789. This section provided that in diversity of citizenship suits at common law the laws of the states shall be utilized as rules of decision by the federal courts. The Marshall Court had loosely intimated that the decisions of state courts could be considered "laws" within the meaning of this section. However, in writing the Taney Court's opinion in *Swift* v. *Tyson,*[19] Justice Story stated that "in the ordinary use of language, it will hardly be contended that the decisions of courts constitute laws." Furthermore, Story ruled that the provisions of section 34 of the Judiciary Act of 1789 do not apply to contracts and other instruments of a commercial nature. For these the true interpretation was to be sought in "the general principles and doctrines of commercial jurisprudence."

It might be assumed that Congress could create a general commercial law on the basis of its power over foreign and interstate commerce. But it had not done so in 1842. Consequently, Story's interpretation opened the way for the development of a general commercial law made solely by federal judges. Wherever this broad doctrine was applied (and its applicability was frequently uncertain), the judicial decisions of state courts on the subject under consideration were ignored or applied at the discretion of the federal justices or judges.[20]

In *Rhode Island* v. *Massachusetts,*[21] the question was raised whether assertion of the power to decide boundary disputes between two states under the grant of original jurisdiction in Article III of the Constitution was an assumption on the part of the Supreme Court of power to determine questions relating to the "political rights" of the states. This argument was rejected by the Taney Court on the ground that the framers had clearly intended that the Court deal with such issues. This assertion of jurisdictional authority, which was repeated four times in other cases involving boundary disputes between states,[22] may be viewed as daring and delicate in an era which heavily emphasized state pride and state "sovereignty."

The Marshall Court had utilized the supremacy clause to establish, in the *McCulloch* case, the doctrine that a state cannot tax an instrumentality of the federal government, a branch of the United States

19. Warren, *History,* II, 362; 16 Peters 1 (1842).

20. Warren, *History,* II, 89; see *Lane* v. *Vick,* 3 Howard 464 (1845); *Williamson* v. *Berry,* 8 Howard 495 (1850); *Pease* v. *Peck,* 18 Howard 595 (1855).

21. 12 Peters 657 (1838).

22. The second case of *Rhode Island* v. *Massachusetts,* 4 Howard 591 (1846); *Missouri* v. *Iowa,* 10 Howard 1 (1850); *Florida* v. *Georgia,* 17 Howard 478 (1854); *Alabama* v. *Georgia,* 23 Howard 505 (1859).

Bank. In *Dobbins* v. *Commissioners of Erie County*[23] the Taney Court extended this doctrine to nullify a state tax levied on the salary of an officer of the United States on the ground that a state tax on such an officer's salary "conflicts" with the congressional law fixing that salary.

This doctrine, extending to the salaries of federal officers immunity from non-discriminatory state taxation, in effect, closed to the states one potentially rich source of tax revenue. And in addition it brought about a situation where persons like Dobbins, who were residents and citizens of the county and state, could enjoy the protection and benefits provided by the county or state governments without assuming a share of "the public burden" equal to those of county and state citizens who were not officers of the United States.

The question whether Congress possessed power under the Constitution to make "internal improvements" had been a controversial one for many years when in 1845 the Taney Court rendered a decision touching indirectly upon the subject. Some time after the construction of the famous Cumberland Road, Congress had turned its upkeep, use and toll collection over to the states through which it passed, reserving by compact certain rights and immunities. Although it did not pass on the vital question whether congressional construction of the road was constitutional, the Taney Court indirectly gave its blessing to this congressional action by applying, in *Searight* v. *Stokes*,[24] the compact between Pennsylvania and the United States which concerned the road.

By the terms of the agreement between Pennsylvania and the United States, the state had been given toll collection privileges on the Cumberland Road in return for the road's upkeep and a guarantee of toll-free passage on the road to all federal mail carriages. In the *Searight* decision, a Pennsylvania tax on vehicles carrying United States mail on the Cumberland Road was held invalid as a violation of this compact.

### BALANCING FEDERAL-STATE AUTHORITY

The foregoing series of decisions represented either defenses or expansions of national authority. In contrast, there were a number of Taney Court decisions in which federal power was not construed broadly. The unifying concept governing the Taney Court in the rendition of the latter cases was an overriding sense of the need to

23. 16 Peters 435 (1842); the Marshall Court's *Weston* v. *Charleston* doctrine was applied in *Bank of Commerce* v. *Commissioners of Taxes and Assessments*, 2 Black 620 (1863).

24. 3 Howard 151 (1845); *Neil, Moore and Company* v. *Ohio*, 3 Howard 720 (1845).

maintain an equilibrium in federal-state relations. The Marshall Court had, of course, given attention to this need in *dicta* in the *McCulloch* and *Gibbons* cases and in decisions such as that of the *Blackbird Creek* case. However, the dominant theme in the Marshall Court period had been the strong defense of federal authority and, in certain areas such as that of the earlier contract clause cases, aggressive expansion of federal authority, usually judicial.

In attempting to maintain a balance between federal and state authority, the Taney Court refrained from holding Congress' power to punish counterfeiting an exclusive one. As had the Marshall Court, it balked at interpreting the commerce clause as a grant of exclusive authority to Congress. It refused to adopt a rule of construction which would have placed submerged lands in navigable rivers within the states in the possession of the national government.[25] In addition, the Taney Court's enforcement of the constitutional prohibitions on the states was less rigorous than that of its predecessor, permitting greater freedom on the part of the state legislatures in the area of economic and social regulation.

### COINAGE AND COUNTERFEITING

Article I, sections 5 and 6, provides, in part, that "The Congress shall have power . . . to coin money, regulate the value thereof, and of foreign coin . . . to provide for the punishment of counterfeiting the securities and current coin of the United States." Congress had, in an act of 1825, made the passing of counterfeit coin a federal offense. In *Fox* v. *Ohio*[26] the validity of an Ohio statute making it a misdemeanor to "utter" or pass counterfeit coin was challenged on the ground that Congress' authority was exclusive. In the majority opinion, Justice Daniel distinguished between the coining and passing of counterfeit money, intimating in one section of his discussion that the punishment of the passing of counterfeit coins in the states was actually outside congressional authority since Congress' power in Article I, sections 5 and 6, was limited to that of "coining and of stamping the standard of value upon what the government creates or shall adopt, and of punishing the offense of producing a false representation. . . ." Elsewhere, however, he conceded that Congress "could rightfully undertake" to punish the passing of counterfeit coin by citizens of a state.

Perhaps because of Daniel's ambiguity in the *Fox* case, Congress'

25. *Pollard's Lessee* v. *Hagan*, 3 Howard 212 (1845).
26. 5 Howard 410 (1847).

authority to punish persons bringing counterfeit coin into the country was challenged a few years later on the ground that the states have exclusive jurisdiction over the control and punishment of passers of counterfeit coin. In *United States* v. *Marigold*,[27] Justice Daniel rejected this argument, maintaining that the power to punish persons introducing counterfeit coin could be traced to the congressional power to coin money "and to the correspondent and necessary power and obligation to protect and preserve in its purity this constitutional currency for the benefit of the nation." The *Fox* and *Marigold* cases provide a good example of the Taney Court's propensity to protect the reserved powers of the state governments without weakening federal authority.

*Commerce Clause*

The Taney Court's early commerce clause decisions, on the other hand, contained a doctrine which not only protected the states in their exercise of reserved powers, but also, by implication, weakened the cardinal principle of federal supremacy. The important case of *City of New York* v. *Miln*[28] embodied its first clear statement.

In this case the Supreme Court seemed to be faced squarely with the issue whether Congress' interstate and foreign commerce powers were exclusive. John Marshall had hinted at, but had not sought to establish, a doctrine of exclusive federal power in the *Steamboat* case. But in *Wilson* v. *Blackbird Creek Marsh Company*[29] he had clearly implied that there was an area of "police power" control in which the states could regulate interstate and foreign commerce.

Some years after the *Miln* decision was handed down, it was disclosed that Justice Thompson had originally been assigned the writing of the opinion, but that upon his completion of the task, a majority of the court was unwilling to accept his commerce power interpretation.[30] Consequently, Justice Barbour was chosen to write a majority opinion which would uphold the New York foreign passenger law solely on the ground that it was a police power regulation within the reserved powers of the state. *Dicta* in Barbour's opinion indicate that he apparently was willing to uphold the New York law as a regulation of the "purely internal commerce of the state." But in order to please all

27. 9 Howard 560 (1850).

28. 11 Peters 102 (1837).

29. *Gibbons* v. *Ogden*, 9 Wheaton 1 (1824); 2 Peters 245 (1829); cf. Felix Frankfurter, *The Commerce Clause under Marshall, Taney, and Waite*, pp. 14-29.

30. See the *License Cases*, 5 Howard 504 (1847); Swisher, *Roger B. Taney*, pp. 394-96.

members of the majority he carefully avoided the question of the exclusiveness of Congress' commerce power, thus enabling the Taney Court temporarily to sidestep that highly controversial issue.

The majority opinion, which was based upon state police power considerations, is a significant illustration of the Taney Court's refusal to consider the existence of any "dormant" federal power as a bar to state action in a field unless, as in the matter of foreign relations, constitutional restrictions or the "nature of the power" demanded such an interpretation. Such refusal did not in itself involve any inconsistency on the part of the Taney Court with its steadfast application of the principle of federal supremacy. And, as a matter of fact, when the Taney Court was faced with a clear-cut conflict between a valid congressional commerce enactment and a state law a few years later in *Sinnot* v. *Davenport*,[31] it unhesitatingly held the state law unconstitutional, stating that

> . . . where an act of the legislature of a state prescribes a regulation of the subject repugnant to and inconsistent with the regulation of Congress, the state law must give way; and this, without regard to the source of power whence the state legislature derived its enactment.

Justice Barbour's opinion in the *Miln* case, however, did incorporate a doctrine which was inconsistent with the supremacy clause. Barbour had defined the police power of the states in the following manner:

> . . . a state has the same undeniable and unlimited jurisdiction over all persons and things, within its territorial limits, as any foreign nation, where that jurisdiction is not surrendered or restrained by the Constitution of the United States. . . . by virtue of this, it is not only the right, but the bounden and solemn duty of a state, to advance the safety, happiness and prosperity of its people, and to provide for its general welfare, by any and every act of legislation, which it may deem to be conducive to these ends; where the power over the particular subject, or the manner of its exercise is not surrendered or restrained, in the manner just stated . . . all those powers which relate to merely municipal legislation, or what may, perhaps, more properly be called internal police, are not thus surrendered or restrained; and . . . consequently, *in relation to these, the authority of a state is complete, unqualified and exclusive.*

Viewed in the context of the times, Barbour's reference to state police powers as "exclusive" was probably intended to be defensive of state powers rather than restrictive of those of the federal government. At no time during the entire Taney Court period had the federal gov-

31. 22 Howard 227 (1959).

ernment attempted to exercise its commerce power in areas previously left to state police power control. But attempts had been made to persuade the Supreme Court to interpret the commerce clause in a manner restrictive of state authority. In any case, the idea that the "police powers" of the states were exclusive cannot be reconciled with the principle of federal supremacy. For the existence of an irreducible block of state police powers limiting the expansion of otherwise constitutional federal powers via the necessary and proper clause is inconsistent with that principle. Moreover, Barbour's doctrine was predicated upon an essentially static concept of the American federal system. Consequently, it ignored both the spirit and hopes of the constitutional framers, which embraced a dynamic concept, and the physical and social factors which inexorably made for change.

The Taney Court never had the occasion to apply the doctrine of the exclusiveness of state police power so as to limit federal power,[32] but Barbour's statement of it harbingered the development of the restrictive doctrine of "dual federalism."

*United States* v. *Coombs*[33] presented an opportunity for utilization of Barbour's doctrine to nullify a federal law, but the Taney Court actually employed Marshall's *Ogden* doctrine that the commerce power does not stop at state boundaries. At issue in this case was the constitutionality of a congressional law punishing the pilfering of shipwrecked vessels whether above or below the high water mark. The Taney Court construed Congress' commerce power broadly, holding that it extends to acts "done on land which interfere with, obstruct, or prevent the due exercise of" it.

The question whether the states could regulate interstate and foreign commerce in the absence of congressional law was not decided by the Taney Court majority in the *Miln* case and continued to plague the justices for nearly two decades. In the *License Cases*[34] the Taney Court sustained three state prohibition laws, but the Court's members were sharply divided in their reasons for the decision. Chaos in the interpretation of the commerce clause was further compounded in the *Passenger Cases*.[35] Here, by a five to four decision, the Court declared unconstitutional statutes of New York and Massachusetts taxing alien

32. The doctrine was referred to by some court members in *dicta* in later decisions; see Daniel's characterization of the American federal system as one of "confederated sovereignties," 5 Howard 615; Chief Justice Taney also referred to "the domestic commerce . . . over which Congress can exercise no control. . . ," 5 Howard 575.

33. 12 Peters 72 (1838).

34. 5 Howard 504 (1847).

35. 7 Howard 283 (1849).

passengers arriving in the ports of those states. So diverse was the reasoning of the justices in reaching this conclusion that the Court's reporter was unable to cull out an opinion shared in common by the majority. Justice McLean viewed the laws as unconstitutional regulations of foreign commerce by the states, and reiterated his position on the exclusiveness of federal commerce authority. Justices Wayne, Catron, McKinley, and Grier came to the same conclusion regarding the constitutionality of the state laws, but refrained from applying a doctrine of the exclusiveness of congressional commerce authority. Chief Justice Taney and Justices Nelson, Woodbury, and Daniel dissented. Taney relied heavily on the *Miln* decision in which Justice Barbour had ruled that persons were not subjects of commerce. State police power and state authority to regulate immigration provided the essential bases for each dissent, although Daniel and Woodbury also wrote separate opinions heavy in emphasis on state sovereignty. Woodbury's opinion is particularly interesting for its statement of the doctrine of "selection exclusiveness" later adopted by the Court in 1852. Justice Nelson simply concurred in the opinion of Chief Justice Taney.

The outcome of the *Miln, License,* and *Passenger* cases made it quite evident that the two most extreme doctrines of commerce clause interpretation were unacceptable to a majority of the Taney Court. In the next major commerce clause case, *Cooley* v. *Board of Port Wardens,*[36] only McLean and Wayne united in claiming that the commerce power was wholly exclusive. Conversely, only Daniel supported a doctrine of "exclusive" state police powers and a definition of congressional commerce power so narrow as to limit it to commercial contracts, "traffic," and "the permission to trade in any subject."

A doctrine acceptable to a majority of the Taney Court which avoided both extremes was handed down by Justice Curtis. The central issue in the *Cooley* case was the question whether the states under any circumstances could regulate interstate or foreign commerce. In particular the validity of a Pennsylvania river pilotage law was considered. Curtis based the majority opinion on three arguments. First, the Constitution did not indicate that Congress' power was exclusive or expressly prohibited state action. Second, the first Congress, many members of which had participated in the framing of the Constitution, had by the act of August 7, 1789, indicated that it did not view the power as an exclusive one. And third, the power did not by its very nature demand exclusive congressional control. Elaborating on this third assumption, Curtis upheld the state law and laid

36. 12 Howard 299 (1851).

down the far-reaching interpretative ruling that where the subjects of regulation demand diversity, state regulation would be permitted in the absence of congressional action, but where the subjects were national or needed uniform treatment, Congress' authority could be considered exclusive.

The *Cooley* doctrine not only successfully permitted freedom of state action in matters unregulated by Congress and susceptible to local control, but also successfully avoided the recognition of any implied limitations on federal commerce power. Consequently, it safeguarded the vitality of the states without weakening either the commerce power of Congress or the cardinal principle of federal supremacy. In addition, it actually enhanced federal judicial power, for it was the Supreme Court itself that ultimately decided whether a matter needed national or local regulation.

Justice Barbour's *Miln* doctrine concerning the "complete, unqualified and exclusive" police powers of the state has, of course, had its influence upon subsequent doctrinal developments. However, in most of the commerce clause cases decided by the Taney Court after the *Cooley* case, the doctrine of "selective exclusiveness" was applied although its application was not always noted in the opinions.[37] During this period, the *Cooley* doctrine was determinative in the constitutional law of the commerce clause. Significantly, Chief Justice Taney and Justices Catron, McKinley, Nelson, and Grier gave their unqualified support to Justice Curtis' statement of that doctrine. A balanced appraisal of the Taney Court's commerce clause determinations must rank the *Cooley* case as its final product, doctrinally speaking.

### CONSTITUTIONAL LIMITATIONS ON THE STATES

An outstanding characteristic of the Marshall Court had been its broad interpretation of the constitutional limitations on the states. By way of contrast, the Taney Court was less rigorous in the enforcement of such limitations. But, interestingly enough, it accomplished this reversal of judicial policy without actually overruling the Marshall Court's broad interpretations of the limitations on state power.

#### *Bills of Credit*

Article I, section 10, provides that "no state shall . . . emit bills of credit. . . ." In *Craig* v. *Missouri*,[38] the Marshall Court had held that

37. Cf. Benjamin F. Wright, *The Growth of American Constitutional Law*, pp. 72-73; see *Veazie* v. *Moore*, 14 Howard 568 (1852); *Smith* v. *Maryland*, 18 Howard 71 (1855); *Withers* v. *Buckley*, 20 Howard 84 (1857).

38. 4 Peters 410 (1830).

certificates issued by loan offices established and operated by the state of Missouri, and made receivable as tax payments to the state or salary payments to state employees, were bills of credit prohibited by that constitutional provision. The Taney Court was asked to apply the same constitutional limitation to notes issued by a public corporation of the state of Kentucky in *Briscoe* v. *The Bank of Kentucky*.[39] A majority of the Court, over the vigorous dissent of Justice Story, upheld the action of the Kentucky corporation by making a careful distinction between state agencies and public corporations. The decision in this case, in effect, enabled the states to take steps to insure the stability of their economies through the establishment of state banks empowered to issue notes. State power to determine its domestic economic policies was thereby preserved without abandonment by the Taney Court of the constitutional prohibition.

*Contract Clause*

The Taney Court did not directly repudiate the Marshall Court's tradition of broad construction of the contract clause limitation. In fact, examples are not lacking to show that in some instances the Taney Court actually outdid its predecessor in enforcement of the prohibition. *Bronson* v. *Kinzie* and *Gelpcke* v. *Dubuque* fall into this category. Nevertheless, there was sufficient modification in cases such as *Christ Church Hospital* v. *County of Philadelphia, Phalen* v. *Virginia,* and the *Charles River Bridge* case to warrant the judgment that the state legislatures enjoyed greater freedom from federal judicial restraint under the Taney Court than they had under its predecessor. New doctrines, such as those laid down in *West River Bridge* v. *Dix, Butler* v. *Pennsylvania,* and *East Hartford* v. *Hartford Bridge Company,* serve to substantiate this view.

The three broadest interpretations of the contract clause prohibition by the Marshall Court were applied without change by the Taney Court. The doctrines of *Fletcher* v. *Peck,* the *Dartmouth College* case, and *New Jersey* v. *Wilson*[40] were as firmly entrenched in American constitutional law at the end as at the beginning of the Taney Court period. Actually only the third of these doctrines was directly challenged by a minority of the Taney Court.[41] In a number of cases in-

39. 11 Peters 257 (1837). The *Briscoe* doctrine was applied by the Taney Court in *Woodruff* v. *Trapnell,* 10 Howard 190 (1850); *Darrington* v. *Bank of Alabama,* 13 Howard 12 (1851); *Curran* v. *Arkansas,* 15 Howard 304 (1853).

40. 6 Cranch 87 (1810); 4 Wheaton 518 (1819); 7 Cranch 164 (1812).

41. Woodbury did refuse to accept the *Dartmouth* doctrine in a concurring opinion in the *Dix* case; 6 Howard 507 (1848).

volving applications of the *Fletcher* and *Dartmouth* doctrines, there were sharp dissents. However, the dissenters did not challenge the Marshall doctrines, but rather disapproved of the construction given the charters under consideration.[42] The situation was quite different in *Piqua Branch Bank* v. *Knoop*.[43] Here the Taney Court was called upon to answer whether a state could bargain away its vital taxing power by granting permanent tax exemptions and, like the Marshall Court in the case of *New Jersey* v. *Wilson*, answered affirmatively. In writing the majority opinion Justice McLean held that granting tax exemptions did not barter away the sovereign power of a state, but rather represented an "essential" exercise of such power. Justice Catron, dissenting, countered with the argument that:

> . . . according to the Constitution of all the states of the Union . . . the sovereign political power is not the subject of contract so as to be vested in an unrepealable charter of incorporation, and taken away from and placed beyond the reach of future legislatures. . . . the taxing power is a political power of the highest class, and each successive legislature having vested in it, unimpaired, all the political powers previous legislatures had, is authorized to impose taxes on all property in the state that its constitution does not exempt.

In subsequent cases involving tax exemption contracts the majority view prevailed,[44] although by the following year Catron gained the support of Justice Daniel.[45] By the logic of the majority position in these decisions, the Supreme Court would insist upon the fulfillment of contract obligations even if the contract involved the bargaining away of a power indispensable to the existence of a state. It would appear that the Taney Court's doctrinal approach in regard to tax exemption contracts was inconsistent with its general policy of preserving the vitality of the states within the constitutional framework of the federal system.

However, its rigorous enforcement of tax exemption contracts was actually softened by two modifying doctrines. In two decisions involving such contracts, the Taney Court avoided applying the *Knoop* doctrine by utilizing the *Charles River Bridge* rule of construction.

42. *Planter's Bank of Mississippi* v. *Sharp*, 6 Howard 301 (1848); *Woodruff* v. *Trapnell*, 10 Howard 190 (1850); *Curran* v. *Arkansas*, 15 Howard 304 (1853).

43. 16 Howard 369 (1853).

44. See *Ohio Insurance Company* v. *Debolt*, 16 Howard 416 (1853); *Dodge* v. *Woolsey*, 18 Howard 331 (1855); *Mechanics' and Traders' Bank* v. *Debolt*, 18 Howard 380 (1856); *Jefferson Branch Bank* v. *Skelly*, 1 Black 436 (1862); *Wright* v. *Sill*, 2 Black 544 (1862).

45. *Ohio Insurance Company* v. *Debolt*, 16 Howard 416 (1853).

Ambiguity in a tax exemption contract was resolved in favor of the state or public interest in each case.[46] But this policy was not consistently adhered to by the Taney Court, for in *Gordon* v. *Appeal Tax Court*,[47] it decided a doubtful tax exemption contract question against the public interest.

The most important qualification of the *Knoop* doctrine by the Taney Court was the doctrine stated by Justice Campbell in his opinion in *Christ Church Hospital* v. *County of Philadelphia*.[48] Under this doctrine, a state legislative tax exemption granted as a favor rather than for some consideration could be repealed at the pleasure of the legislature without violating the contract clause. To this extent at least, the state legislatures were permitted greater freedom of action in dealing with tax exemptions granted by their predecessors.

The *Bronson* and *Gelpcke* cases stand out as instances where the Taney Court out-Marshalled the Marshall Court in rigorous enforcement of the contract clause. In *Bronson* v. *Kinzie*[49] the Supreme Court for the first time applied the contract clause to disallow a state law in a case involving a private rather than a public contract. In the case of *Sturges* v. *Crowninshield*[50] the Marshall Court had established the doctrine that the remedy of a contract might be modified if the contract itself was not impaired. This doctrine was utilized by the Taney Court in the *Bronson* case to nullify an Illinois law which prevented extinguishment of the equitable estate of a mortgagor for twelve months after a sale under a decree in chancery, and permitted redemption by him upon payment of ten percent of the value of the property. Chief Justice Taney held that such modification of the remedy of a contract impaired the obligation of the contract by so altering the conditions for sale as to damage the interests of the mortgagee. The existence of a severe economic depression, which had precipitated adoption of the "stay" law by the Illinois legislature, evidently did not play a part in Taney's determination.

The second decision referred to above, *Gelpcke* v. *Dubuque*,[51] was a diverse citizenship case involving a contract violation not by state law, but by a state judicial decision. The Taney Court majority admitted

46. *Armstrong* v. *Athens County*, 16 Peters 281 (1842); *Philadelphia and Wilmington Railroad Company* v. *Maryland*, 10 Howard 376 (1850).

47. 3 Howard 133 (1845).

48. 24 Howard 300 (1860).

49. 1 Howard 311 (1843); reaffirmed in *McCracken* v. *Haywood*, 2 Howard 608 (1844), and *Howard* v. *Bugbee*, 24 Howard 461 (1860).

50. 4 Wheaton 122 (1819).

51. 1 Wallace 175 (1863); reaffirmed in *Meyer* v. *Muscatine*, 1 Wallace 384 (1863).

that "in cases involving the construction of a State law or Constitution, this court is bound to follow the latest adjudication of the highest court of the state." However, "there have been . . . many exceptional cases." Here contracts entered into under earlier decisions of the Iowa courts would be impaired if a later decision of the Iowa Supreme Court was applied. On this ground the latest Iowa judicial decision was held void. And further, this was done in the face of Story's statement in *Swift* v. *Tyson*[52] that "in the ordinary use of language, it will hardly be contended that the decisions of courts constitute laws." Secondly, the *Gelpcke* decision represents the assumption by the Supreme Court, under Article XXXIV of the Judiciary Act of 1789, of the power to determine state law rather than simply to apply state law impartially between litigants in diverse citizenship cases.[53] Charles Warren's researches have shown that the drafters of the Judiciary Act of 1789 had intended to give the inferior federal courts jurisdiction in diverse citizenship cases only for the latter purpose where no federal question was raised. The *Gelpcke* decision seriously infringed state judicial independence in cases falling within the diverse citizenship jurisdiction of the federal courts which involved contracts but did not involve bona fide contract clause issues.

In sharp contrast to the *Bronson* and *Gelpcke* decisions was the Taney Court's decision in *Charles River Bridge* v. *Warren Bridge*.[54] The case concerned the question whether state legislative incorporation of a new bridge company to build what eventually would become a toll-free bridge in close proximity to a toll bridge previously incorporated (and renewed) by the state violated the contract clause.

Counsel for the oldest bridge company contended that the earlier legislative grants had bestowed an exclusive privilege upon that company. They admitted that this was not explicitly spelled out in the grants, but was an implication which necessarily followed from the nature of the grants. They argued that charters, such as the present one, which are ambiguous must be construed liberally by the courts in favor of the corporate investors. This rule of construction was based, according to counsel, upon the need for maintaining confidence among corporate investors. To decide otherwise, it was suggested, would create fear in business circles and cause general economic stagnation. These arguments comprised the essence of Justice Story's long dissent.

52. 16 Peters 1 (1842).

53. See Westel W. Willoughby's account of the major criticisms of this decision, *The Constitutional Law of the United States*, II, 1249. Hereinafter cited as *Constitutional Law*.

54. 11 Peters 420 (1837).

Chief Justice Taney was unimpressed by the dire predictions of economic atrophy. The absence of a large body of American judicial precedents provided him the rare opportunity for the utilization of what Benjamin Cardozo was wont to call the "method of sociology" in judicial decision-making. The question whether the rule of construction should be strict or liberal in regard to interpretation of corporate charters involved primarily a question of public policy. And just as the defenders of the economic interests of the bridge incorporators urged one course of action because of the alleged economic dangers inherent in its rejection, so did Taney follow his own conception of public policy. Among the fruits of a doctrine of implied contracts, predicted Taney, would be an awakening of the old turnpike corporations, "... calling upon this court to put down the improvements which have taken their place." The "millions of property which have been invested in railroads and canals, upon lines of travel which had before been occupied by turnpike corporations, will be put in jeopardy." And "we shall be thrown back to the improvements of the last century and obliged to stand still, until the claims of the old turnpike corporations shall be satisfied. . . ."

The problem, Taney recognized, was one requiring a balancing of private rights and the interest of the community. Taney's statement that "while the rights of private property are sacredly guarded, we must not forget that the community also have rights, and that the happiness and well-being of every citizen depends on their faithful preservation" indicated the cast of his political thought. Pointing out that the Massachusetts act of incorporation contained no grant of exclusive privilege over the waters of the Charles River, he upheld the new charter under the doctrine that "in grants by the public, nothing passes by implication." This doctrine had, of course, been stated and applied by the Marshall Court on four occasions.[55] Nevertheless, in one of these, the *Providence Bank* case, the Marshall Court had also stated that any power of the state "which may, in effect, destroy [a] charter, is inconsistent with it, and is impliedly renounced by granting it. Such a power cannot be exercised without impairing the obligation of the contract." The Marshall Court almost certainly would have applied this latter doctrine and not the doctrine of strict construction of contracts in the *Charles River Bridge* case.[56]

55. *Jackson* v. *Lamphire,* 3 Peters 289 (1830); *Beaty* v. *The Lessee of Knowles,* 4 Peters 152 (1830); *Providence Bank* v. *Billings,* 4 Peters 514 (1830); *United States* v. *Arredondo,* 6 Peters 691 (1832).

56. Justice Story, in a dissent concurred in by Justice Thompson, took this position; 11 Peters 583-650.

The Taney Court's *Charles River Bridge* decision ranks as its most important modification of Marshall Court judicial policy. As a result, the state legislatures enjoyed a correspondingly broader area of freedom in dealing with social and economic problems. Professor Wright takes the position that the influence of the *Charles River Bridge* case "was not felt until after Taney's death."[57] Yet, in addition to the widespread publicity given this doctrine soon after its first application in 1837, it was applied in seven contract clause decisions handed down by the Taney Court.[58]

Further limitation of the contract clause as a restraint on state regulatory activity was effectuated by Justice Woodbury in *East Hartford* v. *Hartford Bridge Company*[59] in which he held, for the Court, that political subdivisions of a state could not challenge the legislative revocation of a privilege as a contract violation.

A doctrine protecting the states in the control of their public servants was laid down in *Butler* v. *Pennsylvania*.[60] It was argued that an appointment to public office under conditions set down by a state legislature was a contract entered into by a state. It was further contended that a change of salary during the term of office by legislative enactment was a contract violation, and, therefore, was null and void. On the ground that such a doctrine would be destructive of the freedom and efficiency of state administration, Justice Daniel ruled that appointment to public office bestowed no contractual or property right to such office.

In *West River Bridge* v. *Dix*[61] the Supreme Court was called upon to determine for the first time the validity of a state exercise of the power of eminent domain in the face of the contention that such exercise violated the contract clause. Despite the fact that the Fifth Amendment recognizes that the power of eminent domain is vested in the national government, counsel for the company, Daniel Webster, argued that the power was a "foreign" engraftment on American law

57. Wright, *Contract Clause*, p. 63.

58. In addition to the *Charles River Bridge* case itself, the doctrine was applied in *Armstrong* v. *Athens County*, 16 Peters 281 (1842); *Mills* v. *St. Clair County*, 8 Howard 569 (1850); *Philadelphia and Wilmington Railroad Company* v. *Maryland*, 10 Howard 376 (1850); *Richmond, Fredericksburg and Potomac Railroad Company* v. *Louisa Railroad Company*, 13 Howard 71 (1851); *Fanning* v. *Georgoire*, 16 Howard 524 (1853); *Bridge Proprietors* v. *Hoboken Company*, 1 Wallace 116 (1864). In *Baltimore and Susquehanna Railroad Company* v. *Nesbit*, 10 Howard 395 (1850), the Taney Court applied the doctrine that where a company failed to fulfill its charter, no contract existed.

59. 10 Howard 511 (1850); see *Maryland* v. *Baltimore and Ohio Railroad Company*, 3 Howard 534 (1845).

60. 10 Howard 402 (1850).

61. 6 Howard 507 (1848).

unknown to the framers of the Constitution. Significantly, however, Justice McLean, who with Story had remained close to the Marshall tradition in judicial interpretation, wrote the majority opinion sustaining the state's authority. In so doing he held, in effect, that a state cannot bargain away its power of eminent domain.

The doctrine of the inalienability of the power of eminent domain established in the *Dix* case is one of the most important contributions in federal-state relations of the Taney Court. It protected completely the power of the states to facilitate internal improvements through the taking of land or property upon payment of just compensation. And not only was this vital power shielded from contract clause interference, but in a subsequent decision, the Taney Court, with characteristic self-restraint, refused to assume the role of federal judicial supervisor of state highways in order to determine whether the power had been abused. One of the issues in *Mills* v. *St. Clair County*[62] involved a charge that in exercising the acknowledged state power of eminent domain, state road commissions had "grossly abused" their power by taking too much land for a proposed road. The Taney Court ruled, significantly, that

> To the width of needful roads and ferry landings, property can undoubtedly be taken, for the purpose of such easements, and necessarily, the state authorities must decide (as a general rule) how much land the public convenience requires. That the power may be abused, no one can deny. . . . It rests with the state legislature and state courts to protect their citizens from injustice and oppression of this description. . . .

In *dicta* in the case of *Phalen* v. *Virginia*[63] the Taney Court hinted very strongly at the doctrine that a state cannot bargain away its police power, thus paving the way for the important decision of *Stone* v. *Mississippi*.[64]

The *Phalen* case is, of course, important largely because of its influence upon future doctrinal developments. However, it does belong with the large number of Taney Court contract clause decisions in which the constitutional prohibition was construed narrowly. That the Taney Court's policy of avoiding rigorous enforcement of the limitation was not aimed at destroying property rights or corporate stability was amply illustrated by its *Bronson, Knoop,* and *Gelpcke* decisions. Basically the Taney Court's purpose was to interpret the clause so as to preserve to the states the full measure of their legislative control over

62. 8 Howard 569 (1850).
63. 8 Howard 163 (1850).
64. 101 U.S. 814 (1880).

internal social and economic problems without condoning clear-cut contract violations.

## THE RELATIONS OF THE STATES TO EACH OTHER

### *Full Faith and Credit Clause*

Among the provisions of the Constitution designed to govern, to some extent, the relations of the states to each other, Article IV, section 4, states, in part, that "Full faith and credit shall be given in each state to the public acts, records, and judicial proceedings of every other state. . . ." The Marshall Court, in *Hampton* v. *McConnell,*[65] held that under this provision

> the judgment of a state court shall have the same credit, validity and effect, in every other court in the United States, which it had in the state where it was pronounced, and whatever pleas would be good in a suit thereon in such state, and none others, could be pleaded in any other court in the United States.

However, in 1839 the Taney Court refrained from applying this doctrine in *McElmoyle* v. *Cohen.*[66] Instead it held that the clause did not "materially . . . interfere with the essential attributes of the *lex fori.*" In other words, the full faith and credit clause did not materially alter the doctrine of private international law that the courts of one country will recognize and apply the laws and judicial decisions of another country, except where they conflict with local policy or doctrine. This decision left to the states, subject, of course, to Congress' overriding power to regulate the manner of proving the authenticity and the effect of the acts or proceedings of one state in another, the power to refuse to give full faith and credit to the laws or judicial decisions of other states which were inconsistent with local policy.

### *Privileges of State Citizenship*

A question which had tremendous implications for the future of corporate enterprise in America and for the power of the states to control their internal economies was raised in *The Bank of Augusta* v. *Earle.*[67] Justice McKinley had decided, while holding circuit court in the southern district of Alabama, that a bank incorporated under the laws of Georgia could not lawfully purchase bills of exchange in Alabama. Later, Chief Justice Taney, writing for a majority of the Court, reversed this decision, holding that while corporations could not claim the right to operate in other states under the privileges and

65. 3 Wheaton 234 (1818).
66. 13 Peters 312 (1839).
67. 13 Peters 519 (1839).

immunities of state citizenship possessed by the individuals owning its stock, each state could permit or prohibit the entry of foreign corporations as it chose. In the event that a state remained silent on this point it would be assumed by the Court that permission to enter was implicit.

The *Earle* decision supplements the many contract clause decisions of the Taney Court which left the states the greatest possible freedom of action in the regulation of their internal economic affairs.

### *Rendition of Fugitives from Justice*

Another provision of the Constitution dealing with the relations of the states to each other is found in Article IV, section 2:

> A person charged in any state with treason, felony, or other crime, who shall flee from justice, and be found in another state, shall, on demand of the Executive authority of the state from which he fled, be delivered up, to be removed to the State having jurisdiction of the crime.

In *Kentucky* v. *Denison*[68] the Taney Court ruled that the duty imposed upon state governors was ministerial, not discretionary. However, Taney then intimated that a "mandatory and compulsory" interpretation of the clause would result in an unconstitutional invasion of the reserved powers of the states, for the assignment of federal duties to a state officer "might overload [him] . . . and disable him from performing his obligations to the state. . . ." On this ground Taney held that there was no power delegated to the national government to compel Denison, the Governor of Ohio, to return a fugitive from Kentucky justice as requested by the governor of that state.

Unlike Barbour's statement of the doctrine of state police power in the *Miln* case or Taney's own assertion of it in the *License Cases,* Taney's *Denison* reasoning did not refer directly to any "exclusive" reserved powers of the states. Strictly speaking, the statement quoted above emphasizes the federal government's lack of power, but this narrow construction of Article IV, section 2, was, in Taney's eyes, necessary for the preservation of the federal system.

### *Republican Form of Government and Domestic Violence in a State*

*Luther* v. *Borden*[69] represents the first interpretation by the Supreme Court of Article IV, section 4, of the Constitution. This provides, in part, that "the United States shall guarantee to every State in this Union a Republican form of government . . . and upon application of the

68. 24 Howard 66 (1860).
69. 7 Howard 1 (1849).

Legislature or of the Executive (when the Legislature cannot be convened) against domestic violence." Fundamental to the decision of the case was the question of the legitimacy of either the revolutionary or old charter governments of Rhode Island. This question, held the Taney Court, was a political one to be decided by "the political department." Under Article IV, section 4, of the Constitution, intervention by the federal government when a state is torn by domestic violence must be by the appropriate political branch. Under Article IV, section 4,

> it rests with Congress to decide what government is the established one in the state. For as the United States guarantee to each state a republican government, Congress must necessarily decide what government is established before it can determine whether it is republican or not.

By admitting senators and representatives into its membership, Congress recognizes both the legitimacy and the republican character of a state government.

By an act of 1795, Congress had authorized the President to call forth the militia of any other state or states to suppress an insurrection against a state government. In carrying out this duty he must decide which of the contending governments is the legitimate one. The federal courts must follow his decision both during and after the insurrection. Therefore, the Supreme Court, under the doctrine of political questions, had to recognize the charter government of Rhode Island.

Taney's opinion in this case has usually been heralded as a model of judicial self-restraint, and so it was up to this point in the decision. However, the Attorney General of the United States, Nathan Clifford, had argued before the Court that the state had no right to declare martial law. And even though Article IV assumes that the states can put down domestic violence, the lone dissenter, Justice Woodbury, had asserted that this power was vested exclusively in "the general government." Presumably, under the doctrine of political questions, the issue whether the power to declare martial law could be constitutionally exercised by the states should have been resolved by the appropriate political branch of the national government. But here Taney felt free to state that, while Congress would have the duty to declare a permanent state military government, non-republican, martial law might be enforced temporarily. For

> . . . the power is essential to the existence of every government, essential to the preservation of order and free institutions, and is as necessary to the

states of this union as to any other government. The state itself must determine what degree of force the crisis demands.

The argument that such power belongs exclusively to the federal government was not directly answered by Taney.

In regard to the questions whether a state government is republican or not, or which of two competing governments shall be recognized by the federal executive when he is requested to put down domestic violence within a state, the Taney Court, by use of the doctrine of political questions, left its determination to the appropriate political branch of the federal government. Federal authority under Article IV, section 4, was not weakened. Conversely, the Taney decision carefully sought to safeguard state autonomy by its adoption of the view of the state courts on the question of the legitimacy of the charter government and by its subtle disposal of Justice Woodbury's argument that the "general government" possessed exclusive power to declare martial law. However, the doctrine of political questions as here applied was potentially dangerous to state autonomy, since it provided a basis for tacit acceptance of the post-Civil War Reconstruction Acts in *Texas* v. *White*.[70]

### *Slavery Issues*

That the Supreme Court was anxious to avoid embroilment in the bitter slavery controversy was amply indicated by its ruling in *Strader* v. *Graham*.[71] In this case the Court held that it did not have jurisdiction over the question "whether slaves who had been permitted by their masters to pass occasionally from Kentucky into Ohio acquired thereby a right to freedom after their return to Kentucky." The case raised many issues that were later to become important questions in the ill-fated *Dred Scott* case. Chief Justice Taney ruled that the question stated above could only be decided by Kentucky and further held that the Northwest Ordinance of 1787 was no longer operative except where enforced by state constitutions and laws.

The members of the Taney Court, like people throughout the country, were sharply divided on the slavery issue. In an early commerce clause case involving a question of slavery, Justice McLean, a justice who ordinarily tended to hew closely to the nationalistic doctrines of the late John Marshall, took the rather extreme position that

Each state has a right to protect itself against the avarice and intrusion of the slave dealer; to guard its citizens against the inconveniences and dangers

70. 7 Wallace 700 (1869). 71. 10 Howard 82 (1850).

of a slave population. . . . The right to exercise this power, by a state, is higher and deeper than the Constitution. . . .[72]

Other members of the Court, while not favoring slavery as an institution, took strong positions concerning the rendition of fugitive slaves and other matters.

Unfortunately for the Taney Court's enviable record for judicial self-restraint, these fundamental differences boiled to the surface in the emotion-charged case of *Dred Scott* v. *Sanford*.[73] Dred Scott, a Negro slave, based a claim for freedom on the fact that he had been carried by his owner from the slave state of Missouri into a free state and a free territory.

The researches of Charles Warren show that a majority of the Taney Court had first planned to render a decision, to be written by Justice Nelson, only on the question whether the federal circuit court had jurisdiction. However, when it became known that the dissenters, McLean and Curtis, intended to deal with the constitutionality of the Missouri Compromise, the majority also felt impelled to deal with that question.[74] Chief Justice Taney then wrote the majority opinion. Six justices followed the Chief Justice, although they wrote separate concurring opinions. Justice Nelson agreed in regard to the determination of the jurisdictional questions, but did not deal with the Missouri Compromise. Justices McLean and Curtis dissented from the three jurisdictional determinations and from the majority's holding regarding the Missouri Compromise.

With regard to the jurisdictional questions, Chief Justice Taney held that the circuit court in Missouri, which had denied Scott's claim for freedom, lacked jurisdiction on three grounds. Under Article IV, section 2, the Constitution provided that the "citizens of each State shall be entitled to all Privileges and Immunities of Citizens in the several states." However, Taney held that the fact that a state bestows the rights and privileges of state citizenship upon a person does not entitle him to United States citizenship, to the right to sue in the federal courts, or to the privileges of state citizenship protected by the Constitution. Taney assumed, in effect, that in order to enjoy the latter, a person must be a United States citizen. Negroes, ruled Taney, could not attain United States citizenship because the framers of the Constitution had treated them as property and had not extended United States citizenship to either slaves or freedmen at the time of the

72. In *Groves* v. *Slaughter*, 15 Peters 449, 508 (1841).
73. 19 Howard 393 (1856).
74. Warren, *History*, II, 277-97.

formation of the Constitution. Congress likewise, through its exclusive power of naturalization, had refrained from making available the privilege of United States citizenship to Negroes, whether free or slave. Consequently, even if Scott were a freedman, the federal circuit court could not take his suit under its diverse citizenship jurisdiction.

Taney's approach to the second jurisdictional question involved Scott's claim that his removal from the slave state of Missouri to free territory vested him with freedom. Congress, in the famous Missouri Compromise, had prohibited the holding and owning of slaves in the territory north of the thirty-six-thirty parallel. Taney held that Congress' power over the territory and property of the United States was not unlimited and was intended to be exercised within the bounds of the Constitution. Since the act violated the rights of private property in slaves recognized by the Constitution in the Fifth Amendment, it was null and void. Thus Scott's removal to the Northwest Territory gave him "no title to freedom." It was in this discussion that Taney introduced the concept of substantive due process, a concept which was destined to play a very important part in the judicial process of determining federal and state powers and limitations.

The third jurisdictional argument based on Scott's removal to the free state of Illinois similarly failed to move the Court to rule in favor of Scott's freedom. For here Taney merely applied the doctrine of the *Strader* case, holding that the question of Dred Scott's status was one to be determined by the laws of Missouri. Since the highest Missouri Court had held that he was a slave, the Supreme Court again ruled that Scott had no standing in a federal circuit court on the basis of diverse citizenship.

In his dissent, Justice Curtis made two points worthy of attention in regard to the jurisdictional question. He disagreed with Taney's assertion that free Negroes were not considered citizens by any state at the time of the adoption of the Constitution, and he asserted the doctrine that the acquisition of state citizenship automatically brought with it federal citizenship. In regard to this second point, Taney's opinion actually enhanced federal power, for he held that the actions of the states have no relation to questions concerning the acquisition of national citizenship or of state citizenship where the privileges of the latter are protected by the Constitution.

Both McLean and Curtis strongly opposed Taney's ruling regarding the constitutionality of the Missouri Compromise. Curtis' view is particularly interesting inasmuch as he invoked the doctrine of political questions. He argued that since Congress had the power to make "all" needful rules and regulations concerning the territory and property of the United States, it and not the Supreme Court should determine whether slaves could be introduced into the territories. In his words, "to engraft [on the Constitution] a substantive exception not found in it . . . upon reasons purely political, renders its judicial interpretation impossible—because judicial tribunals, as such, cannot decide upon political considerations."[75]

Insofar as Taney's *Dred Scott* opinion limited federal legislative authority, it did so to protect the rights of citizens in their property in slaves and not the rights of states. Nevertheless, although the Missouri Compromise had already been repealed, the decision potentially bolstered the slave states in their losing struggle to maintain their economic and political position in the federal system. For Congress no longer could exclude slavery from the territories. The decision did, of course, also enhance federal judicial authority, and did establish unmistakably the doctrine that acquisition of state citizenship does not, *ipso facto,* result in the acquisition of national citizenship.

### CONCLUSION

In conclusion, these characteristics of the Taney Court stand out. Contrary to the charges of contemporary critics and some later historians, the Taney Court did not abandon or even weaken the cardinal principle of federal supremacy. Actually, it asserted the doctrine under conditions as trying and as dangerous to paramount federal authority as any faced by the Marshall Court. Admittedly, Barbour's doctrine of the exclusiveness of state police power was antithetical to the principle of federal supremacy. Yet not only was it never applied to limit federal power, but also in cases involving clear-cut conflicts of state police power and federal commerce power, the Taney Court applied the principle of federal supremacy. The *Sinnot* and *Coombs* cases are illustrative.

In some areas of constitutional interpretation, the Taney Court was perhaps more concerned with balancing state and federal authority than had been the Marshall Court. Its commerce clause and counterfeiting clause decisions illustrate this point. But its *Genesee Chief, Swift,* and *Prigg* decisions just as clearly embodied doctrines expanding broadly federal authority. It is particularly difficult to reconcile the *Prigg* decision with the idea of maintenance of an equilibrium in federal-state relations.

75. 19 Howard 620; for full and accurate accounts of the background of the case and the political and emotional storm raised by it, see Warren, *History,* II, 279-319, and Swisher, *Roger B. Taney,* pp. 476-523.

The Taney Court decisions involving the application of constitutional limitations on the states offer an interesting study of how the judicial process of interpretation can be utilized to modify the more rigorous doctrines inherited from the past without rejecting them. Without condoning violations of these limitations, the Taney Court generally tempered the older doctrines of the Marshall Court sufficiently (in addition to adopting some new ones) to enable it to follow a policy of leaving to the states the fullest possible freedom of control of their social and economic affairs. Doctrines such as those laid down in the *Knoop* and *Gelpcke* decisions are, of course, important qualifying exceptions.

In its decisions under the various constitutional clauses dealing with the relations of the states to each other, a similar desire on the part of the Taney Court to preserve to the states their autonomy in the federal system is evident. In this respect the *Earle* and *McElmoyle* decisions serve as pertinent examples.

The Taney Court generally exercised more self-restraint as arbiter of federal-state relations than did the Marshall Court, although, unfortunately, the *Dred Scott* decision did not enhance its reputation in that respect. Taken in the context of its entire judicial history, the Taney Court fulfilled the role as final arbiter of the federal system with a keener awareness of the need to maintain the vitality of the state governments than had its predecessor. Yet it did this without weakening the cardinal principle of federal supremacy.

## CHAPTER V

# *The Chase Court, 1864-1873*

Seldom have the Presidents who have successfully led their political parties to electoral victory been afforded the opportunity to carry their revolution in public opinion to full control of the judicial branch of the national government. The constitutional provision for judicial tenure on good behavior and fate combined to thwart all of Thomas Jefferson's hopes after his great electoral victory of 1800. His successors, Madison and Monroe, were able to appoint a Jeffersonian Republican majority, but for reasons yet to be clearly indicated by judicial biographers, these appointees generally behaved like Federalists of the Marshall school when dealing with the great constitutional problems of the period. Before Lincoln, only President Andrew Jackson had been able to appoint a majority to the Court. Now, in 1865, President Lincoln achieved the same distinction as Jackson.[1] With his appointment of Salmon Portland Chase as Chief Justice in 1864, and with the death in the following year of Justice Catron, a new era in judicial interpretation began.

The supremacy and stability of the federal government had been underscored during the opening years of the Chase period by the victorious Union armies. The constitutional division of powers between the federal government and the states meant very little to the Radical

1. Throughout the period of Taney's tenure as Chief Justice, Jacksonian Democrats comprised a majority. Of the members appointed prior to Taney's appointment, three were chosen by Jackson himself—Justices McLean, Baldwin, and Wayne. Barbour was chosen with Taney in 1836, while Justices Catron, McKinley, and Daniel were chosen by Jackson's successor, President Van Buren, the first two in 1837, the latter in 1841. Justice Nelson was appointed by a nominal Whig—President Tyler. Justices Woodbury and Grier were appointed by Democratic President Polk in 1845 and 1846, respectively. Whig President Fillmore appointed Justice Curtis in 1851, while Democratic Presidents Pierce and Buchanan appointed Justices Campbell (1853) and Clifford (1857). The remainder—Justices Swayne, Miller, Davis (all 1862), and Field (1863) were appointed by Republican President Lincoln. Lincoln appointed Chief Justice Chase in 1864. During the remainder of the Chase Court period, President Grant appointed Justices Bradley and Strong in 1870 and Justice Hunt in 1872.

Republicans in Congress, who, flushed with victory, were bent on enforcing a conqueror's peace upon the South. The moderate policies proposed by Lincoln and Johnson were brushed aside, and a militarily enforced reconstruction program imposed upon the former Confederate States. In 1868 the constitutional status of the states was altered by the adoption of the 14th Amendment, ratification of which had been forced upon the Southern states as the price for the seating of their senators and representatives in Congress.[2] In this era of accentuated nationalism and extra-legalism, the position of the states became precarious. President Johnson had been unable to stem the tide of extreme nationalism, and President Grant had neither the will nor the ability to do so. Among the coordinate branches of the national government, only the Supreme Court was able to take positive action to restore the balance in the federal system. This it did in cases where a direct clash with Congress could be avoided.

### JUDICIAL CAUTION AND THE RECONSTRUCTION ACTS

Particularly serious in their implications for the federal system were the three theories which more or less influenced congressional thinking on the problems of reconstruction. For Sumner, the Southern states had committed suicide and were left legally in the status of territories. Even more extreme was the view of Thaddeus Stevens. To him the Southern states were simply conquered provinces, completely stripped of their constitutional rights. And among most congressmen the theory prevailed that the former Confederate states had forfeited their rights through secession, and, consequently, it was a matter of congressional discretion as to when those rights would be restored.[3]

The Chase Court never ruled on the constitutionality of the Reconstruction Acts, although several attempts were made by Southern states to bring the issue before it. In the first attempt, the state of Mississippi filed a bill perpetually to enjoin President Johnson and General Ord of the military district comprising Mississippi and Arkansas from executing these acts. Counsel for Mississippi first asserted that the state had never left the Union because legal secession was impossible. Congress, they further argued, may not expel a state. The Reconstruction Acts, it was contended, "annihilate the state and its government" and the attendant imposition of military rule stripped the people of the state of their constitutional safeguards. In *Mississippi* v. *Johnson,*[4] the Chase Court refused to rule on these contentions

2. J. G. Randall, *The Civil War and Reconstruction,* pp. 689-798.
3. Dunning, *Essays on the Civil War and Reconstruction,* pp. 99-121.
4. 4 Wallace 475 (1866).

because the President's duty was "purely executive and political" rather than ministerial. Any judicial attempt to interfere with the performance of such duties would be unwarranted judicial meddling with the concerns of a political branch.

Next, the state of Georgia brought an original suit in the Supreme Court to enjoin Secretary of War Stanton in the enforcement of the Reconstruction Acts, thus avoiding the difficulty experienced by Mississippi in its suit against the President. Georgia's arguments against the Acts were similar in most respects to those used by Mississippi. The Chase Court again refused to take jurisdiction, this time on the ground that Georgia's plea that the acts would unconstitutionally "annul and totally abolish the existing State Government" called for its "judgment upon political questions."[5]

The Reconstruction Acts undoubtedly would have been construed by the Court in its consideration of the case of the Mississippi editor, McCardle, but Congress hurriedly withdrew the Supreme Court's appellate jurisdiction in the class of cases under which it arose and thus precluded further action. In *Ex Parte McCardle*[6] the Chase Court acknowledged that Congress could validly strip it of this portion of its appellate jurisdiction under Article III, section 2, of the Constitution. Considered together with the *Mississippi* and *Georgia* cases, the *McCardle* episode made it clear that no avenue remained for the opponents of the Reconstruction Acts to test them before the Supreme Court. The Chase Court had refused to permit states to bring suit under its original jurisdiction in the first two cases, while actions brought by individuals under the Supreme Court's appellate jurisdiction could be nullified by congressional intervention. In effect, Congress could abolish state governments, substitute new ones and enforce its action by military occupation virtually secure against Supreme Court interposition. The constitutional position of the states in the early post-Civil War period was indeed precarious.

It was in its consideration of another issue, somewhat less controversial than the question of the constitutionality of the Reconstruction Acts, that the Supreme Court, in *Texas* v. *White*,[7] discussed the constitutional status of the former Confederate states and Congress' authority to establish new governments in them. Incidental to the question of the ownership of certain bonds given by the Confederate government of Texas for military supplies, Chief Justice Chase felt it necessary to discuss the constitutional status of the formerly rebellious

5. *Georgia* v. *Stanton*, 6 Wallace 50 (1867).

6. 6 Wallace 318 (1867).

7. 7 Wallace 700 (1869).

Southern states. Two determinations of the Chase Court majority were quite significant. First, the doctrine that "the Constitution looks . . . to an indestructible Union, composed of indestructible states" rejected by implication the two most extreme theories set forth by Radical Republican legislators—the state suicide theory of Sumner and the conquered province theory of Stevens. But at the same time, Chase's doctrine that Congress had power derived from its authority to determine whether a state government is republican in form to establish state governments in the former Confederate states, in effect, vindicated Congress' Reconstruction Acts. Thus while the doctrines in *Texas* v. *White* assured the continued existence of the states *qua* states, they contributed nothing toward re-establishment of the autonomy of the state governments in the federal system. Actually, congressional power to control such governments under the pretext of guaranteeing to the states republican forms of government was given a stamp of approval by the decision.

### THE PRIVILEGES AND IMMUNITIES CLAUSE OF THE FOURTEENTH AMENDMENT

The Chase Court scrupulously avoided clashing head on with the Radical Republican Congress over the Reconstruction Acts, but was willing to take a stand for state autonomy in regard to certain other issues. Undoubtedly the greatest contribution of the Chase Court toward maintaining the autonomy of the states in the federal system was its determinative decision in the *Slaughterhouse Cases.*[8] This decision embodied the first judicial interpretation of the privileges and immunities clause of the Fourteenth Amendment. A group of independent butchers in the city of New Orleans challenged the constitutionality of a slaughterhouse monopoly law passed by the reconstructed Louisiana legislature. This challenge was based on the Thirteenth Amendment as well as the privileges and immunities, due process, and equal protection clauses of the Fourteenth Amendment. However, it was the immunities clause which received the fullest attention of the Court.

Counsel for the butchers, former Supreme Court Justice Campbell, argued that the immunities clause had revolutionized federal-state relations—"The States in their closest connection with the members of the state have been placed under the oversight and restraining and enforcing hand of Congress." And the phrase "privileges and immuni-

8. 16 Wallace 36 (1872).

ties" applied to all persons, whether former slaves or not, and embraced, in effect, every subject within the police power of the states.

Justice Miller, spokesman for the Chase Court majority, recoiled from such an interpretation. Contradicting Campbell on nearly every point, Miller distinguished between United States citizenship and state citizenship, holding that it is only the privileges and immunities of the former that are protected by the Fourteenth Amendment. The privileges and immunities of United States citizenship do not embrace the vast catalogue of social, economic and political rights presently regulated by the states under their police power. Rather, Miller held, they include only those protected under the original privileges and immunities clause in section 4 of the Articles of Confederation, in the similar clause in Article IV, section 2, of the Constitution, and under the doctrine of *Crandall* v. *Nevada.* In other words, this clause of the Fourteenth Amendment protected no rights which had not been protected before 1868, the year of its adoption.

Justice Field commented, in dissent, that if this were the case, adoption of the amendment "was a vain and idle enactment, which accomplished nothing, and most unnecessarily excited Congress and the people of its passage." However, Justice Miller insisted that because of the serious consequences for the federal system that would follow from a broad interpretation of the clause, the majority must hold that such a construction was not intended unless it was stated in "language which expresses such a purpose too clearly to admit of doubt."

The effect of the adoption by the Court of the broad interpretation of the clause presented by Campbell would be, wrote Miller,

> . . . to fetter and degrade the state governments by subjecting them to the control of Congress, in the exercise of powers heretofore universally conceded to them of the most ordinary and fundamental character. . . . [The Supreme Court will become] a perpetual censor upon all legislation of the states, on the civil rights of their own citizens, with authority to nullify such as it did not approve of as consistent with those rights.

As is noted above, the privileges and immunities protected, under the majority doctrine, were only those attaching to United States citizenship. The rights claimed by the butchers of New Orleans, ruled Miller, were privileges and immunities of state citizenship and, consequently, were not protected by the Fourteenth Amendment.

The *Slaughterhouse* decision virtually emasculated the privileges and immunities clause within five years of its adoption. Students of government have been divided on the question whether the Chase Court was justified in substituting its narrow interpretation for the broad one intended by the amendment's framers.[9] But regardless of this question, there remains little doubt that this decision represents the most important single action, whether for good or evil, taken by the Supreme Court for the preservation of state autonomy within the federal system. The contents of the Civil Rights Act passed by Congress in 1875 made it evident that the dangers to the states enumerated by Miller were not fanciful ones.

Miller's positions on the due process and equal protection contentions raised in the case were also negative. In the long run they proved him to be a poor prophet. In later years the Supreme Court, by developing a body of substantive due process limitations on state action, virtually became "a perpetual censor upon all legislation of the states," and corporations rather than Negroes found in both the due process and equal protection clauses bulwarks against state legislative regulation, at least until 1937. In 1875, three years after the *Slaughter-house* decision and the year that the Civil Rights Act was adopted, the due process and equal protection clauses were as important as potential threats to state autonomy as the privileges and immunities clause. For not only could all three of them provide a basis for judicial censorship of state action, but all similarly were sources for congressional enforcement power as stipulated in section 5 of the amendment. Given a broad interpretation of the amendment such as that presented by Campbell, it is difficult to imagine that the due process and equal protection clauses would provide bases for a congressional civil code less broad than one based upon the immunities clause.

Miller's narrow construction of the privileges and immunities clause was reaffirmed in *Bradwell* v. *Illinois*[10] to repudiate a contention raised by a woman that the right to obtain a license to practice law was a privilege of United States citizenship, and in *Bartemeyer* v. *Iowa*[11] to negate a claim that the right to sell intoxicating liquor was a similar constitutionally-protected privilege.

### INTERGOVERNMENTAL TAX IMMUNITY

It is perhaps one of the ironies of judicial history that it was a Court composed of appointees of Lincoln rather than those of Jackson

9. Compare, for example, Willoughby, *Constitutional Law,* I, 237, and Burgess, *Political Science and Constitutional Law,* I, 228-30.

10. 16 Wallace 130 (1872).

11. 18 Wallace 129 (1873).

which first held a portion of a federal law invalid on the ground that it invaded the reserved powers of the states. The occasion was the Chase Court's decision in *Collector* v. *Day*.[12] Here application of a federal income tax law to the salary of a state judge was held void under the doctrine that the immunity of federal instrumentalities from state taxation was a reciprocal one. Justice Bradley wrote a lone but telling dissent, stating in part that since "no man ceases to be a citizen of the United States by being an officer under [a] state government," federal taxes could be imposed upon such officers. He also noted that "the taxation by [a] State Government of the instruments employed by the General Government . . . involves an interference with the powers of a government in which other States and their citizens are equally interested with the State that imposes the taxation." This observation was similar to one made by Marshall in the *McCulloch* case.

A more basic criticism of the majority doctrine has been raised by Professor Willoughby. He pointed out that implicit in the doctrine is the assumption that the states and the national government are constitutional equals, while in fact the national government has been recognized, in conflicts of authority such as the *McCulloch* case, as having a constitutional status superior to that of the states.[13]

In *United States* v. *Baltimore and Ohio Railroad Company*,[14] the Chase Court held that municipal corporations were exempt from federal taxation because they shared a portion of state governmental power. While the Chase Court exempted the salaries of state officers and municipal corporations from federal taxation, it also laid down a doctrine which, to a certain extent, set limits on federal immunity from state taxation. Several state taxes had been held void by the Chase Court under the Marshall Court's doctrine of the *Weston* case.[15] And in *People* v. *Board of Supervisors*,[16] it had recognized that Congress could validly exempt legal tender notes issued under its authority from state taxation. However, in several other cases, state taxing power was sustained even though such power touched upon federal securities. For example, in *Society for Savings* v. *Coite*,[17] the Chase Court ruled

12. 11 Wallace 113 (1870).

13. Willoughby, *Constitutional Law*, I, 167.

14. 17 Wallace 322 (1872).

15. See *The Bank Tax Case*, 2 Wallace 573 (1864); *Van Allen* v. *The Assessors*, 3 Wallace 584 (1865); *Bradley* v. *The People*, 4 Wallace 459 (1866); *The Banks* v. *The Mayor of New York*, 7 Wallace 16 (1868).

16. 7 Wallace 26 (1868).

17. 6 Wallace 594 (1867); applied also in *Provident Institution* v. *Massachusetts*, 6 Wallace 611 (1867); *Hamilton Company* v. *Massachusetts*, 6 Wallace 632 (1867).

that the fact that the society had invested part of its deposits in United States securities did not exempt those deposits from a state franchise tax on the privilege to do business which was measured by investments.

The case of *National Bank* v. *Kentucky*[18] brought an attempt by the Chase Court to clarify its position on the question whether or not federal agencies or federal bonds were immune from state taxation. Justice Miller wrote the Court's opinion. Speaking of various federal exemptions from state taxation, he pointed out that the doctrine of federal immunity from state taxation is based on the proposition that state legislation actually interferes with agencies of the federal government. To carry it beyond this would be "an unjustifiable invasion of states' rights." On the basis of this reasoning, he held that while the capital of a bank cannot be taxed by a state if it is invested in federal bonds, bank shares owned by individual stockholders which were similarly invested could be taxed by a state.

If the Chase Court had applied the latter doctrine to the *Collector* case it would seem that a practical view of the possible effects of a nondiscriminatory federal tax on the salaries of state officials would have brought the realization that such a tax could not "interfere with or impair" the efficiency of the state governments.

Of all the cases dealing directly with the relationship between federal taxing power and state power, *Veazie Bank* v. *Fenno*[19] represents perhaps the strongest assertion of federal authority made in the Chase Court period. In this case, the constitutionality of a congressional tax of 10 per cent on state bank notes was attacked on two grounds. First, it was argued that the tax was a direct one and had to be apportioned among the states according to their respective populations. Chief Justice Chase, after summarizing the pertinent historical evidence, ruled that only taxes on land and capitation taxes were direct taxes.

The second contention regarding the constitutionality of the 10 per cent tax held deeper significance for the problem of federal-state relations. Congress, it was charged, had imposed a tax impairing a franchise granted by a state, thus invading the reserved powers of the states. Chief Justice Chase first stated that "the reserved rights of the states, such as the right to pass laws, to give effect to laws through executive action, to administer justice through the courts, and to employ all necessary agencies for legitimate purposes of State government, are

18. 9 Wallace 353 (1869); see *Thomson* v. *Union Pacific Railroad*, 9 Wallace 579 (1870); *Union Pacific Railroad* v. *Penison*, 18 Wallace 5 (1873).

19. 8 Wallace 533 (1869).

not proper subjects of the taxing power of Congress." He then established a doctrine basically inconsistent with this statement. For the import of his decision was the far-reaching doctrine that national taxing power might be used to destroy notes issued under state authority and, provided such utilization implemented a valid exercise of congressional authority, it also assumed that the taxing power might be employed to destroy the issuing agency itself even though the agency was created by a state.

The *Veazie Bank* decision stands in sharp contrast to the Chase Court tax immunity decision in *Collector* v. *Day*. For while the latter was based upon the assumption that the existence of the states could in certain circumstances limit national authority, the former was based upon the tacit assumption that the existence of the reserved powers of the states in no way limited an otherwise constitutional exercise of congressional power.

### STATE INTERFERENCES WITH FEDERAL AUTHORITY

Lest the sensitivity of the Chase Court toward the problem of maintaining the states as autonomous entities in the federal system, as illustrated in the *Slaughterhouse* and *Day* cases, be mistaken for complete adherence to an extreme theory of states' rights, it should be noted that the judicial record for the Chase Court also displayed some extremely nationalistic tendencies as well. Several obvious attempts by states to interfere with legitimate federal functions were, of course, declared unconstitutional. Thus in *McGoon* v. *Scales*[20] the sale of land for state taxes while the land was still owned by the United States was held invalid. Again, in *Gibson* v. *Chouteau*,[21] the power of the national government to dispose of public lands free from state interference was reaffirmed.

By far the most serious state obstruction of federal authority, however, was considered in *Tarble's Case*.[22] Here a judge of the state of Wisconsin interfered with the military recruiting of the national government by taking jurisdiction under *habeas corpus* in a case involving the propriety of federal enlistment of an under-age volunteer. The state judge's action was ruled inconsistent with the supremacy clause. And further, the question of the validity of enlistments in the United States Army was held to be a question solely for federal courts. Consequently, the judge of the state of Wisconsin had acted outside the jurisdiction of his court.

20. 9 Wallace 23 (1869).

21. 13 Wallace 92 (1871).

22. 13 Wallace 397 (1871); in addition the Marshall Court decision in the *Osborne* case was reaffirmed in *Davis* v. *Gray*, 16 Wallace 203 (1872).

*Contract Clause*

Unlike the Marshall and Taney Courts, the Chase Court, with one important exception, developed no new doctrines in its determinations under the contract clause. However, it compiled a scarcely to be equaled record for harsh and rigorous enforcement of this formidable prohibition as a brake on state social and economic legislation. Nearly 60 per cent of the state laws considered under the contract clause were declared unconstitutional.[23] In cases involving private contracts the Chase Court remained within the rigorous enforcement tradition of its predecessors.[24]

The conditions which persuaded state judges to attempt to safeguard the interests of state and municipal taxpayers are vividly described by Charles Fairman in his judicial biography of Justice Miller. After the Civil War, states and municipalities often issued bonds to aid in the construction of railroads. Clever promoters would argue persuasively that railroads were merely highways built under state authority and were thus sufficiently "public" in nature to be supported by taxation. In innumerable instances unscrupulous promoters persuaded municipalities to over-invest. Whole communities mortgaged their future in railroad aid bonds. When a municipality sought to evade payment or was unable to raise the necessary amounts through ordinary taxation, the railroad corporation would invoke the contract clause.[25]

Similarly, corporations often secured contracts from states, counties or municipalities which exempted them from taxation. Such exemption was sometimes purchased from dishonest legislators. When new legislators took office and attempted to repudiate such exemptions for the benefit of the community, the corporations would claim the protection of the contract clause. The attitude of the Supreme Court in regard to cases falling within this second category is readily illustrated by the majority opinion in the first *Rouse* case in which the Taney Court's *Knoop* doctrine that general tax exemption laws were constitutionally protected contracts was rigidly applied.[26]

23. Wright, *Contract Clause*, p. 93.

24. The Taney Court's *Bronson* doctrine was applied in *Hawthorne* v. *Calef*, 2 Wallace 10 (1864). See *Gunn* v. *Barry*, 15 Wallace 610 (1872); *Walker* v. *Whitehead*, 16 Wallace 314 (1873).

25. Charles Fairman, *Mr. Justice Miller and the Supreme Court, 1862-1890*, pp. 207-36; hereinafter cited as *Justice Miller*. See *Von Hoffman* v. *City of Quincy*, 4 Wallace 535 (1866); *The Binghamton Bridge*, 3 Wallace 51 (1865).

26. See *Home of the Friendless* v. *Rouse*, 8 Wallace 430 (1869); *Washington University* v. *Rouse*, 8 Wallace 439 (1869); *McGee* v. *Mathis*, 4 Wallace 143 (1866); *Wilmington Railroad Company* v. *Reid*, 13 Wallace 264 (1871).

The case of *Salt Company* v. *East Saginaw*[27] was, however, an important exception. For here the Chase Court sustained a revocation by the Michigan legislature of a general tax exemption extended to any individual or company which would undertake salt manufacturing within the state. In so doing it laid down the doctrine that "General encouragements held out to all persons indiscriminately, to engage in a particular trade or manufacture, whether such encouragements be in the shape of bounties or drawbacks, or other advantage, are always under the legislative control and may be discontinued at any time."

Several attempts by state judges to develop new doctrines designed to safeguard and preserve intact state and municipal taxing power were disallowed under the *Gelpcke* doctrine because the majority of the Chase Court deemed them judicial attempts at contract violation.[28] The over-all effect of the Chase Court's rigid enforcement of the contract clause was the safeguarding of private enterprise and investment from state or municipal enactments or ordinances and state court decisions designed to modify contracts for the protection of the taxpayers of the state or city. State, county, and municipal taxing power was weakened by some of these decisions. And, of greater importance, such rigid enforcement limited to a certain extent state control of its economy in a period when decisive legislative action was frequently needed. The *Salt Company* case was, of course, an important but isolated exception.

### *Commerce Clause*

In regard to the uses of the commerce clause as a basis for federal action, the Chase Court was disposed to sustain such utilization provided the exercise of power was not too remote in its relationship to an enumerated power of Congress. In *Thomson* v. *Union Pacific Railroad*,[29] for example, the Chase Court sustained Congress' power to support or instigate the building of a transcontinental railroad system under the broad constructionist interpretation of the implied powers clause and the commerce, postal, and war powers. This decision indi-

27. 13 Wallace 373 (1872).

28. *Havenmeyer* v. *Iowa County*, 3 Wallace 294 (1866); *Thompson* v. *Lee County*, 3 Wallace 327 (1866); *Mitchell* v. *Burlington*, 4 Wallace 270 (1867); *Larned* v. *Burlington*, 4 Wallace 275 (1867); *Butz* v. *Muscatine*, 8 Wallace 575 (1869); *Kenosha* v. *Lamson*, 9 Wallace 477 (1870); *Olcott* v. *Supervisors of Fond du Lac County*, 16 Wallace 678 (1873); *Pine Grove Township* v. *Talcott*, 19 Wallace 666 (1873); in *Lee County* v. *Rogers*, 7 Wallace 181 (1868), the Chase Court ruled that the *Gelpcke* doctrine was not open for re-examination. See also *Yates* v. *Milwaukee*, 10 Wallace 497 (1870), where the Chase Court interposed to protect private property rights against municipal regulation under the doctrine of *Swift* v. *Tyson*.

29. 9 Wallace 579 (1870).

cated unmistakably that the question of the constitutionality of congressional efforts at internal improvement through federal public works or federally financed projects no longer represented a serious constitutional issue.

However, in *United States* v. *Dewitt*,[30] the Chase Court held section 29 of the Internal Revenue Act of 1867 unconstitutional on the ground that it was "a police regulation, relating exclusively to the internal trade of the states. . . ." The section in question made it a misdemeanor, punishable by fine and imprisonment, to mix for sale or to sell illuminating oils which were dangerously inflammable. In defending the constitutionality of the section, the Assistant Attorney General of the United States observed that "instances of the exercise of police power over certain instruments or agencies of commerce, for the protection of life and property, are found in various acts of Congress." He then pointed out that the disputed section may have been enacted to protect transportation companies engaged in interstate and foreign commerce from danger to life and property and to protect revenue officers engaged in examining and marking oil products in the assessment of federal excise taxes. On these grounds, he argued, the regulation was necessary to the exercise of both the commerce and taxing powers. In dismissing these arguments, Chief Justice Chase interpreted the commerce power as "a virtual denial of any power to interfere with the internal trade and business of the separate states."

The case of *The Daniel Ball*[31] involved questions concerning the Court's admiralty jurisdiction and Congress' commerce power. With regard to the latter, the Chase Court ruled that the vessel in question in the case, the *Daniel Ball,* was an instrument of interstate commerce subject to congressional legislation because it carried commodities which had begun to move from one state to another on a river which, though located entirely within one state, was "a continued highway over which commerce is or may be carried on with other states or foreign countries. . . ." *Dicta* in this decision harbingered some congressional control of the internal commerce of the states such as that sustained in the *Shreveport Rate* case many years later. For in reference to an expression by counsel of fear[32] that a doctrine such as

30. 9 Wallace 41 (1869).

31. 10 Wallace 557 (1870); see *Gilman* v. *Philadelphia,* 3 Wallace 713 (1865); *The Montello,* 11 Wallace 411 (1870).

32. This view reflected a long prevalent assumption on the part of many early political leaders that federal commerce power was narrower in regard to land transportation than in regard to water transportation. See Frank J. Goodnow, *Social Reform and the Constitution*, pp. 112-13.

that adopted in the present case would open the way for congressional regulation of land transportation on highways wholly within a state, the Court refused to commit itself to a limiting doctrine and intimated that under certain circumstances regulation of land transportation could be upheld.

The Chase Court's uses of the commerce power as a limitation on state action were based upon older doctrines such as those of the *Cooley* case and *Brown* v. *Maryland*. Conflicts of state taxing power and federal commerce power were involved in two important Chase Court decisions. *The State Freight Tax Cases*[33] raised the issue whether a Pennsylvania tax on freight shipped in interstate commerce violated the commerce clause of the Constitution. Justice Strong ruled in the affirmative on the basis of the *Cooley* doctrine. However, a state tax on the gross receipts of domestic railroad corporations including revenue derived from interstate commerce but assessed in proportion to the mileage in the state was sustained in *Philadelphia and Reading Railroad Company* v. *Pennsylvania*.[34] Since the tax was not levied until after the receipts had become mingled with the other property of the corporations it was considered "a tax on business carried on within the state and without discrimination between its citizens and citizens of other states." Thus while the Chase Court ruled out state interference with interstate commerce through use of the taxing power, state taxing power was permitted to extend to domestic corporations engaged in such commerce, provided it did not impede it or discriminate against the products or citizens of other states.

A particularly significant Chase Court commerce clause decision was that of *Woodruff* v. *Parham*.[35] One of the arguments raised in this case concerned the applicability of the "original package" doctrine to interstate rather than foreign commerce. In concluding his opinion in *Brown* v. *Maryland*[36] Chief Justice Marshall had remarked that "we suppose the principles laid down in this case [concerning state taxing power] apply equally to importations from a sister state." Counsel for Woodruff contended that a non-discriminatory municipal tax on merchandise sold at auction fell within the prohibition set down in the "original package" doctrine because it was levied on goods "imported" from a sister state.

This argument was rejected on two grounds. First, the word "import" referred to articles imported from foreign countries, not the

33. 15 Wallace 232 (1872).
34. 15 Wallace 284 (1872); see *Osborne* v. *Mobile*, 16 Wallace 479 (1872).
35. 8 Wallace 123 (1868); *Hinson* v. *Lott*, 8 Wallace 148 (1868).
36. 12 Wheaton 419 (1827).

states. And second, Marshall's "casual remark" was simply *obiter*. Justice Miller, who wrote the majority opinion, did indicate, however, that a tax which discriminated against the products of other states would be held unconstitutional. Similarly, the Chase Court tended to sustain police power regulation of interstate carriers by the states. In *Railroad Company* v. *Fuller*[37] it upheld as a valid exercise of state police power an Iowa act requiring the annual fixing of rates by railroad companies, the posting of such rates, and the consistent adherence to them by the companies.

From the foregoing cases, it would appear that the Chase Court was not strongly disposed to expand the uses of the commerce clause as a limitation on the states and particularly as a limitation on state taxing power. It was, however, disposed toward invalidation of state interference with interstate or foreign commerce via the taxing power or of state discriminatory taxation.

The case of *Crandall* v. *Nevada* could have been decided under the commerce clause,[38] since the *Passenger Cases*[39] had established that the carrying of persons is commerce. The Nevada law levied a tax on the transportation of persons out of the state. The law was not held invalid as an interference with interstate commerce or an "impost on exports," however. Instead it was held void on the ground that the right of free ingress and egress among the states and of coming to the seat of government was a right of national citizenship, and interference with it by a state was inconsistent "with the objects which the Union was intended to attain." The Chase Court, in effect, established this right as a privilege of national citizenship before the adoption of the Fourteenth Amendment. For the first time the Supreme Court invalidated a state law, not on the ground that it interfered with a valid exercise of federal power, or the right of an individual based upon an express constitutional limitation on state power, but rather because it interfered with an individual right implied from the nature of the Union itself.

The case of *Paul* v. *Virginia*[40] is important not only in the interpretation of the commerce clause, but in the development of Article IV, section 2, of the Constitution as well. The latter clause provides that "the citizens of each state shall be entitled to all privileges and immunities of citizens in the several states." A Virginia law requiring

37. 17 Wallace 560 (1872).

38. 6 Wallace 35 (1867). This case would probably be decided under the commerce clause today. See *Edwards* v. *California*, 314 U.S. 160 (1941).

39. 7 Howard 283 (1849).

40. 8 Wallace 168 (1868); affirmed in *Ducat* v. *Chicago*, 10 Wallace 410 (1870).

deposit of a bond by out-of-state insurance companies desiring to do business within the state was challenged under the "indisputable citizenship of the stockholders" theory. This theory held that a corporation is to be treated as a citizen of the state that chartered it.[41] For the purpose of Article IV, section 2, this was rejected by the Chase Court. Leaning heavily upon *Bank of Augusta* v. *Earle,* Justice Field objected to the notion that corporations, "the creatures of local laws," were citizens within the meaning of the clause, stating that such a ruling would place the states at the mercy, economically, of out-of-state corporations. State authority in the regulation of such corporations was held to include power to ". . . exclude the foreign corporation entirely; . . . restrict its business to particular localities; or . . . exact . . . security for the performance of its contracts. . . ."

It was also contended that the Virginia license tax discriminated against foreign corporations in violation of the commerce clause. Evidently impelled by the same considerations for the freedom of the states to control their domestic economic affairs that governed his determination in regard to Article IV, section 2, Justice Field construed the commerce clause narrowly, holding that "a policy of insurance was not a transaction of commerce but a purely local one governed by local law." It is noteworthy that the federal government did not regulate insurance in this period. In the absence of state regulation the business would have been uncontrolled.

The net effect of these two doctrines of *Paul* v. *Virginia* was to insure to the states, as far as the two constitutional provisions involved were concerned, complete discretion in dealing with foreign insurance companies. The decision was a significant contribution to the preservation of state autonomy in a very crucial period. For not only was the constitutional position of the states threatened by extremists in the Radical Republican Congress, but the economic independence of some of the financially weaker states was seriously threatened by generally unrestrained corporate power.

## SUMMARY AND CONCLUSION

Throughout the Chase Court period, tremendous forces had operated to weaken and even destroy the autonomy of states in the federal system. The most important of these had been the Radical Republican Congress. The Chase Court's reaction to various congressional threats to state autonomy was contradictory. It cautiously evaded the question

41. Gerard Henderson, *The Position of Foreign Corporations in American Constitutional Law,* p. 69.

of the constitutionality of the Reconstruction Acts. And in the case of *Texas* v. *White,* the Court, in effect, gave its blessing to these acts and the state governments set up under them. Conversely, in the *Slaughterhouse Cases,* the Chase Court went to the other extreme, and in an unprecedented decision virtually emasculated the privileges and immunities clause of the Fourteenth Amendment in order, in its judgment, to preserve the federal system.

A second force operating to weaken state governments in the Chase Court period was the multiplicity of largely unregulated corporations. In order to deal with this threat, the state legislatures needed rather complete freedom to grapple with internal economic problems. Here the record of the Chase Court is somewhat contradictory also. For while decisions like that in *Paul* v. *Virginia* contributed a great deal toward preserving states' control of their internal economies, the Chase Court's contract clause and diverse citizenship cases involving contracts seriously weakened state, county and municipal taxing power.

In other areas of constitutional law, particularly those relating to governmental tax immunity and the commerce clause, the Chase Court sometimes evidenced a strong desire to preserve state autonomy and in some instances, such as *Collector* v. *Day,* so fulfilled that desire as to imply that the existence of the states limited otherwise valid exercises of federal taxing power. On the other hand, some of the Chase Court decisions involving federal taxing power embodied exceedingly broad interpretations of federal power. *Veazie Bank* v. *Fenno* well illustrates this point.

In conclusion, it might be noted that although the Chase Court strongly upheld federal authority against state encroachment in decisions such as that in *Tarble's Case,* it weakened federal authority in its *Slaughterhouse* and *Day* decisions. In some of its commerce clause decisions such as that of the *Fuller* case the Chase Court permitted state regulation of matters later found to require uniform national regulation.

As arbiter in federal-state relations the Chase Court lacked the balanced statesmanship that characterized both the Marshall and Taney Courts, but it did have an awareness of the need to preserve intact the states as part of the federal system. In carrying out this purpose it went a good deal further than the Taney Court in restricting federal authority in order to protect state autonomy. Undeniably the pressures upon the states were much greater in the Chase Court period than in that of its predecessor. But whether this fact justified the Chase Court's unwise restriction of federal taxing power in the *Collector* case or its virtual nullification of the privileges and immunities clause of the Fourteenth Amendment is open to question. In any case it might be said that it was the Chase Court rather than the Taney Court which was truly the outstanding "states'-rights" court in American judicial history.

CHAPTER VI

# *The Waite Court, 1874-1888*

THE PASSING OF Chief Justice Chase and the subsequent appointment of Morrison R. Waite as his successor produced no immediate revolution in doctrinal development.[1] But after the first few years of the Waite Court period, important doctrinal innovations, some extending, others limiting state authority, made their appearance in such different areas as the law of the commerce and contract clauses. And of far greater importance, several significant decisions relating to the due process and equal protection clauses of the Fourteenth Amendment were handed down.

## CONSTITUTIONAL LIMITATIONS ON THE STATES

### *The Privileges and Immunities Clause of the Fourteenth Amendment*

As far as the privileges and immunities clause of the Fourteenth Amendment was concerned, the Waite Court displayed no desire to overturn the narrow interpretation of the clause laid down by Justice Miller in the *Slaughterhouse* decision. However, opportunities for reversal were not lacking. For Justice Miller's hasty catalogue of the privileges of national citizenship opened the way for further inquiries. In *Minor* v. *Happersett*,[2] the Waite Court rejected a contention that the right to vote was a privilege of national citizenship which was violated by a state constitutional provision limiting this right to males. Similarly, it ruled in *Walker* v. *Sauvinet*[3] that the right to trial by jury

1. In terms of personnel, the Waite Court period produced many changes, although it might be noted that as in the Chase Court period all of the appointments were made by Republican Presidents. John Marshall Harlan replaced David Davis in 1877; William B. Woods took Justice Strong's place in 1880; Stanley Matthews replaced Noah H. Swayne in 1881; Horace Gray replaced Nathan Clifford in the same year; and Samuel Blatchford replaced Ward Hunt in 1882.

2. 21 Wallace 162 (1874).

3. 92 U.S. 90 (1875); see *Kirtland* v. *Hotchkiss*, 100 U.S. 491 (1879); *Presser* v. *Illinois*, 116 U.S. 252 (1886); *Mugler* v. *Kansas*, 123 U.S. 623 (1887).

in suits at common law in state courts was not a privilege of United States citizenship protected by the Fourteenth Amendment.

*Extent of Congressional Authority under Fourteenth Amendment*

Justice Miller had been particularly concerned, in the *Slaughter-house Cases,* over the possibility that a broad interpretation of the privileges and immunities clause of the Fourteenth Amendment would open the way for the imposition by Congress of a federal civil code upon the people of the states, replacing the innumerable state police power laws which had previously governed individual behavior. Section 5 of the Fourteenth Amendment provides that "The Congress shall have power to enforce, by appropriate legislation, the provisions of this article." As was noted in the preceding chapter, this enforcement section embraces the whole amendment. Congress, in 1875, recognized this when it utilized the due process and equal protection clauses as well as that pertaining to privileges and immunities as a basis for a comprehensive federal code of individual conduct. The Thirteenth Amendment was also invoked. A legislative code entitled the "Civil Rights Act" was drawn up which attempted to do three things. First, it subjected state officials to certain penalties if they deprived any citizen of the rights secured by the two amendments mentioned above. This did not raise any serious constitutional problem.[4] Second, it penalized private individuals who deprived Negroes of certain rights safeguarded by the amendments. And third, and perhaps of greatest significance for federal-state relations, the Act spelled out in detail the rights which Congress believed were protected by the amendments.

The constitutionality of the Act was questioned before the Waite Court in the *Civil Rights Cases*[5] in 1883. The issue was whether Congress, under the Thirteenth and Fourteenth Amendments, could constitutionally protect colored people from private as distinguished from state or public discrimination, and whether it could, though enactment of a civil rights code, supersede the state legislatures in regard to the control of private conduct. In determining the scope of congressional authority under the Act, the Waite Court held that Congress cannot adopt "general" legislation governing individual conduct, but only "corrective" legislation designed to counteract state laws or actions contravening the rights safeguarded by the amendment. Since sections

4. See *Strauder* v. *West Virginia,* 100 U.S. 303 (1879); *Ex Parte Virginia,* 100 U.S. 339 (1879).

5. 109 U.S. 3 (1883). This decision had been harbingered to some extent by the earlier Waite Court decisions in *United States* v. *Reese,* 92 U.S. 214 (1875) and *United States* v. *Cruikshank,* 92 U.S. 542 (1875).

1 and 2 of the Civil Rights Act fell into the category of the former, they were "repugnant to the Tenth Amendment."

It had been argued that racial discrimination practiced by private persons imposed a badge of slavery upon colored people in violation of the Thirteenth Amendment. Congress, it was claimed, merely acted under that amendment's enforcement provision to prohibit such violation. Significantly, the Court recognized that the scope of congressional enforcement authority was broader under the Thirteenth than under the Fourteenth Amendment, for under the former, Congress could legislate against individual as well as state action. The discriminations prohibited by the Civil Rights Act, however, were held to have "nothing to do with slavery or involuntary servitude." Consequently, the Thirteenth Amendment could not be properly invoked as a basis for the Act.

The Waite Court's decision in the *Civil Rights Cases* decisively defeated a congressional attempt at creating a federal civil rights code designed to supersede the various laws of the state legislatures governing such matters. As in the *Slaughterhouse Cases,* an affirmative decision by the Supreme Court would have opened the way for a fundamental alteration of the federal division of powers with perhaps irreparable harm to the autonomy of the states. However, the Waite Court's *Civil Rights* decision is different from the Chase Court's *Slaughterhouse* decision in one important respect. For while the latter achieved its purpose by practically erasing the privileges and immunities clause, the former limited the scope of congressional enforcement power, but did not destroy it.

Actually, the Waite Court had sustained portions of the Civil Rights Act which were "corrective" of state legislation or action in several cases decided before the *Civil Rights Cases.* In *Strauder* v. *West Virginia,*[6] a state law which denied to all colored citizens the right to act as jurors, because of race, although they were otherwise qualified to participate, was held to violate the equal protection clause of the Fourteenth Amendment. And in *Ex Parte Virginia*[7] the constitution-

6. 100 U.S. 303 (1879).

7. 100 U.S. 339 (1879). The case of *Virginia* v. *Rives,* 100 U.S. 313 (1879), established the principle that while a colored man awaiting trial is entitled to a jury selected without racial discrimination, it is not essential to the requirements of the equal protection clause that in a particular case a mixed jury be selected; in *Neal* v. *Delaware,* 103 U.S. 370 (1880), the Court reaffirmed the doctrines of the *Strauder* and *Rives* cases and *Ex Parte Virginia.* Here, consistent refusal by state judicial officers to appoint Negro jurors because allegedly there were none in a population of 26,000 who could qualify intelligently as jurors was held to be state action in violation of the equal

ality of a section of the Civil Rights Act authorizing federal prosecution of state officials for discriminating racially in the selection of jurors was sustained.

In decisions like those in the *Strauder* and *Virginia* cases, the Waite Court made it clear that the equal protection clause of the Fourteenth Amendment would be construed as a source of both judicial and legislative authority for the federal government. State laws or actions were held subject to federal judicial review and state officials were held subject to congressional "corrective" legislation. Thus, unlike the Chase Court's privileges and immunities clause decision, the Waite Court was able to safeguard state autonomy in the *Civil Rights Cases* as well as in others discussed above without emasculating the other clauses of the Fourteenth Amendment. And while it rejected the extreme interpretation presented by the Congress which enacted the Civil Rights Act, the Waite Court recognized clearly that the amendment was truly a limitation on state action, and, within bounds, a fruitful source of federal authority. The Waite Court's interpretative solution is undeniably the more statesmanlike of the two.

### *The Evolution of Substantive Due Process*

The period of the Waite Court, 1874-88, was one of cautious expansion of the scope of the due process clause. In the main, the Waite Court professed to view the due process limitation with caution and reserve.[8] Nevertheless, many of its decisions dealing with the clause were characterized by a curious inconsistency. While the Waite Court's actual decisions were liberal in the sense that state legislative power was not unduly circumscribed under its due process holdings, these decisions often contained doctrines, stated by way of *dicta,* which intimated that the due process clause limited state power substantively as well as procedurally. To put it another way, the Waite Court itself did not, in its due process decisions, seriously hamper state legislative authority, but in evolving the concept of due process as a substantive limitation, it paved the way for rigorous federal judicial interference in later years.

Before the Civil War the Supreme Court had, with the single exception of the *Dred Scott* decision, consistently refrained from viewing the Fifth Amendment's due process limitation on congressional legislation as anything more than a procedural safeguard. However,

---

protection clause. Under this holding, the Court quashed an indictment found by a jury chosen in a manner to exclude Negroes.

8. See Justice Miller's remarks in *Davidson* v. *New Orleans,* 96 U.S. 97 (1878).

Professor Corwin has indicated that by the 1850's the New York courts were stating and applying the doctrine that the due process clause in the state constitution restrained the state legislature substantively.[9]

Early in the Waite Court period, a decision was handed down which, while not based upon the due process clause of the Fourteenth Amendment at all, indicated unmistakably that the Waite Court justices were disposed to limit state legislative activity substantively. In *Loan Association* v. *Topeka*[10] the Court established the doctrine that taxes can be levied only for public purposes. Although the due process clause of the Fourteenth Amendment was already available in 1874, the *Topeka* doctrine was not based on any express constitutional provision, but on the natural law theory that "There are limitations on such power which grow out of the essential nature of all free governments; implied reservations of individual rights, without which the social compact could not exist. . . ." Within a few years, other justices were to discover that the due process clause could serve as a more defensible substantive limitation than natural law.

*Munn* v. *Illinois*[11] is outstanding in the Waite Court's evolution of due process doctrines which, while sustaining state authority in the short run, embodied potentially serious limitations on such authority. State regulation of the prices or rates of grain elevators and railroads had been a natural consequence of intense agrarian reaction to the unscrupulous price manipulation characteristic of the 1860's and 1870's.[12] In the *Munn* case the constitutionality of an Illinois law regulating the rates of privately owned grain elevators was tested under the due process clause of the Fourteenth Amendment, and secondarily under the commerce clause. The law was sustained by a majority of the Waite Court under the doctrine, introduced by the chief justice, that private business which is "affected with a public interest" may be validly subjected to state legislative rate-making. And further, once state power to regulate was established under the public interest doctrine the question whether rates were excessive or regulations oppressive did not raise a judicial issue under the due process clause. For protection against such abuses by legislatures "the people must resort to the polls, not to the courts."

Viewed as an affirmative doctrine, that of the *Munn* case apparently opened the way for state regulation of the rates of any business "affected with a public interest." But it is difficult to imagine why the

9. "Due Process Before the Civil War," 24 *Harvard Law Review* 370, 460.
10. 20 Wallace 655 (1874); applied in *Cole* v. *LaGrange*, 113 U.S. 1 (1884).
11. 94 U.S. 113 (1877).
12. Solon J. Buck, *The Agrarian Crusade*, pp. 43-59.

Waite Court did not simply sustain the rate regulations as valid exercises of state police power unless the Waite justices wanted to establish, via the due process clause, definable limits to that power in the field of price regulation. Thus, from Chief Justice Waite's discussion it is evident that the majority assumed that the due process clause limited state legislative power substantively.[13] For as Justice Field's dissent indicated, if a business was found by the court not to be affected with a public interest, state legislative rate regulation would violate the due process clause.

Even though the *Munn* doctrine itself, by implication, set limits to state regulatory power, it was considered much too broad a basis for state authority by the dissenters, Justices Field and Strong. In Field's words, the doctrine was "subversive of the rights of private property." After the *Granger* cases, the doctrine was applied again by the Waite Court in *Spring Valley Waterworks* v. *Schottler*.[14] But in other cases the Waite Court justices began to temper the doctrine. In 1886, Chief Justice Waite, for example, retreated from his broad statement in the *Munn* case that legislative abuse of the power to regulate rates must be corrected at the polls, not in the courts. In *Stone* v. *Farmer's Loan and Trust Company*,[15] he noted, by way of *dicta*, that "From what has thus been said it is not to be inferred that this power of limitation or regulation is itself without limit. This power to regulate is not a power to destroy, and limitation is not the equivalent of confiscation." This statement hinted at stricter federal judicial control of state legislative or administrative rate-making. And, furthermore, it might justifiably be termed an important step in the evolution of the doctrine of reasonableness.

The case of *Mugler* v. *Kansas*[16] provides an excellent illustration of how the Waite Court, while attaining a record unequaled by later courts for sustaining state regulatory legislation in its due process decisions, developed a number of doctrines which were potentially highly restrictive of state police power. In its *Mugler* decision, the Waite Court sustained a Kansas law prohibiting the manufacture and sale of intoxicating liquor as a valid exercise of state police power. But in doing so laid down the following significant doctrine:

13. *Cf.* Wright, *The Growth of American Constitutional Law*, pp. 99-100.

14. 110 U.S. 347 (1883).

15. 116 U.S. 307 (1886).

16. 123 U.S. 623 (1887); see *Davidson* v. *New Orleans*, 96 U.S. 97 (1878); *Missouri, Pacific Railroad Company* v. *Humes*, 115 U.S. 512 (1885); *Dow* v. *Beidelman*, 125 U.S. 680 (1888); *Powell* v. *Pennsylvania*, 127 U.S. 678 (1888); or *Hurtado* v. *California*, 110 U.S. 516 (1884).

If . . . a statute purporting to have been enacted to protect the public health, the public morals or the public safety, has no real or substantial relation to these subjects, or is a palpable invasion of rights secured by the fundamental law, it is the duty of the courts to so adjudge and thereby give effect to the constitution.

The Mugler *dicta* are important in three respects. For not only did they incorporate a full acceptance by the Waite Court of the role of censor of the substance of state legislation, but they also contained a definition of state police power in which reference to power to provide for the general welfare was conspicuously absent. And, in addition, it was intimated that the Court itself would decide whether conditions existed which justified legislative action, thus opening the way for judicial determination of the wisdom of or necessity for such action.

Another doctrine which broadened greatly federal judicial authority to determine the constitutionality of state regulatory legislation was that which held that a corporation is a person within the meaning of the Fourteenth Amendment. This was established in *Santa Clara County* v. *Southern Pacific Railroad Company*.[17] In the decision the Waite Court flatly refused to hear argument on the question of the validity of this doctrine. Actually, the Court had tacitly extended the protection of the Fourteenth Amendment to corporations in several earlier cases.[18]

The extension of the protection of the Fourteenth Amendment to artificial corporate entities, plus the Waite Court's assumption, in *dicta* in the *Mugler* and other cases, that the due process clause limited state power substantively as well as procedurally, paved the way for later development of the clause as the greatest single constitutional limitation on state power and the greatest single bulwark of private property as well.

Throughout the entire period 1874-88, the Waite Court invalidated only one state law under the due process clause. And it did so on purely procedural grounds.[19] However, the Waite Court generally took a liberal view of the permissible scope of state legislative authority in regard to procedural due process questions. For in *Hurtado* v. *Cali-*

17. 118 U.S. 394 (1886).

18. See *Chicago, Burlington and Quincy Railroad Company* v. *Iowa*, 94 U.S. 155 (1877); *Richmond, Fredericksburg and Petersburg Railroad Company* v. *Richmond*, 96 U.S. 521 (1878).

19. The case was *Pennoyer* v. *Neff*, 95 U.S. 714 (1878), in which the Waite Court held that the rendering of a judgment by a state court against a person who did not reside in the state without providing adequate notice of the proceeding violated the due process clause.

*fornia,*[20] it held that procedural innovations did not violate the Fourteenth Amendment if they fulfilled the basic requirements of a fair judicial proceeding.

However, as the foregoing cases indicated, the Waite Court, through the subtle processes of interpretation, paved the way for a remarkable revolution in federal-state relations. By assuming that the Fourteenth Amendment's due process clause limited state power substantively, it placed the federal judiciary in the position of censor of all the legislation of the states. In utilizing the tremendous judicial power that it assumed under this clause, the Waite Court exercised a great deal of self-restraint. But it laid the basis for enforcement by its successors of judicial policies which considerably weakened state authority, particularly under the police power. This it did, not as traditional arbiter in conflicts of federal and state authority, but as arbiter of the relations of each state to its people under the due process clause of the Fourteenth Amendment.

### *Equal Protection Clause*

That the Waite Court would hold void, as in conflict with the equal protection clause, state legislation of a racially discriminatory nature has been discussed above in cases such as *Strauder* v. *West Virginia.* The Court maintained this attitude in *Yick Wo* v. *Hopkins,*[21] a case involving a San Francisco ordinance which vested arbitrary power in the hands of administrators who exercised it in a racially discriminatory manner. All the state statutes or actions declared unconstitutional under this clause by the Waite Court involved racial discrimination of some kind. However, the Waite Court did not confine itself to racial discrimination issues but considered state taxation and other policies under the equal protection clause.[22]

### *Contract Clause*

Although its record was somewhat contradictory, the Waite Court definitely enlarged the permissible scope of state police power in its contract clause decisions. This judgment is, of course, subject to certain important qualifications. For while the Waite Court period is definitely one of liberalization from the standpoint of state powers, the contract clause still remained the greatest single source of federal judicial censorial power over state social and economic legislation.[23] Even for a court as aware of the pressing needs for judicial innovation to meet

20. 110 U.S. 516 (1884). 21. 118 U.S. 356 (1886).

22. *San Bernardino County* v. *Southern Pacific Railroad Company,* 118 U.S. 417 (1885).

23. Wright, *Contract Clause,* p. 95.

rapidly changing conditions as was the Waite Court, the sheer force of long-established precedents set definable limits to the area susceptible of interpretative change.[24]

However, the use of older doctrines only partly filled the interpretative needs of the times. The social pressures that caught up the Waite Court and, figuratively speaking, demanded modification of the Supreme Court's formerly rigorous application of the *Dartmouth College* doctrine are admirably illustrated in the case of *Fertilizing Company* v. *Hyde Park*.[25] In this case the Waite Court sustained a municipal ordinance forbidding the transportation of offal through the municipal limits to a fertilizer company which had been established in the locality before it had become urbanized. The state had granted the company a fifty-year charter, but the Waite Court ruled that this charter was not an irrevocable contract but must be viewed as a "sufficient license until revoked." The extreme offensiveness of the nuisance enabled the Court to invoke the common law principle that private property must be so used as to avoid injuring others. The *Hyde Park* decision was an important contribution to state police power in a period when rapid industrialization and urbanization created serious health problems.

Just as the *Hyde Park* decision of the Waite Court enhanced state police power in the area of public health, so did its decision in *Stone* v. *Mississippi*[26] broaden appreciably the permissible scope of state police power in the area of public morals. For in this case the doctrine that a state cannot bargain away its vital police power in regard to morals was applied for the first time. In *New Orleans Gas Company* v. *Louisiana Company*,[27] however, the court indicated that it was unwill-

24. Some of the older doctrines such as those of the *Knoop, Kinzie, Gelpcke* and *Von Hoffman* decisions were restrictive of state action. See *Farrington* v. *Tennessee*, 95 U.S. 679 (1877); *Edwards* v. *Kearzery*, 96 U.S. 595 (1877); *University* v. *People*, 99 U.S. 309 (1878); *Wolff* v. *New Orleans*, 103 U.S. 358 (1880); *Burgess* v. *Seligman*, 107 U.S. 20 (1882); *Nelson* v. *St. Martin's Parish*, 111 U.S. 716 (1883). However, others like the *Charles River Bridge* doctrine were permissive of state action. See *Erie Railway Company* v. *Pennsylvania*, 21 Wallace 492 (1874); *Home Insurance Company* v. *Augusta*, 93 U.S. 116 (1876); *Railroad Company* v. *Hecht*, 95 U.S. 168 (1877); *Turnpike Company* v. *Illinois*, 96 U.S. 63 (1877); *Memphis Gas Company* v. *Taxing District of Shelby County*, 109 U.S. 398 (1883); *C. & O. Ry. Co.* v. *Miller*, 114 U.S. 176 (1884).

25. 97 U.S. 659 (1878).

26. 101 U.S. 814 (1880); see *Beer Company* v. *Massachusetts*, 97 U.S. 25 (1877); *Butchers' Union Company* v. *Crescent City Company*, 111 U.S. 746 (1883). In *Boyd* v. *Alabama*, 94 U.S. 645 (1877), the doctrine was stated by way of *dicta*, but not applied.

27. 115 U.S. 650 (1885); see *New Orleans Waterworks Company* v. *Rivers*, 115 U.S. 674 (1885); *St. Tammany Waterworks* v. *New Orleans Waterworks*, 120 U.S. 64 (1886).

ing to extend the doctrine to other areas in the vast catalogue of state police powers. Since a grant by the Louisiana legislature to the New Orleans Gas Company of exclusive monopoly privileges in supplying gas did not, in the eyes of the Court, raise a problem involving the public health or safety, the state could not grant the privilege of supplying gas to another company in the same city without violating the contract clause.

That the Eleventh Amendment could under certain circumstances thwart the purposes of the contract clause was illustrated in *Louisiana* v. *Jumel* and *Ex Parte Ayers*.[28] These cases involved situations where state officials actually represented a state and fulfilled its legislative or constituent policy. Thus a suit against such an officer was considered a suit against the state forbidden by the Amendment. However, where a state official exceeded his authority or acted under color of an unconstitutional statute, a suit for an injunction could lie against him as an individual without violating the Eleventh Amendment.[29]

By and large the Waite Court's contract clause decisions modified in several important aspects the restrictions on state police power established by its predecessors. Its most important contributions were in decisions such as *Stone* v. *Mississippi,* where state power to safeguard public health and morals was enhanced.

### GRANTS OF POWER TO THE NATIONAL GOVERNMENT

Although the Waite Court was generally inclined to expand the permissible scope of state authority in its enforcement of the constitutional limitations on the states, it was not disposed to permit state interference with valid exercises of federal power. And in some areas it actually expanded federal authority.

#### *The Commerce Clause*

The Waite Court's treatment of the commerce clause is largely a story of expanding federal judicial and legislative power. As early as the Chase Court period, the states, generally under the urgent insistence of agrarian organizations, had begun to regulate the rates and policies of interstate carriers. The Supreme Court had only begun to cope with the problem when Chief Justice Chase died in 1873. The basic question which emerged for the consideration of the Waite Court and which was fundamental to practically every major commerce clause case coming before it was whether a matter requiring national regulation could be regulated by the states in the absence of congres-

28. 107 U.S. 711 (1882); 123 U.S. 443 (1887).
29. *Board of Liquidation* v. *McComb,* 92 U.S. 531 (1876).

sional action. The Waite Court did not come up with an immediate answer, but evolved what was destined to become a determinative constitutional doctrine between the years 1874 and 1887.

In the first year of Waite's tenure as Chief Justice, the Court discussed the problem of state obstruction of interstate commerce in a case in which the authority of the state was sustained. In *Railroad Company* v. *Maryland*,[30] a stipulation in a state railroad charter to the effect that the company must pay a bonus from its earnings to the state was held a valid exercise of state power over internal improvement facilities set up under its auspices and authority. Justice Bradley's *dictum* on the possibility of meeting state obstruction was particularly interesting. He suggested that serious state obstruction to private railroad development could be met by congressional competition through the use of its commerce, postal and military powers.

The cast of Waite Court thinking concerning the doctrinal solution for state interference with interstate commerce seemed to be clearly set in the case of *Welton* v. *Missouri*[31] in which a Missouri act which required payment of a license fee by peddlers of merchandise produced outside the state, but not by peddlers of state-produced merchandise, was held to be an unconstitutional discrimination against the products of other states under the *Cooley* doctrine. Congress, it was pointed out, had power under the commerce clause to lay down uniform national regulations on the exchange of interstate products and this was a situation calling for uniformity. The absence of such regulations was "equivalent to a declaration that interstate commerce shall be free and untrammelled."

The *Welton* and other early decisions indicated that where uniform national regulation of interstate and foreign commerce was necessary the states could not act even if Congress had not acted. However, in the year following the *Welton* decision, the *Granger Cases* seemed to suggest an entirely different approach on the part of the Waite Court. Although the commerce clause questions raised in *Munn* v. *Illinois* were dealt with summarily in the majority opinion, this case and the related *Granger Cases* are of perhaps as great interest in the development of the constitutional law of the commerce clause as in that of the due process clause. Evidently the due process clause contentions involving the constitutionality of the grain-elevator rate regulations overshadowed all other considerations. When Chief Justice Waite

30. 21 Wallace 456 (1874).

31. 91 U.S. 275 (1875). The *Cooley* doctrine was also applied in *Henderson* v. *Mayor of New York*, 92 U.S. 259 (1875); and in *Chy Lung* v. *Freeman*, 92 U.S. 275 (1875); *People* v. *Compagnie Generale Transatlantique*, 107 U.S. 59 (1882).

characterized the great midwestern grain storage companies as toll-takers at a vital "gateway of commerce," he apparently did so to prove that such companies could be subjected to state rate regulation without doing injury to the due process safeguard. For while he recognized the vital role the companies played in interstate and foreign commerce, he held that their regulation was

> . . . of domestic concern, and certainly, until Congress acts in reference to their interstate relations, the state may exercise all the powers of government over them, even though in so doing it may indirectly operate upon commerce outside its immediate jurisdiction.

In another *Granger* case, *Peik* v. *Chicago and Northwestern Railway Company,*[32] Waite applied this doctrine to an interstate carrier. These comments on the commerce power in the *Munn* and *Peik* cases seemed to modify the Court's earlier holdings in the *Welton* and *Henderson* cases. But in spite of the apparently divergent tendency evidenced in the *Granger Cases,* most of the subsequent Waite Court commerce clause decisions followed the *Welton* doctrine.[33]

The developmental climax came in 1886 with Justice Miller's opinion in *Wabash, St. Louis and Pacific Railway Company* v. *Illinois.*[34] The importance of the *Wabash* case can scarcely be overestimated, for it represents in many respects a landmark in the Court's long and sometimes unpredictable evolution of the law of the commerce clause. In terms of federal-state relations it definitely enhanced federal authority while curtailing that of the states. At issue in the case was the constitutionality of an Illinois statute regulating the rates of interstate railroads. In this instance the state legislature attempted to put an end to the ruinous rate discrimination practiced by profit-conscious railroad companies. The Court held that despite the "obvious injustice" of the discriminatory rate, the state of Illinois could not regulate the rates of interstate carriers without violating the commerce clause. The doctrine upon which this ruling was based held that even where Congress had not acted, whenever the subject to be regulated required "general and national" supervision, the states cannot act.

The *Wabash* decision is credited with spurring congressional adop-

32. 94 U.S. 164 (1877).

33. See *Railroad Company* v. *Husen,* 95 U.S. 465 (1877); *Hall* v. *Decuir,* 95 U.S. 485 (1877); *Guy* v. *Baltimore,* 100 U.S. 434 (1879); *Tierman* v. *Rinker,* 102 U.S. 123 (1880); *Webber* v. *Virginia,* 103 U.S. 344 (1880); *Cooper Manufacturing Company* v. *Ferguson,* 113 U.S. 727 (1884); *Walling* v. *Michigan,* 116 U.S. 446 (1885); *Gloucester Ferry Company* v. *Pennsylvania,* 114 U.S. 196 (1884).

34. 118 U.S. 557 (1886).

tion of the Interstate Commerce Act in 1887.[35] However, the decision not only enhanced federal legislative power but also expanded federal judicial power. For in a decision invalidating an Iowa liquor prohibition requiring interstate carriers to procure a certificate from the auditor of the county of destination before bringing liquor into the state, Justice Matthews laid down the rule that the Supreme Court would decide in each case whether, in the absence of congressional legislation, state statutes affecting interstate or foreign commerce would be sustained.[36] From the point of view of the states, the *Wabash* decision definitely and decisively limited state power, precluding state railroad rate regulation in a period when many farm state legislators felt strongly that state action was necessary to protect the people of their states from railroad exploitation. Moreover, the substitution of congressional control through the Interstate Commerce Commission proved relatively ineffective for a number of years.[37]

Many of the commerce clause decisions of the Waite Court which were discussed or cited above in themselves indicated an important expansion of the scope of the commerce clause as a limitation on state power. But in addition, the Waite Court opened the way for serious curtailment of the Chase Court's *Woodruff* v. *Parham* doctrine. In that case it had been held that the "original package" doctrine did not apply to state taxes on "imports from a sister state" but was limited to foreign imports. However, when the Waite Court was called upon to consider the constitutionality of a state prohibition law which interfered with interstate commerce in intoxicating liquor, it ruled, in *Bowman* v. *Chicago and Northwestern Railroad Company,*[38] that "transportation between the states, including the importation of goods from one state to another" required uniform, national regulation. Consequently, the absence of congressional action was "equivalent to its [Congress'] declaration that commerce in that matter shall be free." This doctrine, as applied to interstate commerce in liquor, in itself seriously hampered state officials in the enforcement of state prohibition laws. The *Bowman* decision in turn paved the way for the Fuller Court's application of the "original package" doctrine to interstate commerce in *Leisy* v. *Hardin*[39] two years later.

*Pensacola Telegraph Company* v. *Western Union Telegraph Com-*

35. Charles Fairman, *Justice Miller,* p. 314.

36. *Bowman* v. *Chicago and Northwestern Railway Company,* 125 U.S. 465 (1887).

37. Arthur M. Schlesinger, *The Political and Social Growth of the American People, 1865-1940,* pp. 134-35.

38. 125 U.S. 465 (1887).

39. 135 U.S. 100 (1890).

*pany*[40] provides an excellent example of the Supreme Court's ability to adapt constitutional interpretation to fundamental social and technological changes, if it wants to do so. A grant by Florida of exclusive telegraphic privileges to a single company was held "inoperative" because it interfered with Congress' commerce and postal powers. These powers were interpreted broadly so as to include modern as well as old instrumentalities of commercial and postal communication. In short, Congress' regulatory authority was not confined to those modes of communication familiar to the framers of the Constitution.

One question in the *Pensacola* case which had far-reaching implications for state control of internal economy was whether in the absence of congressional legislation a state could constitutionally exclude an individual or a corporation engaged in interstate commerce from the state. The Waite Court held that it was unnecessary to answer this question, but in referring to *Paul* v. *Virginia,* intimated that a negative answer might be anticipated should it actually arise.

The preceding commerce clause cases indicate clearly that the Waite Court's primary purpose in utilizing the commerce clause as a limitation on state power was to prevent state interference with interstate and foreign commerce. However, the Waite Court refrained from voiding state police power legislation which only remotely affected such commerce. The case of *Smith* v. *Alabama*[41] reflected accurately its attitude on this point. This decision sustained an Alabama police power regulation requiring the examination and licensing of locomotive engineers engaged in interstate commerce by a state board to safeguard the public safety. Laws like this, said the Court, which affect transactions of commerce "only indirectly, incidentally and remotely" but do not burden or impede them, do not violate the commerce clause.

In regard to the purely internal commerce of the states, the Waite Court showed little disposition to interfere judicially with state police and taxing regulations even when state action affected to some extent

40. 96 U.S. 1 (1877). Other state interferences with interstate commerce in telegraphic messages were invalidated in *Western Union Telegraph Company* v. *Pendleton,* 122 U.S. 347 (1886); *Ratterman* v. *Western Union Telegraph Company,* 127 U.S. 411 (1887); *Leloup* v. *Mobile,* 127 U.S. 640 (1888). However, in *Western Union Telegraph Co.* v. *Massachusetts,* 125 U.S. 530 (1888), the Court indicated, by way of *dicta,* that telegraph companies were not exempt from state taxation which did not obstruct interstate or foreign commerce.

41. 124 U.S. 465 (1887); see *Quachita Packet Company* v. *Aiken,* 121 U.S. 444 (1886); *County of Mobile* v. *Kimball,* 102 U.S. 691 (1880); *Turner* v. *Maryland,* 107 U.S. 38 (1883); *Wiggins Ferry Company* v. *East St. Louis,* 107 U.S. 365 (1882); *Morgan's Steamship Company* v. *Louisiana Board of Health,* 118 U.S. 455 (1885).

interstate commerce. Thus in *Coe* v. *Errol*[42] a tax on goods originating within the state imposing the tax was sustained even though the goods being taxed were destined for transportation in interstate commerce. The case of *McCready* v. *Virginia*[43] indicates similar Waite Court self-restraint concerning state regulation of its property. In this decision a Virginia law prohibiting the "planting" of oyster beds in Virginia waters by persons who were not citizens of Virginia was sustained as a proper exercise of state authority over property held in common for all the citizens of the state. It was held to be neither an unconstitutional regulation of commerce nor a violation of a privilege of "inter-state citizenship."

Furthermore, the Waite Court, like its immediate predecessor, was firmly opposed to expansion of congressional regulatory authority over the internal commerce of the states. Consistent with this viewpoint is its decision in the *Trade Mark Cases,*[44] in which a congressional act providing for the punishment of persons counterfeiting trade-marks registered according to the laws of the United States was held unconstitutional under the Tenth Amendment as an invasion of the internal commerce of the states.

Under the doctrine of the Marshall Court's *Blackbird Creek* case the Waite Court sustained various state obstructions of navigable streams.[45] However in *Cardwell* v. *American Bridge Company,*[46] the Court adopted the doctrine that a state, in this case California, can, in the absence of congressional legislation to the contrary, obstruct a navigable river by authorizing the building of a bridge across it. The majority reasoned that if it did not sustain this doctrine, new states like California could be prevented from exercising a power long enjoyed by the older eastern states. This, they felt, would violate the principle of state equality.

In decisions such as those in the *Welton* and *Wabash* cases, the Waite Court undoubtedly enlarged federal commerce power at the expense of the states under the general theory that the states cannot be permitted to burden or obstruct interstate or foreign commerce. Yet, that the Waite Court justices thought that they had a concomitant duty to safeguard the purely internal commerce of the states from

42. 116 U.S. 517 (1885); applied also in *Turpin* v. *Burgess,* 117 U.S. 504 (1885).

43. 94 U.S. 319 (1876); see *Transportation Company* v. *Wheeling,* 99 U.S. 273 (1878).

44. 100 U.S. 434 (1879); an argument attempting to base the act on the patent clause was rejected.

45. See *Huse* v. *Glover,* 119 U.S. 543 (1886); *Sands* v. *Manistee River Improvement Company,* 123 U.S. 288 (1887).

46. 113 U.S. 205 (1884).

federal encroachment was established by their decision in the *Trade Mark Cases.* The over-all effect of the Waite Court commerce clause decisions was to withdraw from state police power, supervision of many activities of interstate carriers, while, at the same time, preserving for the states the control of their "purely internal" commerce. During the Waite Court period, the commerce clause became one of the most important limitations on state power to be found in the Constitution.

*The Postal Clause*

In *Ex Parte Jackson*[47] the Waite Court upheld a pioneering attempt by Congress to regulate public morals by utilizing its enumerated postal power to exclude from the mails lottery tickets or circulars referring to lotteries. After establishing that the postal power included the power to designate the nature, size, weight, form and carrying charges of mail, the Waite Court concluded that "the right to determine what shall be carried necessarily involves the right to determine what shall be excluded." Their decision is of particular interest because it presaged the great development of a federal police power in the twentieth century. Through this development certain aspects of the regulation of public safety, health, morals and general welfare, matters traditionally considered within the reserved or internal police powers of the states, were brought within congressional control through the use of its enumerated postal, commerce, and taxing powers[48]

*Federal Control of National Elections*

It was not until 1870 and 1872 that Congress enacted statutes which regulated comprehensively the conduct of congressional elections. The source of its authority was Article I, section 4, which provides that

> The times, places and manner of holding elections for senators and representatives shall be prescribed in each state by the legislature thereof; but the Congress may at any time, by law, make or alter such regulations, except as to the place of choosing Senators.

The congressional acts, among other things, provided for appointment of federal supervisors in any city with more than twenty thousand inhabitants by a federal circuit judge upon request of any two citizens. Actually the duties of the federal supervisors consisted in large part of enforcement of state election laws concerning national officials.

47. 96 U.S. 727 (1878).
48. See Ernst Freund, *The Police Power, Public Policy, and Constitutional Rights,* pp. 62-64.

The constitutionality of the acts was first tested in *Ex Parte Siebold*[49] and later in *Ex Parte Yarbrough*.[50] In the first case the principle was laid down that Congress could validly make it a federal offense for a state election official to fail to abide by state election laws regulating congressional elections. In the second, it was established that the right to vote in a federal election, once the necessary state qualifications such as those pertaining to age were met, could be protected by congressional legislation even against private interference. Both decisions were destined to play important roles in the twentieth century unfolding of the constitutional law governing primary elections. Moreover, in these decisions the Waite Court sustained important extensions of congressional authority into areas of election regulation which had hitherto been left largely to the states.

*Federal Judicial Authority*

In *Tennessee* v. *Davis*,[51] the Waite Court held that the principle of national supremacy rendered insufficient the argument of the state of Tennessee that removal of the case of a federal revenue officer from a state to a federal court violated the sovereignty of the state. The revenue officer had been prosecuted for murder in a state court for killing a man while performing his official federal duties.

### SUMMARY AND CONCLUSION

In conclusion, it is noteworthy that while the Waite Court contributed significantly to the preservation of state autonomy in the *Civil Rights Cases,* it did so without completely emasculating congressional power under section 5 of the Fourteenth Amendment. The states were not deprived of their power to govern the conduct of individuals, but at the same time Congress was not deprived of power to enforce the provisions of the Fourteenth Amendment through the adoption of legislation which was "corrective" of state infringements of the rights of individuals protected under the amendment. In the *Yarbrough* case the scope of congressional authority over national elections under Article I, section 4, was held broad enough to permit congressional prohibition of private interferences with the right to vote in national elections.

While it remained aware of the need to preserve state autonomy, the Waite Court was disposed to sustain what it considered to be valid

49. 100 U.S. 371 (1879); applied in *Ex Parte Clarke,* 100 U.S. 399 (1879); and *United States* v. *Gale,* 109 U.S. 65 (1883).

50. 110 U.S. 651 (1885).

51. 100 U.S. 257 (1879).

expansion of federal authority. Thus while it sought to protect the internal commerce of the states in the *Trade Mark Cases,* it sustained broad expansions of federal interstate commerce authority in the *Wabash* and *Pensacola* cases. In its *Bowman* decision, it seriously curtailed state police power on the ground that its exercise in regard to interstate transportation in intoxicating liquor interfered with matters requiring uniform, national regulation by Congress.

In its contract clause decisions, the Waite Court broadened considerably the scope of state police power in decisions such as *Stone* v. *Mississippi,* the *Fertilizer Company* case and *Louisiana* v. *Jumel.* However, the Waite Court's commerce clause decisions had quite a different result. In a series of decisions climaxed by that of the *Wabash* case, the commerce clause became, as was noted above, a tremendously effective limitation on state regulatory authority involving carriers in interstate commerce.

Nevertheless, by far the most significant developments for federal-state relations were the doctrines developed by the Waite Court concerning the due process and equal protection clauses. In regard to the latter clause, the Waite Court invalidated a number of state laws or actions which involved racial discrimination. However, it also considered a number of other cases involving the rights of private property, thus disproving Justice Miller's prediction in the *Slaughterhouse Cases.*

In both the equal protection clause and the due process clause, corporations found bases for claiming constitutional protection against state regulation of one kind or another. The Waite Court itself did not intervene to any great extent in its actual decisions to protect corporations against state regulation, but it paved the way for such intervention by its successors. This it did in a number of cases by assuming, as, for example, in the *Munn* and *Mugler* cases, that the due process clause limited state legislative power substantively as well as procedurally.

By and large the Waite Court's actual decisions in the field of federal-state relations were characterized by caution and self-restraint. Many of its decisions indicated a keen awareness of the need to preserve state autonomy without destroying or weakening federal authority. Yet in its due process cases, the Waite Court evolved doctrines which were destined to revolutionize federal-state relations by opening the way for federal judicial censorship of the legislation of the states.

# CHAPTER VII

## *The Fuller Court, 1888-1910*

By the time President Cleveland appointed Melville Weston Fuller Chief Justice of the United States, that judicial tribunal had functioned for almost a century. No longer could a new chief justice approach constitutional problems with the feeling of freedom and challenge of the new and unknown enjoyed by predecessors such as John Jay, Oliver Ellsworth, and John Marshall. To be sure, the everchanging problems of modern industrial society and the seemingly inexorable enlargements of federal authority raised new questions of constitutional import. And, of course, the Court could always "change its mind."[1] Nevertheless, a century of precedents did not fail to exert its influence upon the Fuller Court.

### CONSTITUTIONAL LIMITATIONS UPON THE STATES

#### *Contract Clause*

The influence of established doctrines was perhaps strongest in regard to the Fuller Court's contract clause decisions, for in contrast to the Waite Court, the Fuller Court developed no new contract clause doctrines; and whereas this clause had figured in 40 per cent of the cases involving the validity of state legislation during the Waite

1. Changes in membership also brought some changes in judicial temperament. With the exception of four, all were appointed by Republican Presidents. Justice Lucius Q. C. Lamar was appointed as Justice Woods' successor in 1887. The new Chief Justice, Melville Weston Fuller, was appointed in 1888. David J. Brewer succeeded Justice Matthews in 1889. Henry B. Brown succeeded Justice Miller in 1890. After Justice Bradley's death in 1892, George Shiras, Jr., was appointed. Howell E. Jackson succeeded Justice Lamar in 1893, while Edward D. White succeeded Justice Blatchford in 1894. In 1895 Justice Jackson died and was replaced by Rufus W. Peckham. Next, Justice Field retired in 1897 and was succeeded by Joseph McKenna in 1898. Oliver Wendell Holmes succeeded Justice Gray in 1902. William R. Day replaced Justice Shiras in 1903. And William H. Moody replaced Justice Brown in 1906. Horace H. Lurton succeeded Justice Peckham in 1909. Charles Evans Hughes replaced Justice Brewer in 1910, and Edward D. White was promoted to the Chief Justiceship in the same year.

Court period, it played a part in only 25 per cent of such cases in the long Fuller Court period.[2] The Fuller Court was not unduly rigorous in its determinations under the clause, but at the same time it never indicated a disposition to liberalize the doctrines which it inherited in order to permit greater legislative freedom for the states in economic matters.

### *Due Process Clause of the Fourteenth Amendment*

Perhaps the outstanding reason for the sharp decline in contract clause litigation during the Fuller Court period was the fact that the due process clause, under doctrines evolved by the Waite Court, provided a much broader base for the protection of the rights of private property. A true measure of the theoretical road traversed by the Supreme Court during the period 1873-92 can perhaps be gotten by contrasting Justice Miller's *Slaughterhouse* opinion with *dicta* by Justice Brewer in *Budd* v. *New York*.[3] In the former, Justice Miller was largely concerned with preventing the destruction of the federal system, but in the latter Brewer was especially interested in preserving the laissez faire economic system and was little disposed to consider the consequences of such a policy on the states.

In the *Budd* case Brewer had written that "The paternal theory of government is to me odious. The utmost possible liberty to the individual, and the fullest possible protection to him and his property, is both the limitation and duty of government." Although this was written in a dissenting opinion, the record of the Fuller Court, particularly in its application of the due process clause of the Fourteenth Amendment, indicates that a majority of the justices not only shared this view, but frequently enforced it in their judicial determinations.

By the 1890's the regulatory needs of the era of giant industrialization had become tremendous. The state legislatures frequently pioneered in new fields of social legislation, enacting more rigorous statutes regulating the rates of certain businesses and seeking to protect the health and safety of workers directly and the community indirectly by establishing safety regulations in some industries or by limiting daily working hours in others. The judicial policy of the Fuller Court in the face of these developments wrought a fundamental alteration in the relationship of the states to the federal government by making the federal courts censors of the state legislatures. This revolution had been ushered in, it is true, by the Waite Court in *dicta* in a number of its

2. Wright, *Contract Clause,* pp. 95-96.
3. 143 U.S. 517 (1892).

due process clause decisions. But the Waite Court had been quite cautious in its use of the new doctrines. Not so the Fuller Court.

Utilizing the doctrines developed by its predecessor and several which it created itself, the Fuller Court revolutionized federal-state relations by making the due process clause so broad a base for litigation that practically every effort at state legislative regulation of business, in effect, had to run the gauntlet of federal judicial censorship. Furthermore, the Fuller Court frequently substituted its own judgment concerning the necessity for or wisdom of state police power regulations for that of the state legislatures. These developments seriously weakened state autonomy in the federal system. For federal judicial supervision of state regulatory legislation not only frequently blocked needed state regulations, but also tended to discourage state legislative experimentation in the midst of an era in which state legislative initiative and daring were sorely needed.

A number of key due process clause decisions of the Fuller Court illustrate the drastic nature of the change wrought in federal-state relations. The old *Munn* doctrine was not overruled by the Fuller Court and in fact was even applied in a few scattered cases.[4] However, in several cases involving state rate regulation a narrower doctrine was substituted for it. For example, it was held that a rate regulation by a Georgia railroad commission could constitutionally extend to a company affected with "a public use." Businesses became so affected when they incurred an obligation to the public by accepting privileges from the state legislature or a municipal council in return for rendition of a public service. This doctrine was established by Justice Field in *Georgia Railroad and Banking Company* v. *Smith*.[5] The *Munn* doctrine had permitted state regulation of any business "affected by a public interest," while the doctrine of the *Smith* case was narrower, permitting state regulation only of businesses devoted to public service such as trolley lines or gas and electric utilities.

One of the most significant decisions in the Fuller Court's development of a broad supervisory power over state legislation was made in 1890. For just as the *Wabash* case set the stage for broader assumption of congressional power over interstate commerce, so did *Chicago, Milwaukee and St. Paul Railway Company* v. *Minnesota*[6] open the way

4. See *Brass* v. *Stosser,* 153 U.S. 391 (1894); *Budd* v. *New York,* 143 U.S. 517 (1892).

5. 128 U.S. 174 (1888); see *Charlotte, Columbia and Augusta Railroad Company* v. *Gibbs,* 142 U.S. 386 (1891); *New York* v. *Squire,* 145 U.S. 175 (1891).

6. 134 U.S. 418 (1890); see *Minneapolis Eastern Railway Company* v. *Minnesota,* 134 U.S. 467 (1890).

for greater federal judicial control of state regulatory legislation. Warren points out that direct legislative rate regulation, although constitutionally valid under the *Munn* doctrine, presented several practical difficulties. Railroad directors frequently refused to extend their lines in states employing such methods, and where midwestern farmers had formerly been plagued with exorbitant railroad rates, they later were faced with the impossibility of getting transportation for their crops. As a compromise measure, several states created special railroad commissions to make and administer rates.[7] It had been in its consideration of such an early railroad commission that the Waite Court, in *Stone* v. *Farmer's Loan and Trust Company,* had hinted at the doctrine that it was part of the judicial duty of the Supreme Court to determine the reasonableness of state rate-making regulations. The hint became a ruling under the Fuller Court. For in holding the Minnesota Railroad Commission Act void, the majority spokesman, Justice Blatchford, laid down the doctrine that the question of the reasonableness of railroad rates is eminently a question for judicial determination.

There is evidence in other portions of Justice Blatchford's opinion that he was particularly concerned about the exercise of judicial functions by what he believed to be a completely non-judicial body. But regardless of the implications of the decision concerning the Court's distrust of administrative procedures, the case is of the utmost importance in the ever-changing relationship of federal authority to state power. The doctrine enunciated laid the groundwork for a subsequent expansion of federal judicial supervision of state regulatory activities in the field of rate fixing. A tremendous increase in federal judicial power resulted.

Another step in the steady tendency of the Fuller Court to assume broader censorial power over state regulatory and especially rate fixing agencies was the case of *Reagan* v. *Farmer's Loan and Trust Company.*[8] Here the Court held that federal courts of equity may restrain the enforcement of rates made by state commissions if they deem the rates unreasonable or unjust. The climax came in 1898, when in *Smyth* v. *Ames*[9] the doctrine that the federal courts, and particularly the Supreme Court, shall determine whether the railroad rates set by state legislatures or state administrative boards of experts are reasonable was carried to its logical conclusion. The Fuller Court, in effect,

7. Warren, *History,* II, 580-90.

8. 154 U.S. 362 (1893).

9. 169 U.S. 466 (1898); see *Lake Shore and Michigan Southern Railway Company* v. *Smith,* 173 U.S. 684 (1899).

superseded a Nebraska administrative Board of Transportation provided for by legislative enactment, by establishing its own criteria for the reasonableness of such rates. A complicated formula was adopted by the Court to govern the present and future determinations of this kind, the Court holding that the basis for all calculations concerning the reasonableness of railroad rates imposed under state legislative sanction was "the fair value of the property" being used by the railroad "for the convenience of the public."

Intelligent men may differ over the question what is "fair," just as they might differ over the question what is "reasonable." The answers given to these questions generally are influenced by the particular social and economic philosophy motivating those who give the answers. Thus the formula of a "fair return" on a "fair value" could be challenged on social and economic grounds. However, the doctrine provided frequent opportunities for the Supreme Court justices to enshrine their personal economic and social predilections in the body of American constitutional law.[10]

Another doctrine which enhanced federal judicial supervisory power over state legislation or state action was laid down in *Allgeyer* v. *Louisiana,*[11] in which a state act prohibiting the sale of "open" marine insurance contracts was held void as a violation of "liberty of contract," a liberty purportedly guaranteed by the due process clause of the Fourteenth Amendment. The doctrine was originally stated in the following manner:

> The liberty mentioned in that amendment means not only the right of the citizen to be free from the mere physical restraint of his person, as by incarceration, but the term is deemed to embrace the right of the citizen to be free in the enjoyment of all of his faculties; to be free to use them in all lawful ways; to live and work where he will; to earn his livelihood by any lawful calling; to pursue any livelihood or avocation, and for that purpose to enter into all contracts which may be proper, necessary and essential to his carrying out to a successful conclusion the purposes above mentioned.

In its introductory statement the doctrine of liberty of contract appeared innocent enough. The need for balancing such individual liberty with compliance with law was recognized. But the tribunal enunciating this doctrine reserved the power to decide which laws were valid. Like the doctrine of reasonableness, that of liberty of contract repre-

10. Cf. Frankfurter, *The Public and Its Government,* pp. 101-9. For other extreme applications of the doctrine of "reasonableness," see *Norwood* v. *Baker,* 172 U.S. 267 (1898); *Dewey* v. *Des Moines,* 173 U.S. 193 (1899); *Chicago, Burlington and Quincy Railroad Company* v. *Chicago,* 166 U.S. 226 (1897).

11. 165 U.S. 578 (1897).

sented another constitutional engraftment further enlarging the powers of the federal judiciary, and commensurately subjecting the states to further federal judicial supervision of their legislative and administrative affairs.

The potentialities of the doctrine of liberty of contract were clearly recognized by the Fuller Court in the case of *Holden* v. *Hardy*.[12] In sustaining a Utah statute fixing eight hours as the maximum daily work period for miners as a reasonable exercise of state police power to protect the health and safety of a class of workers engaged in a hazardous occupation, the Court significantly pointed out that "The question in each case is whether the legislature had adopted the statute in exercise of a reasonable discretion, or whether its action be a mere excuse for an unjust discrimination, or the oppression, or spoliation of a particular class." The tribunal having the last word in the determination of such a question was, of course, the federal Supreme Court.

The case of *Lochner* v. *New York*[13] indicates clearly the uses to which a doctrine such as liberty of contract may be put by a court determined to enforce, whenever judicially possible, its own social and political philosophy. In its essentials, this decision, by a margin of 5 to 4, held void as a violation of the liberty of contract of employees a New York law limiting working hours in bakeries to ten hours daily and sixty hours weekly.[14] The Attorney General of New York had argued that the law was necessary to protect the health of both bakery workers and the public. Particularly in regard to the first argument, he cited voluminous medical reports supporting the judgment of the New York legislature. However, Justice Peckham and the other members of the majority preferred their own judgment on this matter to that of the state legislature.

Two dissenting opinions were written in the *Lochner* case. Justice Harlan, supported by Justices White and Day, attacked the majority's view on the public health question. The majority's substitution of its own view on the healthfulness of the baker's trade was, in Harlan's eyes, a judicial usurpation of the function of the state legislature. Justice Holmes' separate dissent has, of course, become a classic. Justice Peckham's opinion had been filled with indications that the majority had chosen the bakery case as the one in which the line would be drawn against further state legislative regulation of wages and hours. Holmes put his finger on this with his observation that

12. 169 U.S. 366 (1898).

13. 195 U.S. 45 (1905).

14. The majority opinion was, of course, also based on the premise that bakery workers and their employers bargained on a basis of equality.

. . . the word liberty in the Fourteenth Amendment is perverted when it is held to prevent the natural outcome of a dominant opinion, unless it can be said that a rational and fair man necessarily would admit that the statute proposed would infringe fundamental principles as they have been understood by the traditions of our people and our law.

Aside from Justice Holmes' well-taken criticism of the majority's incorporation of its own social and economic philosophy into the Constitution, his dissent intimated that the court should return to the older doctrine that doubtful state legislation shall be presumed valid. However, the Fuller Court majority did not do so. In *Muller* v. *Oregon*[15] a state law limiting the daily working hours of women employed in manufacturing concerns and laundries was sustained. But the presentation of a factual brief by Louis Brandeis is generally credited with convincing the Fuller Court that the law was a valid exercise of state police power designed to protect the health of women. The physical structure and maternal functions of women were recognized by the court to "place her at a disadvantage in the struggle for subsistence." The state law was upheld, but on the Fuller Court's own terms and only after the Court had satisfied itself concerning the relationship of the law to the health of women workers.

Bare statistics have in themselves little analytical value, but the fact that the Fuller Court decided 130 due process clause issues in the period 1900-10 is an accurate indication of the tremendous pressures put upon it by anti-regulatory forces. In fairness to the Fuller Court, it should be noted that it sustained a number of important state regulatory acts as valid exercises of state police power. Among them were laws requiring the observance of safety regulations in the operation of coal mines and oil and natural gas wells,[16] laws prohibiting combinations in restraint of trade,[17] zoning laws, and statutes prohibiting the use of the national flag for advertising purposes, false labeling of manufactured products, dealings in grain "futures" as well as several other

15. 208 U.S. 412 (1908).

16. *Ohio Oil Company* v. *Indiana* (No. 1), 177 U.S. 190 (1900); *Wilmington Mining Company* v. *Fulton*, 205 U.S. 60 (1907); *Chadwick* v. *Kelley*, 187 U.S. 540 (1903); *Schaefer* v. *Werling*, 187 U.S. 616 (1908); *Hibbon* v. *Smith*, 191 U.S. 310 (1903); *Shepard* v. *Burrow*, 194 U.S. 553 (1904); *Field* v. *Barber Asphalt Company*, 194 U.S. 618 (1904); *Seattle* v. *Kelleher*, 195 U.S. 351 (1904).

17. *National Cotton Oil Company* v. *Texas*, 197 U.S. 115 (1905); *Southern Cotton Oil Company* v. *Texas*, 197 U.S. 134 (1905); *Jack* v. *Kansas*, 199 U.S. 372 (1905); *Carrol* v. *Greenwich Insurance Company*, 199 U.S. 401 (1909); *Waters-Pierce Oil Company* v. *Texas* (No. 1), 212 U.S. 86 (1909); *Hammond Packing Company* v. *Arkansas*, 212 U.S. 322 (1909); *Grenada Lumber Company* v. *Mississippi*, 217 U.S. 433 (1910).

important subjects.[18] But as in the *Muller* case, the Fuller Court upheld these acts on its own terms.

Although the Fuller Court stated in *Northwestern Life Insurance Company* v. *Riggs*[19] that the "liberty guaranteed by the Fourteenth Amendment against deprivation without due process is the liberty of natural, not artificial persons," this did not, in fact, seriously hamper its activities in defense of economic laissez faire, for the doctrine of liberty of contract could be invoked to protect corporations as well as the "freedom" of individual employees to contract to work for outrageously long hours, and in addition the broader test of reasonableness was still a protective barrier for the property of corporate as well as natural persons.

There is reason to believe that the true measure of the effectiveness of the Fuller Court's rigorous supervision of state regulatory legislation via the due process clause of the Fourteenth Amendment is not the number of state enactments which were held void. For taking the decision in *Coppage* v. *Kansas* as an example, the federal judicial invalidation of a Kansas law prohibiting "yellow dog" contracts under the doctrine of "liberty of contract" not only annulled the particular legislative product of Kansas but pulled the rug, so to speak, from under the similar laws of twelve other states.[20]

In the cases discussed above, the Fuller Court insisted upon deciding for itself whether conditions warranted state legislative intervention. These cases all involved situations in which state regulatory legislation threatened economic laissez faire. State autonomy was weakened by the Fuller Court's substitution of its judgment on the wisdom of such legislation for the judgment of the state legislators. However, in another class of cases arising under the due process clause of the Fourteenth Amendment, those involving non-economic human

18. *L'Hote* v. *New Orleans,* 177 U.S. 587 (1900); *Minnesota Iron Company* v. *Kline,* 109 U.S. 593 (1905); *Martin* v. *Pittsburgh and Lake Erie Railroad Company,* 203 U.S. 284 (1906); *Bacon* v. *Walker,* 204 U.S. 311 (1907); *Brown* v. *Walling,* 204 U.S. 320 (1907); *Halter* v. *Nebraska,* 205 U.S. 34 (1907); *Heath and Milligan Manufacturing Company* v. *Worst,* 207 U.S. 338 (1907); *Lemieux* v. *Young,* 211 U.S. 489 (1909); *McLean* v. *Arkansas,* 211 U.S. 539 (1909); *Boston Chamber of Commerce* v. *Boston,* 217 U.S. 189 (1910); *Booth* v. *Illinois,* 184 U.S. 425 (1902); *Smiley* v. *Kansas,* 196 U.S. 447 (1905); *Aikens* v. *Wisconsin,* 195 U.S. 194 (1904).

19. 203 U.S. 243 (1906); *Western Turf Association* v. *Greenberg,* 204 U.S. 359 (1907). See also *Orient Insurance Company* v. *Daggs,* 172 U.S. 557 (1899), in which the Fuller Court held that a corporation was not a citizen within the meaning of the privileges and immunities clause of the Fourteenth Amendment.

20. 236 U.S. 1 (1915); the *Coppage* case was actually decided in the White Court period. California, Colorado, Connecticut, Idaho, Louisiana, Massachusetts, Minnesota, Nevada, New Jersey, New York, Oklahoma, and Oregon were affected; George C. S. Benson, *The New Centralization,* p. 106, note 2.

rights, the Fuller Court scrupulously refrained from enforcing its views on social policy upon the states. In these cases all attempts to broaden the scope of the Fourteenth Amendment to include some or all of the protections for individual non-property rights included in the first eight amendments were thwarted by the Fuller Court. Most were disposed of simply by invocation of the *Hurtado* doctrine;[21] others required a return to the principle of *Barron* v. *Baltimore* or the *Slaughterhouse Cases*;[22] but all were in marked contrast to the Fuller Court's customary eagerness to discover limitations, such as the doctrine of reasonableness, to safeguard economic rights.

*Equal Protection Clause*

The doctrine of reasonableness found a place in the constitutional law of the equal protection of the laws clause during the Fuller Court period. Thus the test of constitutionality under this clause could generally be summed up in the question, is the classification adopted by a state legislature a reasonable one? For example, in *Gulf, Colorado and Santa Fe Railway Company* v. *Ellis*,[23] a Texas law which required railroad companies to pay the attorneys' fees of litigants who successfully opposed them in stock damage suits was declared an unreasonable categorization because the companies were denied a commensurate right in the event that they won.

The Fuller Court's treatment of equal protection clause cases involving the Negro race offers an accurate indication of its primary concern with property rights and the preservation of economic laissez faire and its comparative disinterest in protecting human non-property rights. Ironically, the Fourteenth Amendment had been adopted primarily to protect the emancipated Negroes after the Civil War. In time, and partly because of the persuasive arguments of men like Roscoe Conkling,[24] this Amendment became the legal bulwark of giant corporations, while the few Negroes who could afford the costs of litigation found that the Court was all too willing to interpret away

21. *Bolen* v. *Nebraska*, 176 U.S. 83 (1900); *Maxwell* v. *Dow*, 176 U.S. 581 (1900); *West* v. *Louisiana*, 194 U.S. 258 (1904); *Rogers* v. *Peck*, 199 U.S. 425 (1905); *Howard* v. *Kentucky*, 200 U.S. 164 (1906); *Felts* v. *Murphy*, 201 U.S. 123 (1906); *Rawlins* v. *Georgia*, 201 U.S. 638 (1906); *Ballard* v. *Hunter*, 204 U.S. 241 (1907); *Coffey* v. *Harlan County*, 204 U.S. 659 (1907); *Patterson* v. *Colorado*, 205 U.S. 454 (1907).

22. *Lloyd* v. *Dollison*, 194 U.S. 445 (1904); *Barrington* v. *Missouri*, 205 U.S. 483 (1907); *Maxwell* v. *Dow*, 176 U.S. 581 (1900); *Hunter* v. *Pittsburgh*, 207 U.S. 161 (1907); and *Twining* v. *New Jersey*, 211 U.S. 78 (1908).

23. 165 U.S. 150 (1897); see *Cotling* v. *Kansas City Stockyards Company*, 183 U.S. 79 (1901).

24. *San Mateo County* v. *Southern Pacific Railroad Company*, 116 U.S. 138 (1885); *cf.* Swisher, *American Constitutional Development*, pp. 404-5.

their civil and political rights. To be sure, the Waite Court decisions limiting the scope of the protection afforded Negroes by the Fourteenth Amendment were based upon the idea of preserving the federal system. However, for the three major Fuller Court determinations in the area no such justification can be found. The doctrines laid down in *Plessy* v. *Ferguson, Williams* v. *Mississippi,* and *Cumming* v. *Richmond Board of Education*[25] indicated an amazing judicial indifference toward discriminatory practices that were matters of common knowledge. This judicial indifference to the facts of racial discrimination in education and the exercise of the suffrage, for example, was obviously inconsistent with the same court's keen interest in the facts of state legislative or administrative railroad rate determinations.

The case of *Plessy* v. *Ferguson* involved the constitutionality of a Louisiana statute segregating colored from white passengers, but nominally providing equal facilities for both. After dismissing a contention based on the Thirteenth Amendment, Justice Brown, the majority spokesman, pointed out that "so far . . . as a conflict with the Fourteenth Amendment is concerned, the case reduces itself to the question whether the statute is a reasonable regulation, and with respect to this there must necessarily be a large discretion on the part of the legislature." Holding that the legislature may act with due regard for the established usages, customs and traditions of its people and with a view to the preservation of public peace and good order, Brown concluded that the separate but equal requirement was not unreasonable.

In *Williams* v. *Mississippi* the Supreme Court sustained a Mississippi voting qualification against a charge that it discriminated against Negroes in violation of the equal protection clause. Mississippi citizens, in order to qualify as legal voters, were required by a state constitutional provision to read any portion of the state constitution or to understand it when read. It was submitted to the Court that the framers of this constitutional requirement intended to exclude Negroes and that the discretion vested in white election officials would be used to accomplish such a purpose. However, the majority held that the constitutional provisions ". . . do not on their face discriminate between the races, and it has not been shown that their actual administration is evil, only that evil was possible under them."

*Cumming* v. *Richmond Board of Education* concerned the validity of a Georgia school board order suspending the maintenance of a high school for colored children, while continuing that of a white high

25. 163 U.S. 537 (1895); 170 U.S. 213 (1898); 175 U.S. 528 (1899).

school. The reason for the suspension given by the board and accepted by a state court was economic. Negro taxpayers had challenged the suspension as racially discriminatory. When the issue reached the Fuller Court on writ of error, that tribunal evidenced no interest in determining the "facts" for itself. And further, it asserted a respect for state autonomy that was generally absent in its determinations involving conflicts of corporations with state regulatory authority.

It would appear that the state legislatures could enact laws in the field of race relations as well as other subjects which did not involve curtailment of economic laissez faire, with the assurance that the Fuller Court would apply the presumption of validity doctrine in cases of doubtful constitutionality. This policy was not in itself reprehensible, and if adhered to consistently would have prevented undue judicial interference with state legislative policies. However, where state regulatory legislation threatened economic laissez faire, the Fuller Court decided for itself whether conditions warranted state legislative intervention.

### THIRTEENTH AMENDMENT

In fairness to the Fuller Court, it should be noted that it did not totally disregard human non-economic rights in its decisions, for in *Clyatt* v. *United States,*[26] it sustained one Clyatt's conviction under a congressional statute forbidding peonage by applying the doctrine that the protection of the Thirteenth Amendment extended against individual as well as state action.

### THE COMMERCE CLAUSE AND STATE POLICE POWER

Not only did the Fuller Court employ vigorously the commerce clause doctrines of the Waite Court which were restrictive of state police power,[27] but in *Leisy* v. *Hardin*[28] it applied the Marshall Court's "original package" doctrine in a situation involving interstate rather than foreign commerce. With regard to products, such as the beer in question, transported in interstate commerce, the state could regulate

26. 197 U.S. 207 (1905).

27. See *Western Union Telegraph Company* v. *Pennsylvania,* 128 U.S. 39 (1888); *Western Union Telegraph Company* v. *Alabama Board of Assessment,* 132 U.S. 472 (1889); *McCall* v. *California,* 136 U.S. 104 (1889); *Norfolk and Western Railroad Company* v. *Pennsylvania,* 136 U.S. 114 (1889); *Harman* v. *Chicago,* 147 U.S. 396 (1893); *Illinois Central Railroad Company* v. *Illinois,* 163 U.S. 142 (1895); *Brimmer* v. *Rebman,* 138 U.S. 78 (1890); *Minnesota* v. *Barber,* 136 U.S. 313 (1889); *Voight* v. *Wright,* 141 U.S. 62 (1890); *Brennan* v. *Titusville,* 153 U.S. 289 (1893).

28. 135 U.S. 100 (1890); see *Lying* v. *Michigan,* 135 U.S. 161 (1889); *Schollenberger* v. *Pennsylvania,* 171 U.S. 1 (1898).

them only after their importation was completed and they had "mingled with and become a part of the general property of the state." The effect of this application of the original package doctrine was practically to defeat the attempts of a number of states to protect the health and morals of their inhabitants against the ravages of excessive indulgence in intoxicating liquor. This application was intended to protect congressional commerce power.[29] Later, Congress itself circumvented this judicial doctrine in the Wilson and Webb-Kenyon Acts.

### FEDERAL POLICE POWER

#### *Narrow Construction of the Commerce Clause*

The Fuller Court's penchant for imposing judicially conceived constitutional restrictions on state police power regulations of economic activities was not to be taken as an indication that the Court favored federal governmental regulation of such matters. On the contrary, a number of cases decided in the early period of the Fuller Court indicate unmistakably that basically the spirit of the Fuller Court justices was anti-regulatory rather than pro-nationalistic. Although the language in the cases restricting national regulatory power frequently was that of federal-state relations, it would seem that the fundamental and underlying issue for the justices was actually that of federal regulation versus economic laissez faire. Chief among these cases were *United States* v. *E. C. Knight Company, Counselman* v. *Hitchcock,* and *Cincinnati, New Orleans and Texas Pacific Railway Company* v. *Interstate Commerce Commission.*

In *United States* v. *E. C. Knight Company,*[30] an important question concerning the legitimate scope of the Sherman Anti-Trust Act under Congress' interstate commerce power was considered. In a decision highly significant for the effectiveness of congressional attempts at regulation of business under the commerce power, the Fuller Court held that the Act could not be validly applied to a merger establishing a virtual monopoly in the refining of sugar because any resultant restraint on interstate commerce would be "indirect" and because the manufacture of refined sugar was not commerce. To hold that Congress' commerce power extends to "all contracts and combinations in manufacture, agriculture, mining, and other productive industries whose ultimate result may affect interstate commerce" would, con-

29. The Fuller Court occasionally sustained state police power regulations which affected interstate commerce, but did not interfere with congressional regulations; *Reid* v. *Colorado,* 187 U.S. 137 (1902). See *Crossman* v. *Turman,* 192 U.S. 189 (1904).
30. 156 U.S. 1 (1894).

cluded Fuller, leave "comparatively little of business operations and affairs" to state control.

In a lone and vigorous dissent, Justice Harlan argued that Congress had full power to deal with combinations, such as the Sugar Trust, because of the intimate relationship of monopolistic price fixing with free trade among the states. Particularly telling was Harlan's argument that he was unable to perceive how congressional control of such monopolies "would imperil the autonomy of the states, especially as that result cannot be attained through the action of any one state." Harlan's comment pointed up succinctly the basic problem created by the Fuller Court majority. By denying to Congress the power to curb a nationwide manufacturing monopoly, the Fuller Court actually created areas where private corporations could operate free from governmental regulation of any kind. The states were generally incapable of coping with nationwide monopolies, while under the doctrine of the *Knight* case the federal government was powerless to act.

A similar result stemmed from several early Fuller Court determinations regarding the statutory powers of the Interstate Commerce Commission. In 1886 the Waite Court's *Wabash* decision had decisively precluded any further direct state regulation of interstate carriers. In the following year Congress acted to fill the regulatory void by creating the Commission. But in 1892 the Fuller Court held that the Interstate Commerce Commission lacked power to compel witnesses to give testimony before it. For in *Counselman* v. *Hitchcock*[31] the Court held that the statutory provisions giving the Commission power to compel the giving of testimony opened the way for the use of such testimony to uncover further evidence in violation of the prohibition against involuntary self-incrimination in the Fifth Amendment.

In 1894 the Fuller Court upheld the creation of the Interstate Commerce Commission as a necessary and proper exercise of congressional commerce power in *Interstate Commerce Commission* v. *Brimson*.[32] However two years later in *Cincinnati, New Orleans and Texas Pacific Railway Company* v. *Interstate Commerce Commission*[33] the same court interpreted the act creating the Interstate Commerce Commission narrowly, holding that its provisions neither granted power nor implied that the Commission had power to set reasonable maximum rates when it found those set by an interstate railroad com-

31. 142 U.S. 547 (1892). Subsequently Congress passed new provisions which were sustained by the Fuller Court in *Brown* v. *Walker*, 161 U.S. 591 (1896).

32. 154 U.S. 447 (1894).

33. 162 U.S. 184 (1896).

pany unreasonable. Until the passage of the Hepburn Act in 1906, the Fuller Court decision created a virtual vacuum in the field of railroad rate regulation. For, as was noted above, under the *Wabash* doctrine the states could not act, and under the Fuller Court's devitalizing doctrines the Interstate Commerce Commission could act only feebly. The effect of the early Fuller Court decisions on the Interstate Commerce Commission is best summed up in the annual report of that Commission for 1897. After pointing out that it could conduct investigations and make reports as well as do a few other things, the Commission observed bluntly:

> But by virtue of judicial decision, it has ceased to be a body for the regulation of interstate carriers. It is proper that Congress should understand this. The people should no longer look to this Commission for a protection which it is powerless to extend.[34]

Particularly after the turn of the century it must have become apparent to the Fuller Court justices that they could not contain indefinitely the rising popular demands for federal governmental regulation in important areas of the national economy hitherto left to the states or left unregulated. The Fuller Court itself undoubtedly contributed to these pro-regulatory pressures by imposing judicially created prohibitions on important state police power regulations and construing federal commerce power narrowly. Fuller Court decisions such as in *Leisy* v. *Hardin* and the *Knight* case created what became known as a twilight zone in the American federal system where corporations could operate free from either state or federal supervision.

### ELIMINATION OF THE TWILIGHT ZONE: INHERENT POWERS V. FEDERAL POLICE POWER

Efforts to extend federal regulatory authority into this twilight zone took two forms. The most extreme was the espousal of the inherent powers doctrine of James Wilson by President Theodore Roosevelt. Less extreme but more effective was the exercise of a federal police power by Congress.

That the Fuller Court was directly responsible for the adoption of the extreme doctrine of inherent powers is shown clearly by President Theodore Roosevelt's speech at the dedication of the Pennsylvania capitol at Harrisburg. In his words,

> . . . Certain judicial decisions have done just what [James] Wilson feared;

34. Cited in Carl McFarland, *Judicial Control of the Federal Trade Commission and the Interstate Commerce Commission*, p. 110.

they have, as a matter of fact, left vacancies, left blanks between the limits of actual national jurisdiction over the control of the great business corporations. . . . Actual experience has shown that the States are wholly powerless to deal with this subject; and any action or decision that deprives the nation of the power to deal with it, simply results in leaving the corporations absolutely free to work without any effective supervision whatever; and such a course is fraught with untold danger to the future of our whole system of government, and, indeed, to our whole civilization.[35]

Interestingly enough, the first judicial test of this far-reaching doctrine involved federal intervention in a dispute between two states over water rights and not an attempt by the federal government to regulate corporations. During the presentation of arguments in *Kansas* v. *Colorado*,[36] Attorney General Charles J. Bonaparte filed a petition of intervention for the United States. In his arguments, Bonaparte pointed out that the individual states were powerless to cope with the problem because their authority or reserved powers extended only to their boundaries. It was suggested that the Federal Government could intervene under the commerce power, but if this were not sufficient, a more extensive power was available, that of the inherent power of national sovereignty.

The petition of intervention was denied and Roosevelt's doctrine of inherent powers was decisively rejected by the Fuller Court. The possibility that a twilight zone might exist was acknowledged by the justices, for, as they put it,

. . . as our national territory has been enlarged, we have within our borders extensive tracts of arid lands which ought to be reclaimed, and it may well be that no power is adequate for their reclamation other than that of the National Government. *But, if no such power has been granted, none can be exercised.*[37]

The doctrine of inherent powers was, in the eyes of the Fuller Court, inconsistent with a constitution of enumerated and implied powers, for any powers not enumerated or implied are reserved to the states or to the people by the Tenth Amendment.

Acceptance of the doctrine of inherent powers by the Fuller Court would have constituted a revolutionary alteration of the relationship of the federal government to the states, for the principle of federalism would have ceased to contain the modern expansion of national power within the bounds of the delegated and implied powers. Presumably,

35. Cited in Westel W. Willoughby, *Constitutional Law*, I, 31.
36. 206 U.S. 46 (1907).
37. Italics mine.

the acceptance of a doctrine of inherent powers could have opened the way for the rapid development of a unitary system.

While the Fuller Court decisively rejected the extreme doctrine of inherent powers presented by the Roosevelt administration in *Kansas* v. *Colorado,* it felt impelled to give its blessing to a milder revolution in federal-state relations instigated in the halls of the national Congress. Just as in the adoption of the doctrine of inherent powers by President Theodore Roosevelt, so in the development of a federal police power did the Fuller Court have an unwilling part in forcing its espousal by Congress.

In regard to the question whether the Fuller Court justices were as unalterably opposed to the latter as they were to the former, the answer seems to be a qualified "no." Federal regulations under the enumerated powers of Congress of matters which fell within the traditional sphere of police power regulation in its narrow sense, i.e., crime and immorality, were readily sustained by the Fuller Court. However, federal police power regulations which interfered with so-called legitimate business and which violated the principles of economic laissez faire were generally subjected to close scrutiny by the Fuller Court. And while the Fuller justices did not refuse to uphold all such federal legislation, they did, to use Professor Wright's apt description, fight "a rear-guard action."[38]

*Postal Clause*

*In Re Rapier* and *Public Clearing House* v. *Coyne* illustrate the Fuller Court's willingness to sustain federal police power regulations based on the postal clause which sought to prevent or punish crime or immorality.

Recognition of the existence of such power came early in the Fuller Court period in *In Re Rapier.*[39] In 1890 Congress in section 3894 of the Revised Statutes provided that ". . . no letter, postal card or circular concerning any lottery, etc. and no lottery ticket or part thereof . . . shall be carried in the mail. . . ." This act was upheld under doctrine that Congress, both as recipient of the delegated postal power and as proprietor, had complete authority to exclude from the mails matter deemed by it injurious to public morals. This, it was added, did not violate freedom of communication.

Further important expansion of federal police power under the postal clause came in *Public Clearing House* v. *Coyne.*[40] This case

38. Benjamin F. Wright, Jr., *The Growth of American Constitutional Law,* p. 112.
39. 143 U.S. 110 (1891); see *Canfield* v. *United States,* 167 U.S. 518 (1897).
40. 194 U.S. 497 (1904).

involved the constitutionality of the far-reaching "fraud order" authority of the Postmaster General of the United States. According to the pertinent congressional act, this official may issue a fraud order barring from final delivery in the mails the letters of individuals or companies engaged in fraudulent activities or in operating lotteries.

The entire set of regulations was sustained under the doctrine established in the *Jackson* case that Congress' postal power is plenary and extends to the exclusion of matter deemed harmful to "the public morality." Two due process objections were dealt with briefly. It was reiterated that due process does not require a judicial hearing in every situation. The Court felt that such a requirement in regard to fraud orders would result in a practical suspension of departmental activities. The power to seize prohibited matter was also upheld on practical grounds, for it was pointed out that since letters cannot be opened, the postal officials would be powerless to act unless they could detain letters sent from individuals or companies engaged in the prohibited activities. Finally it was established that the Postmaster General does not confiscate money under his fraud order authority, but merely refused to extend the facilities of the department to the final delivery of letters falling within the prohibited categories. This power fell, the Court concluded, well within Congress' regulatory authority under the postal clause.

The *Rapier* and *Coyne* cases show that the Fuller Court was prepared to uphold congressional measures passed under the postal clause which quite clearly dealt with crime and immorality—matters traditionally within the sphere of state police power.

The case of *In Re Debs*[41] could be dealt with under either the commerce or postal clauses. Here, the Fuller Court sustained the use of an injunction against the officers of the American Railway Union in their strike against the Pullman Palace Car Company on the ground that the United States could remove obstructions to the exercise of its commerce and postal powers. This judicial vindication of President Cleveland's controversial intervention in the bitter Pullman strike was in itself a far-reaching pronouncement of federal power. But viewed in the light of the controversy between Governor Altgeld and President Cleveland which preceded the Supreme Court decision, it would appear that the *Debs* decision had other important implications for federal-state relations. For Professor Corwin has pointed out that, since this case, Article IV, section 4, of the Constitution, which provides that the United States "shall guarantee [every state] on applica-

41. 158 U.S. 564 (1894).

tion of the Legislature or of the Executive . . . against domestic violence" has become relatively less important. Under the far-reaching *Debs* doctrine the federal government can act to quell domestic violence within a state without awaiting state legislative or executive application whenever interstate commerce, the mails or any violation of federal law are involved.[42]

*Commerce Clause*

In 1884 Congress prohibited the transportation in interstate commerce of livestock infected with contagious diseases. While this regulation was not challenged constitutionally, there is every reason to believe that it would have been sustained as a valid attempt by Congress to protect the health of livestock shipped in interstate commerce or to prevent the use of interstate commerce to endanger the health of stock within a state. In 1895, however, Congress prohibited the transmission through interstate commerce or the mails of lottery tickets or lottery advertisements—articles which in themselves constituted no threat to other products shipped in interstate commerce or through the postal system. The constitutionality of this prohibitory act was tested in the famous *Lottery* case—*Champion* v. *Ames*[43]—in which the Fuller Court, by a narrow margin, sustained the statute under the "harmful effects" doctrine utilized earlier in the postal clause cases.

The writer of the majority opinion, Justice Harlan, intimated that congressional commerce power could be utilized to abolish practically any remaining areas in the twilight zone. However, the closeness of the Court's vote—5 to 4—indicated that any further expansion of congressional police power under the commerce clause would be subjected to close judicial scrutiny. Evidently sensing the implications of the majority doctrine, Fuller in dissent set about devising a doctrine intended to keep congressional interstate commerce authority within limits. This he did by interpreting such authority narrowly and by implying that the reserved powers of the states actually limited federal interstate commerce power.

In one sense the Lottery Act of 1895 simply represented another application of a congressional policy sanctioned by the Fuller Court in *In Re Rahrer*[44] in 1891. That decision sustained the Wilson Act which

42. Edward S. Corwin, *The President, Office and Powers,* pp. 164-166.

43. 188 U.S. 321 (1903).

44. 140 U.S. 545 (1891). The Fuller Court held that Congress, in adopting the Wilson Act, had not delegated legislative authority to the states, but had merely removed a presumption of unconstitutionality which had seriously hampered state police power enforcement.

had sought to mitigate the effects of *Bowman* v. *Chicago and Northwestern Railway* and *Leisy* v. *Hardin* by providing that liquor shipped in interstate commerce should become subject to state police power upon arrival in a state.[45] The principle had been established earlier that Congress may validly remove obstacles to the exercise of state police power created by the existence of its plenary power over interstate commerce. However, while the lottery prohibition act was similar in the narrow sense that it represented another congressional attempt to supplement state police power legislation, it went far beyond the Wilson Act. For Congress did not remove an obstacle to state action in the former act, but actually prohibited the shipment of tickets. In other words, it did not simply clear the way for state action, but exercised a police power of its own.

The Fuller Court decisions involving congressional police power regulation of business activity as distinguished from the narrower concept embracing crime and immorality indicated more reluctance and occasionally outright opposition to the expansion of federal police power. The Fuller Court's two main defenses against congressional regulation or prohibition of business enterprise were the Fifth Amendment's due process clause and an extremely narrow interpretation of the commerce clause.

In regard to the former, the doctrine of liberty of contract, frequently invoked as a judicially engrafted constitutional prohibition against state action, was applied via the due process clause of the Fifth Amendment to void a congressional statute making it a criminal offense for an interstate carrier to discharge an employee solely on the ground that he belonged to a labor union.[46] The *Knight* case was a classic example of narrow interpretation of the commerce clause. However, narrow construction of the commerce clause also accounted for Fuller Court invalidation of the first Employer's Liability Act and a federal quarantine regulation applied to livestock transported in intrastate commerce.[47] In both instances the Court held that Congress had regulated matters outside the scope of its commerce authority.

Nevertheless, in spite of its sometimes obvious reluctance to sustain federal regulations of business activity, the Fuller Court frequently did so after the turn of the century. This reluctant willingness may well attest to the accuracy of Mr. Dooley's famous remark about the

45. However, in rendering an interpretation of the Wilson Act in 1898, the Fuller Court practically defeated the purposes of its enactment; *Rhodes* v. *Iowa,* 170 U.S. 412.

46. *Adair* v. *United States,* 208 U.S. 161 (1908).

47. *The Employer's Liability Cases,* 207 U.S. 463 (1908); and *Illinois Central Railroad Company* v. *McKendree,* 203 U.S. 514 (1906).

relationship of the Court's decisions to the election returns. For the era was that of the progressive Republican drive to break the trusts, to enforce sanitary standards in food-processing, and to inject ethical standards in politics. New appointees also exerted some influence.[48]

In any event, the Fuller Court, in cases such as *Swift and Company* v. *United States, Addyston Pipe and Steel Company* v. *United States,* and *Northern Securities Company* v. *United States,*[49] sustained exercises of federal police power which were of tremendous import to federal-state relations. For in the *Swift* case the Court indicated that at least in certain circumstances it would bypass the narrow construction of commerce given in the *Knight* case.

Shortly after the decision in the *Knight* case, the Fuller Court had sustained an application of the Sherman Anti-Trust Act to a combination by six corporations to control not the manufacture of, but rather the sale and sale prices of, cast iron pipe in *Addyston Pipe and Steel Company* v. *United States.* Here the court held that interstate commerce was affected directly and substantially, not remotely and indirectly. Similarly, in the famous *Northern Securities Company* case, the Fuller Court rejected an argument that the federal government, by prosecuting a holding company under the Anti-Trust Act, was regulating the transference and holding of stock shares issued by state-chartered corporations, a subject reserved to the states under the Tenth Amendment.

In *Swift and Company* v. *United States* the Fuller Court, in an opinion by Justice Holmes, unanimously held that the sending of cattle from other states to Chicago for sale in its stockyards and their subsequent transshipment to other states was "a current of commerce among the states" and that the purchase of cattle at such stockyards was "a part and incident of such commerce." Consequently, a combination among the leading dealers in fresh meat in the United States not to bid against each other in order to regulate prices and to get less than lawful rates from railroads to the exclusion of competitors was a violation of the Sherman Anti-Trust Act of 1890. The effect of such a combination in restraint of trade or interstate commerce was held to be direct, not secondary or incidental. And again in the *Danbury Hatter's* case,[50] the Fuller Court held that a boycott, organized by a labor union to prevent the manufacture of hats which were

48. Schlesinger, *The Political and Social Growth of the American People, 1865-1940,* pp. 296-319; Edward S. Corwin, *The Twilight of the Supreme Court,* p. 40.

49. 196 U.S. 375 (1905); 175 U.S. 211 (1899); 193 U.S. 197 (1904).

50. *Loewe* v. *Lawlor,* 208 U.S. 274 (1908).

to be shipped in interstate commerce, violated the Sherman Anti-Trust Act.

The *Addyston, Swift* and *Hatter's* cases seemed to indicate that the Fuller Court was abandoning the narrow construction of the commerce power established in the *Knight* case. In that case, it had virtually confined federal commerce power to the regulation of actual interstate traffic or transportation. However, in the later cases it apparently recognized the essential unity of the national economy and seemed willing to admit that actions which took place before physical transportation in interstate commerce began or after it ceased could "directly" affect such commerce. Actually, however, only a few of the Fuller Court justices were willing to accept this broad view in all commerce clause cases. The opinion of the dissenters in the *Lottery* case was only one of numerous indications that a number of the Fuller Court justices were not only eager to return to the narrow construction of the *Knight* case, but were prepared to treat the reserved powers of the states as limitations on federal commerce power.[51] However, the denouement did not come until the White-Taft Court period and the *Hammer* case.

*Taxing Clause*

Fuller Court determinations involving the uses of the taxing clause as a basis for a federal police power were far fewer than those under the commerce clause, but in regard to their significance in federal-state relations, they were of equal importance. For in the *Felsenheld* and *McCray* cases, it adopted doctrines which opened an apparently limitless field for federal police power regulation under the taxing clause.

In the Dingley Tariff Act of 1897,[52] Congress forbade the inclusion in packages of tobacco or cigarettes subject to excise taxes of anything except the tobacco or cigarettes. The Fuller Court upheld this regulation in *Felsenheld* v. *United States*[53] on the ground that Congress may constitutionally assume responsibility for assuring the buying public that packages of excised goods contain the goods which under the law they purport to contain.

Professor Cushman has pointed out that under the doctrine laid down in this case, Congress could through regulations incidental to its power to levy excise taxes, accomplish everything in the way of social policy that has been achieved under the Pure Food and Drug

51. See also *dicta* in the majority opinion in *Covington and Cincinnati Bridge Company* v. *Kentucky*, 154 U.S. 204 (1894).

52. 30 STAT. at L. 151.

53. 186 U.S. 126 (1902).

Acts, and do so more thoroughly.[54] The power sustained in the *Felsenheld* case admittedly opened the way for a broad expansion of federal police power under the taxing clause, but, in fact, Congress has generally limited its use of such power to the regulation of habit-forming drugs.

The second important taxing clause case involved the controversial oleomargarine tax law of 1902. Congress, under the pressure of the dairy-interest lobby, enacted a law which levied a tax of ten cents per pound on oleomargarine colored to look like butter. The constitutionality of this tax came before the Supreme Court in *McCray* v. *United States*.[55] The central question for the Court was whether or not Congress had exercised, under the guise of taxation, a regulatory power which properly was reserved to the states. The act was upheld as a valid tax "on its face," the Court holding that it could not inquire into the motives of Congress.

The *McCray* doctrine provided Congress with a means to control through regulatory or destructive tax burdens matters ordinarily entirely outside the scope of any delegated federal power. The oleomargarine act had not been passed by Congress as a revenue-raising measure and had not been enacted, as had the tax on state bank notes in 1866 later upheld in the *Veazie Bank* case, as an aid to the exercise of another delegated power of Congress. Moreover, of particular interest in federal-state relations was the Fuller Court's acceptance of the doctrine that regardless of the consequences for the reserved powers of the states, if the measure was a tax "on its face," it would be considered within the constitutional authority of Congress.

The recognition and acceptance in the foregoing decisions of a broad federal police power based on the commerce, taxing, and postal clauses represented a second great revolution in federal-state relations which took place under the aegis of the Fuller Court. Under doctrines such as those in the *Rapier, Ames,* and *McCray* cases, the Fuller Court gave its sanction to broad federal police power regulations which embraced matters hitherto left to the states. It should be noted, however, that the federal police power regulations sustained generally did not supersede state regulations but rather supplemented them.

### FEDERAL SUPREMACY

In addition to the tremendous enhancement of federal authority represented in its federal police power decisions, the Fuller Court

54. Robert E. Cushman, "Social and Economic Control under the Taxing Clause of the Constitution," in Corwin, Cushman, *et al.*, *Selected Essays on Constitutional Law*, III, 546-47, 552-53.

55. 195 U.S. 27 (1903). See *Schick* v. *United States*, 195 U.S. 65 (1904).

expanded federal power in several other fields as well. The specific terms of the supremacy clause refer to the federal Constitution, laws made in pursuance of it, and treaties made under the authority of the United States. The case of *In Re Neagle*[56] would have fallen into the category of an ordinary supremacy clause case, except for the fact that deputization of Neagle as Justice Field's bodyguard had not been made in pursuance of a specific law of the United States, but had been authorized by the Attorney General. Section 753 of the Revised Statutes provided "that the writ [of habeas corpus] shall not extend to a prisoner in . . . jail unless he is in custody for an act done or committed in pursuance of a law of the United States. . . ."

The decision turned upon the supremacy of a federal "law" over the law of the state of California under which Neagle had been held. It was Justice Miller's extremely broad definition of "law" that established the importance of the *Neagle* case in American constitutional law. He held that,

> In the view we take of the Constitution of the United States, any obligation fairly and properly inferrible (*sic*) from that instrument or any duty of the marshal to be derived from the general scope of his duties under the laws of the United States is "a law". . . .

The *Neagle* decision, although it established what was felt to be a startling precedent, limited state power only in defense of federal authority. The important cases of *Ex Parte Young* and *South Carolina* v. *United States,*[57] on the other hand, subjected the states to federal authority in two important areas.

### *Eleventh Amendment*

The *Young* case represented a particularly broad modification of the Eleventh Amendment. For in it the Fuller Court sustained a federal circuit court contempt citation against the Attorney General of Minnesota for violating a federal court injunction restraining him in the carrying out of his official state duties. According to Minnesota law, Young was required to enforce the rate schedules set by the state railroad commission. A railroad corporation secured an injunction in a federal court to restrain him in the enforcement of such a schedule through proceedings in the state courts. The significance of the decision lies in the fact that the constitutionality of the state law had not been determined when the preliminary injunction had been issued by the lower federal court. The Fuller Court ruling thus precluded any

56. 135 U.S. 1 (1889).
57. 209 U.S. 123 (1908); 199 U.S. 437 (1905).

further state court action to determine the validity of the act. The Court felt that this action was necessary because the validity of the rate law could only have been tested in the state courts at the risk of enormous expense by the railroad companies in the event that they lost. The Minnesota rate law was held unconstitutional by the Fuller Court because the enormous penalties attaching to any unsuccessful tests in the state courts of the reasonableness of rates made under the law precluded, in practical effect, the necessary remedy of state judicial review.

### INTERGOVERNMENTAL TAX IMMUNITY

*South Carolina* v. *United States,* decided in 1905, represented the most important interpretative development in the law of intergovernmental tax immunity since the Chase Court's decision in *Collector* v. *Day*.[58] The South Carolina legislature, in a series of acts, had established dispensaries for the exclusive sale of liquor in the state. The validity of a federal tax levied on such dispensaries was considered. The majority opinion stressed the evil consequences of extension of immunity to such state activities, the intentions of the constitutional framers regarding the scope of the taxing power, and the eighteenth-century common law.

This latter point is of interest because it indicates that to some extent Justice Brown was opposed to the state monopoly of liquor selling not merely because it might cut off a source of federal revenue, but because it conflicted with the theory of economic laissez faire. After stating that the framers were steeped in the common law, he made the historically questionable assertion that "the framers of the Constitution were not anticipating that a state would attempt to monopolize any business heretofore carried on by individuals." It was also intimated that extension of such monopolistic control to public utilities and railroads might violate the constitutional requirement that each state have a republican form of government. The federal tax was upheld under the doctrine that while the federal government "may do nothing by taxation in any form to prevent the full discharge by the [State] of its governmental functions, yet whenever a State engages in a business which is of a private nature that business is not withdrawn from the taxing power of the Nation." Besides insuring to the federal government a lucrative source of tax

58. An extreme extension of the immunity doctrine was presented in the *Pollock* case. Here interest received by private investors from state or municipal bonds were held exempt from federal taxation; *Pollock* v. *Farmers Loan and Trust Company,* 157 U.S. 429 (1895).

revenue, the decision enhanced considerably the power of the Supreme Court. For it was the Court itself which decided in each case of this kind whether a state function was "governmental" or not.

### STATE CONTROL OF THE CHOICE OF ELECTORS

In *McPherson* v. *Blacker,*[59] the Fuller Court ruled that the authority to change the mode of choosing presidential electors had been vested in the states under Article II, section 2, of the Constitution. Neither Amendment Fourteen nor Fifteen diminished this power. Thus state power in this matter was preserved in its entirety.

### SUMMARY AND CONCLUSION

By way of summary, two fundamentally important revolutions in federal-state relations can be in large part credited to the Fuller Court. By utilizing doctrines such as reasonableness and liberty of contract, the Fuller Court made the due process clause of the Fourteenth Amendment the lever for an hitherto unprecedented expansion of federal judicial supervisory power over the legislation and action of the states. It is true that prior to the Fuller Court period the state legislatures were restricted to a limited extent in regard to the substance of their laws. Thus *ex post facto* laws, bills of attainder and laws impairing the obligation of contracts were constitutionally prohibited. With the exception of the last, these were relatively unimportant restrictions. And again with the exception of the contract clause, they had precise technical legal definitions which did not permit judicial interpretative expansion. The contract clause itself, though interpreted to include public as well as private contracts, generally affected, after all, just those pieces of state legislation involving contracts. And doctrines such as that in *Ogden* v. *Saunders* served to mitigate its restrictive effect on state legislative activity.

The breadth given to the meaning of due process in *dicta* in the Waite Court period and in the actual decisions of the Fuller Court subjected, at least potentially, most state legislation or action to the supervision of the federal judiciary. Such supervision was not necessary to the preservation of federal supremacy or to the federal arbiter concept. It, in fact, involved a fundamental alteration in federal-state relations. Since the Fuller Court's substantive due process decisions, the autonomy of the states in the federal system has been diminished considerably. Potentially, all the relations, whether legislative, executive, or judicial, of the states with their people are subject to the censorship of a branch of the national government.

59. 146 U.S. 1 (1892).

In addition, state immunity from federal taxation was limited to essential governmental functions in the *South Carolina* case. In effect, federal power to quell domestic violence within a state without the desire or assent of state authorities where federal law is violated or federal power obstructed was given tacit approval in the broad *Debs* doctrine. And like its predecessor, the Fuller Court found in the commerce clause a broad base for the invalidation of state regulatory legislation. In decisions such as *Leisy* v. *Hardin,* state police power was severely hampered.

So far as the motives of justices can be identified in their constitutional opinions, it appears that the Fuller Court did not rigorously curtail state police power legislation under the commerce clause and the due process clause of the Fourteenth Amendment out of tender regard for federal supremacy. Rather it would seem that considerations stemming from the laissez faire philosophy overrode the need for preserving the vitality of the states in the federal system.

The movement toward creation of a federal police power in Congress had stemmed from the need for regulation in so-called twilight zones in the federal system which were largely created by decisions of the Fuller Court and its predecessor. Although it rejected the inherent powers doctrine, in cases such as *Champion* v. *Ames* and *McCray* v. *United States,* the Fuller Court sustained broad federal police power regulation of matters traditionally left to the states. Its sometimes reluctant acceptance of federal regulation of crime, immorality and business opened a broad new field for federal authority. This expansion of federal power into areas hitherto well within the reserved powers of the states represents the second great revolution in federal-state relations ushered in by the Fuller Court. So far as the federal system was concerned, the Fuller Court wrought a far greater modification of the federal system in the direction of centralization than had any of its predecessors.

# CHAPTER VIII

## *The White-Taft Court, 1911-1930*

TWO AREAS in the constitutional law of federal-state relations were of paramount importance in the White-Taft Court period. First, in continuing the expansion of the broad supervisory powers assumed by the Fuller Court under the due process clause of the Fourteenth Amendment and to a less extent under the equal protection clause of the same amendment, the White-Taft Court further weakened state autonomy. And second, in sustaining, generally speaking, a wide variety of federal police power regulations enacted under the commerce and taxing clauses, the same court gave its blessing, at least tacitly, to the process of federal centralization. However, by construing federal commerce and taxing powers narrowly in a few highly important cases, the White-Taft Court set limits on the expansion of federal police power in certain areas, ostensibly to protect the reserved rights of the states.[1]

### CONSTITUTIONAL LIMITATIONS ON THE STATES

#### *Due Process Clause of the Fourteenth Amendment*

In regard to the first of these developments it may be emphasized that the due process clause of the Fourteenth Amendment lost none of its vitality as a source of judicial supervisory authority under the White-Taft Court. True, many important pieces of state legislation were sustained, such as the Illinois Child Labor Law, the Ohio "Blue

1. There were a great number of personnel changes during the White-Taft period. Willis Van Devanter replaced Edward White, who was promoted to the Chief Justiceship in 1910. Joseph R. Lamar succeeded Justice Moody in the same year. Mahlon Pitney replaced Justice Harlan in 1912. James C. McReynolds succeeded Justice Lurton in 1914. Louis D. Brandeis replaced Justice Lamar in 1916. John H. Clarke succeeded Justice Hughes in 1916. William H. Taft succeeded Chief Justice White in 1921. George Sutherland replaced Justice Clarke in 1922. Pierce Butler succeeded Justice Day in the same year. Edward T. Sanford replaced Justice Pitney in 1923. Harlan F. Stone replaced Justice McKenna in 1925. And Charles Evans Hughes succeeded Chief Justice Taft in 1930.

Sky" Law and the Oregon Maximum Hours Law.[2] But the great revolution in federal-state relations ushered in during the Fuller Court period was not challenged at any time by a majority of the Court. And, in fact, in some areas new interpretations restrictive of state regulatory authority were adopted. The dissenters who supported Justice Holmes' *Lochner* case viewpoint did, of course, criticize severely the manner in which the White-Taft Court employed its supervisory powers over state legislation.

That the White-Taft Court was unwilling to relinquish the broad supervisory powers attained by its predecessor over state regulatory legislation is well illustrated by *Burns Baking Company* v. *Bryan*[3] in which the majority held void a Nebraska law designed to protect the consumer by standardizing the weight of bread loaves. The legislative standard, decided the court, was arbitrary because it allowed a "tolerance" of only two ounces which "owing to normal evaporation due to local weather conditions was not enough to prevent violation of the law unless the loaves were wrapped." Justice Brandeis, supported by Holmes, pointed out in dissent that since there existed wide differences of opinion among experts over this question of "tolerance," resolution of such a debatable issue should be left to the state legislature. To decide such issues, charged Brandeis, is "an exercise of the powers of a super-legislature—not the performance of the constitutional function of judicial review."

In *Price* v. *Illinois*,[4] the White-Taft Court actually accepted the advice of Justice Holmes and his few supporters on the court regarding the need for judicial self-restraint in the determination of due process clause issues. Writing the majority opinion, Justice Holmes was able to apply the doctrine for which he contended valiantly in his classic *Lochner* dissent. At issue was the constitutionality of an Illinois pure food act. This act, as interpreted by a state court, had prohibited the sale of food preservatives containing boric acid. Price's counsel had agreed that the question whether the product was harmful was

2. See *Sturges and Burn* v. *Beauchamp*, 231 U.S. 320 (1913); *Hall* v. *Geiger-Jones Company*, 242 U.S. 539 (1917); *Bunting* v. *Oregon*, 243 U.S. 426 (1917).

3. 264 U.S. 504 (1924); see *Coppage* v. *Kansas*, 236 U.S. 1 (1915); *Adams* v. *Tanner*, 244 U.S. 590 (1917); *Fairmont Creamery Company* v. *Minnesota*, 274 U.S. 1 (1927); *Traux* v. *Corrigan*, 257 U.S. 312 (1921); *Adkins* v. *Children's Hospital*, 261 U.S. 525 (1923), represented an application of the Fifth Amendment's due process clause to a congressional law fixing minimum wages for women and minors in the District of Columbia. Its influence in federal-state relations rests largely on the fact that it indicated a revival of the restrictive *Lochner* doctrine: under the *Adkins-Lochner* doctrine, minimum wage laws of Arizona and Arkansas were held invalid (under the Fourteenth Amendment) in 1925 and 1927, respectively.

4. 238 U.S. 446 (1915).

debatable but still had insisted that the state's interference with its sale was clearly arbitrary. However, Holmes observed that "It is plainly not enough that the subject should be regarded as debatable. If it be debatable, the legislature is entitled to its own judgment. . . ."

Actually this approach was seldom used by a majority of the court during the period 1911-30.[5] It was *Burns Baking Company* v. *Bryan* rather than *Price* v. *Illinois* which was characteristic of the due process clause determinations of the White-Taft Court period. During this period the pressures upon the court to disallow state regulatory legislation under the due process clause of the Fourteenth Amendment were as great or greater than those upon the Fuller Court. In the decade from 1911 to 1921, nearly two hundred cases were decided by the court under this constitutional prohibition.

That the White-Taft Court inherited the Fuller Court's penchant for imposing new judicially-conceived restrictions on state regulatory authority under the broad base of substantive due process is well shown in *Wolff Packing Company* v. *Court of Industrial Relations* and *Gitlow* v. *New York*.[6] In the *Wolff* case, a Kansas law subjecting labor disputes in the state meat-packing industry to compulsory arbitration and wage determination was held unconstitutional on the ground that it fixed wages in an industry which was not sufficiently "clothed with public interest" to warrant such regulation. Writing the majority opinion, Chief Justice Taft held that price-fixing or wage-fixing of this kind was permissible under the due process clause only when a business fell into one of three categories. These included, first, those businesses, like public utilities, which were carried on under a public grant and which were directly under state or municipal regulatory power in the terms of their charters; second, certain occupations, such as inn keeping, which have since very early times been subject to public regulation; and third, those businesses which through devotion to public use, grant "the public an interest in that use." These apparently easy-to-distinguish categories vested, of course, further discretionary power in the Supreme Court itself, for it had the final word as to whether a particular business actually belonged in one of these categories or not.

The White-Taft Court utilized the *Wolff* case doctrine to include and exclude state regulations as a matter of discretion. Held to be

5. It was used, of course, to good effect in a few important cases such as *Village of Euclid* v. *Ambler Realty Company* and *Zahn* v. *Board of Public Works*, 272 U.S. 365 (1926), and 274 U.S. 325 (1927), respectively.

6. 262 U.S. 522 (1923); 268 U.S. 652 (1925).

clothed with a public interest were businesses "akin to banking,"[7] but held not to be clothed with a public interest were mining, ticket brokerage, employment procurement, and gasoline distribution.[8]

In spite of the pressure put upon it in many cases, the Supreme Court, throughout the periods of the Waite and Fuller Courts, had steadfastly refused to hold that the protection of the due process clause extended to all the human non-property rights guaranteed against federal encroachment by the first eight amendments—the "Bill of Rights." And while the White-Taft Court did exhibit a strong inclination to protect human non-property rights against state action in its procedural due process cases,[9] as late as 1922 it stated in *Prudential Insurance Company* v. *Cheek*[10] that "neither the Fourteenth Amendment nor any other provision of the Constitution of the United States imposes upon the states any restrictions about freedom of speech. . . ."

Yet within three years, the same court stated by way of *dictum* in *Gitlow* v. *New York*[11] that

> For present purposes we may and do assume that freedom of speech and of the press—which are protected by the First Amendment from abridgment by Congress—are among the fundamental personal rights and liberties protected by the due process clause of the Fourteenth Amendment from impairment by the states.

This reversal was undoubtedly one of the most important doctrinal developments affecting federal-state relations in this period. Its significance may be illustrated by a comparison of the *Wolff* and *Gitlow* doctrines. Actually the *Wolff* doctrine was similar to that of reasonableness and liberty of contract in that it restricted state regulation of economic activity of some kind. In sharp contrast, the *Gitlow* doctrine related to non-economic rights—those of freedom of speech and press. These matters had hitherto been considered to be entirely within the jurisdiction of state police power. With this expansion of federal judicial censorial authority there remained no major area of state legislative activity immune from the supervisory authority of the judicial branch of the national government.

Three justices—Holmes, Brandeis and Stone—were generally critical of the manner in which the White-Taft Court exercised its super-

7. *Dillingham* v. *McLaughlin*, 264 U.S. 370 (1924).

8. *Dorchy* v. *Kansas*, 264 U.S. 286 (1924); *Tyson and Brothers* v. *Banton*, 273 U.S. 418 (1927); *Ribnik* v. *McBride*, 277 U.S. 350 (1928); *Williams* v. *Standard Oil Company*, 278 U.S. 235 (1929).

9. See *Moore* v. *Dempsey*, 261 U.S. 86 (1923).

10. 259 U.S. 530 (1922).

11. 268 U.S. 652 (1925); see *Fiske* v. *Kansas*, 278 U.S. 380 (1927).

visory power under the due process clause of the Fourteenth Amendment. Their dissents embodied three basic ideas—the need for judicial self-restraint on the part of the majority in the exercise of its broad supervisory authority, the need for intellectual honesty in making substantive due process clause determinations, and the plea that the states be permitted greater freedom from federal judicial control in the conduct of social experiments.[12]

As well taken as these criticisms of the majority were, they did not attack the Court's basic assumption that it could test state legislation substantively as well as procedurally under the Fourteenth Amendment's due process clause. Fundamentally, Holmes' plea that the majority refrain from holding void state-sponsored social experiments was beside the point in regard to the relationship of the states and the federal government. For given the premise that the American federal system envisages the existence of states largely autonomous in regard to their internal affairs, the basic question is, how can the Supreme Court's assumption of virtually complete supervisory authority over state legislative and other activity be reconciled with the concept of state autonomy? This question was not raised by the dissenters for the obvious reason that they shared the basic assumptions of the majority regarding the exercise of such power under the doctrines of substantive due process.

### *Contract Clause*

To a lesser extent the equal protection of the laws clause of the Fourteenth Amendment and the contract clause provided bases for the White-Taft Court's exercise of broad supervisory powers over the legislation of the states. In regard to the latter clause, no new doctrines were developed. However, the case of *Public Service Company* v. *St. Cloud*[13] indicated that at least occasionally the contract clause has been successfully invoked by municipalities to enforce established private utility rates which in the absence of a valid contract would undoubtedly have been declared unreasonable and void under the due process clause of the Fourteenth Amendment. By and large the contract clause, when invoked as a restriction on state legislation, was far overshadowed by the due process and equal protection clauses of the Fourteenth Amendment.[14]

12. Justice Holmes' dissent in *Tyson* v. *Banton,* 273 U.S. 418 (1927), well illustrates the first two arguments, while his dissent in *Traux* v. *Corrigan,* 257 U.S. 312 (1921), illustrates the third.

13. 265 U.S. 352 (1924).

14. Wright, *Contract Clause,* pp. 96-97.

*Equal Protection Clause*

The restrictive uses of the equal protection clause during the White-Taft Court period were in turn often overshadowed by the due process clause issues, since in many cases both clauses were invoked against state action.[15] Nevertheless, like the Fuller Court, the White-Taft Court exercised full discretionary authority to sustain state statutory classifications as "reasonable" or to invalidate them as "arbitrary" or "discriminatory" under the equal protection clause.[16] Moreover, the White-Taft Court showed a greater awareness of the facts of state-sponsored racial discrimination than did the Fuller Court. Thus in *Nixon* v. *Herndon*[17] the court held void as a discriminatory classification based on race a Texas statute barring Negroes from participation in Democratic primary elections.

*Fifteenth Amendment*

Over the years the Southern states had evolved an ingenious variety of laws and administrative policies to strip from Negroes the privilege of voting. Not the least of these was the Oklahoma constitution's requirement that in order to qualify to vote, otherwise eligible persons must read and write any section of the state constitution. Because many Negroes in this state were illiterate, this provision effectively disqualified most colored voters. However, many whites were also illiterate and in order to permit these persons to vote, the framers of the Oklahoma constitution provided that

> No person who was, on January 1, 1866, or at any time prior thereto, entitled to vote under any form of government, or who at that time resided in some foreign nation, and no lineal descendant of such person, shall be denied the right to register and vote because of his inability to so read and write sections of such constitution.

In *Guinn* v. *United States,*[18] the White-Taft Court unanimously held the Oklahoma "Grandfather Clause" to be in violation of the Fifteenth Amendment because it implicitly denied the privilege to vote on the basis of race.

*The Commerce Clause and State Power*

The Waite and Fuller Courts had fully recognized the potentialities of the commerce clause as a barrier to state regulatory activity. Con-

15. See *Finlay* v. *California,* 222 U.S. 28 (1911); *Rosenthal* v. *New York,* 226 U.S. 260 (1912); *Royster Guano Company* v. *Virginia,* 253 U.S. 412 (1920).

16. See *Silver* v. *Silver,* 280 U.S. 117 (1929); *Quaker City Cab Company* v. *Pennsylvania,* 277 U.S. 389 (1928).

17. 273 U.S. 536 (1927).

18. 238 U.S 347 (1915); *Myers* v. *Anderson,* 238 U.S. 368 (1915).

versely, both Courts were firmly opposed to extension of congressional commerce authority into matters intrastate. However, by the very nature of America's complex industrial development many subjects of interstate commerce became so intermingled with the purely internal commerce of the states that any threat or danger from the latter could conceivably burden or endanger the former. Recognition of this development by the White-Taft Court was basic to its famous *Shreveport Rate* case decision in 1914.[19] Although couched in guarded language, the principle that the federal government may regulate the purely internal commerce of a state in order to foster and protect its interstate counterpart was enunciated and applied. The recognition of the interrelationship of the two was basic to the decision.

Throughout the White-Taft Court period, the commerce clause was frequently utilized as a limitation on state power, generally under doctrines enunciated by the Waite or Fuller Courts. Of particular interest in federal-state relations was *McDermott* v. *Wisconsin*,[20] in which the White-Taft Court held void a state police power regulation which provided that goods be labeled accurately, on the ground that it interfered with a congressional regulation enacted under the commerce clause—the Pure Food and Drug Act. By the very logic of the principle of federal supremacy, a valid exercise of federal power not only can enter the traditional area of state police power, but, in effect, can supersede state police power regulations in conflict with it. Professor Corwin felt that under this principle the Hepburn Act of 1906 was probably more destructive of state legislation than any other congressional act.[21]

State autonomy was sharply curtailed in the important case of *Western Union Telegraph Company* v. *Kansas*.[22] In regard to a condition by Kansas that the Western Union Company pay into the state school fund a percentage of its authorized capital (estimated on the basis of its intrastate and interstate holdings) in order to engage in business, the White-Taft Court held that it burdened interstate commerce. The effect of this decision was twofold in regard to the weakening of state autonomy. First, as was noted above, state power to exclude or control foreign corporations was circumscribed where the

19. *Houston, East and West Texas Railway Company* v. *United States*, 234 U.S. 342 (1914); actually its doctrine was harbingered in *Southern Railway Company* v. *United States*, 222 U.S. 20 (1911).

20. 228 U.S. 115 (1913).

21. *The Constitution of the United States*, p. 246, hereinafter cited as *Constitution;* see *Chicago I. & L. Railroad Company* v. *United States*, 219 U.S. 486 (1911); *Southern Railway Company* v. *Reid*, 222 U.S. 424 (1912).

22. 216 U.S. 1 (1910); see *Pullman Company* v. *Kansas*, 216 U.S. 59 (1910).

intrastate transactions of such corporations are an integral part of their interstate transactions. And second, state control of its purely internal commerce was limited where state regulation of intrastate commerce burdened interstate commerce.[23]

### FEDERAL POLICE POWER

The second development of great import for federal-state relations during the White-Taft Court period was the further expansion of federal police power under the commerce and taxing clauses. However, like the Fuller Court, the White-Taft Court also tried to set limits on the extension of federal police authority under these clauses.

#### *Commerce Clause*

In a number of important decisions the White-Taft Court, in broad constructionist interpretations, sustained far-reaching exercises of federal police power under the commerce clause.[24] *Hoke* v. *United States, Hipolite Egg Company* v. *United States,* and *Brooks* v. *United States* serve as excellent examples.

In order to put an end to the sordid traffic in human lives known as "White Slavery," Congress prohibited, in 1910, the transportation in interstate and foreign commerce of women and girls for immoral purposes. The constitutionality of this act was challenged in *Hoke* v. *United States*[25] on the ground that it was a congressional attempt to regulate morality, a subject reserved to state police power under the Tenth Amendment. However, the White-Taft Court sustained the act as a valid regulation of "transportation" under the commerce clause.

Under the general doctrine that Congress may bar from interstate

23. The commerce clause was occasionally utilized in this manner in combination with the due process and the equal protection clauses of the Fourteenth Amendment. For example, in the case of *Bethlehem Motors Corporation* v. *Flynt,* 256 U.S. 421 (1921), the White-Taft Court held unconstitutional a state law discriminating against out-of-state corporations doing business within the state not only because it "interfered" with interstate commerce, but because it violated the equal protection of the laws clause as well.

24. *Wilson* v. *New,* 243 U.S. 332 (1917), sustained the Adamson Act of 1916; *Stafford* v. *Wallace,* 258 U.S. 495 (1922), upheld the Packers and Stockyards Act of 1921; *Board of Trade* v. *Olsen,* 262 U.S. 1 (1923), sustained the Grain Futures Act of 1922; *Clark Distilling Company* v. *Western Maryland Railroad,* 242 U.S. 311 (1917), upheld the Webb-Kenyon Act; *United States* v. *Hill,* 248 U.S. 420 (1919), sustained the "Bone Dry" Amendment to the Post Office Appropriation Act of 1917; *United States* v. *Ferger,* 250 U.S. 199 (1919), upheld a Congressional Act of 1916 prohibiting issuance of fraudulent bills of lading; and *Dayton-Goose Creek Railway* v. *United States,* 263 U.S. 456 (1924), sustained the "recapture clause" of the Transportation Act of 1920.

25. 227 U.S. 308 (1913); *Athanasaw* v. *United States,* 227 U.S. 326 (1913); *Bennett* v. *United States,* 227 U.S. 333 (1913); *Harris* v. *United States,* 227 U.S. 340 (1913); *Caminette* v. *United States,* 242 U.S. 470 (1917).

commerce adulterated products, the White-Taft Court sustained in *Hipolite Egg Company* v. *United States*[26] portions of the Pure Food and Drug Act which permitted not only the prohibition of the shipment of such products, but also their seizure and condemnation in transit or in their original unbroken packages in the state of destination.

And finally, in the third of the illustrative cases referred to above—*Brooks* v. *United States*—the White-Taft Court sustained the constitutionality of a congressional act prohibiting the transportation of stolen automobiles in interstate or foreign commerce. In doing so it used the following far-reaching language:

> Congress can certainly regulate interstate commerce to the extent of forbidding and punishing the use of such commerce as an agency to promote immorality, dishonesty or the spread of any evil or harm to the people of other states from the state of origin. *In doing this it is merely exercising the police power, for the benefit of the public, within the field of interstate commerce.*[27]

The federal police power cases discussed and cited above indicated unmistakably that, generally speaking, the White-Taft Court was willing to sustain a wide variety of such congressional regulations under the commerce clause. In these cases, the fact that congressional regulatory authority entered the area of traditional state police power control apparently presented no problem for the court; and in the *Brooks* case the phrase "police power" was actually used. However, in the controversial case of *Hammer* v. *Dagenhart*,[28] the White-Taft Court indicated that there was a line beyond which congressional regulatory authority under the commerce clause could not go. The majority opinion in this case also made it clear that the court itself would draw that line. In addition, the White-Taft Court followed the Fuller Court's anti-regulatory policy of weakening federal authority by rendering narrow statutory interpretations. The engraftment of the "rule of reason" onto the terms of the Sherman Anti-Trust Act is an outstanding example.

By 1916 nationwide disapproval of the evils of child labor had wrought one of those great revolutions in public opinion very similar to earlier public revulsion to lotteries and later opposition to the manufacture and sale of intoxicating liquor. Congress acted decisively and in that year prohibited the shipment in interstate commerce of goods

26. 220 U.S. 45 (1911); see *Seven Cases of Eckman's Alternative* v. *United States*, 239 U.S. 510 (1915); *Weeks* v. *United States*, 245 U.S. 618 (1918).

27. 267 U.S. 432 (1925); italics mine.

28. 247 U.S. 251 (1918).

made in establishments utilizing child labor. The act was challenged as an invasion of the reserved powers of the states.

In a concise and well-organized brief, President Wilson's Solicitor General, John W. Davis, pointed out that numerous precedents supported the proposition that Congress' power to regulate foreign and interstate commerce included the power to prohibit the shipment in it of products which, while not harmful in themselves, were harmful in their effect. One harmful effect of the shipment of child-made goods was, of course, the damaging effect the manufacture of the products had upon the health and development of the children engaged in such manufacture. However, to emphasize the interstate character of the evil, Solicitor Davis pointed up the fact that "the shipment of child-made goods outside of one state directly induces similar employment of children in competing states." Such competition was deemed by Congress to be unfair and detrimental.

The White-Taft Court majority, in an opinion by Justice Day, rejected these arguments. Day first found it necessary to distinguish the present law from the many regulations previously sustained under the commerce clause. In each of the previous situations, said Day, "the use of interstate transportation was necessary to the accomplishment of harmful results." But here the act aimed "to standardize the ages at which children may be employed in mining and manufacturing within the states," an objective outside federal commerce power. Elsewhere, Day noted that "the nation is made up of states to which are entrusted the powers of local government and to them and to the people the powers not *expressly* delegated to the National Government are reserved." Thus Day engrafted upon the Constitution phraseology from the Articles of Confederation which had, significantly, been omitted by the framers at the Philadelphia Convention.

This interpretation suggested that the reserved powers of the states could serve as a barrier to the exercise of federal constitutional authority, although Justice Day was careful to emphasize the lack of federal authority as well. In justification of this far-reaching decision, the opinion of the five-man majority stressed the allegedly terrible consequences of a contrary opinion in these terms:

> The far-reaching result of upholding the act cannot be more plainly indicated than by pointing out that if Congress can thus regulate matters entrusted to local authority by prohibition of the movement of commodities in interstate commerce, all freedom of commerce will be at an end, the power of the states over local matters may be eliminated, and thus our system of government be practically destroyed.

The regulation of lotteries, prostitution, and robbery (i.e. car thefts) were also traditionally considered matters entrusted to local authority, and yet the same court sustained congressional intervention under the commerce clause.

The *Dagenhart* case again underscored the basic paradox involved in those decisions which invoked the time-honored formula of the need to preserve state autonomy. As far as the ability of the states to regulate or prohibit the employment of child labor was concerned, the Court had done far more to weaken state power in this regard than to strengthen it. In a series of decisions beginning with the *Bowman* case in the 1880's, the Court had made it clear that a state could not, under the commerce clause, prohibit the introduction of goods made in other states. And this judicially-enforced free competition among the states undoubtedly tended to discourage social experimentation because state legislators frequently feared that competing states, by permitting the employment of child labor, for example, would gain economic advantages through the migration of industries or through the ability to sell their products at lower prices.[29]

Frequently, when the White-Taft Court wished to curb federal regulatory power, it avoided a head-on clash such as that in the *Dagenhart* case, and accomplished its anti-regulatory purpose by weakening or emasculating federal authority through narrow statutory interpretation. Thus in *Standard Oil Company* v. *United States*[30] the effect of the Sherman Anti-Trust Act was considerably weakened by the expedient of reading into the statute's provisions the "rule of reason." By the express terms of the Anti-Trust Act all combinations in restraint of trade in interstate and foreign commerce were prohibited. However, drawing upon the history of the English common law, the White-Taft Court held that only those monopolies which "unduly" restrained trade were prohibited by the act.

### *Taxing Clause*

The White-Taft Court did give its blessing to some important expansions of federal police power under the taxing clause, notably in the *Doremus* and *Alexander Theatre Office* cases discussed below. But it also developed the penalty doctrine in the *Child Labor Tax* case. And with this doctrine it often limited further expansion of federal police power under the taxing clause. In the *Hill* case, the Court went

29. This approach was suggested by Professor Benson's discussion of the influence of similar considerations on state taxation policies; *The New Centralization*, pp. 22-25.

30. 221 U.S. 1 (1911); see *United States* v. *American Tobacco Company*, 221 U.S. 106 (1911).

so far as to indicate that it preferred that Congress channel further development of federal police power to the commerce clause. Because the adoption of the restrictive penalty doctrine greatly enhanced the Court's power to supervise congressional police power legislation under the taxing clause, the *Bailey* case will be dealt with first.

In view of the fact that the Supreme Court upheld the Oleomargarine Act in the *McCray* case, it was not surprising that Congress turned to the taxing power when its attempt to restrict the employment of child labor under its commerce power was defeated by the Court in *Hammer* v. *Dagenhart.* Under Title XII of the Revenue Act of February 24, 1919, Congress levied a tax of 10 per cent on the annual net profits of persons or corporations who knowingly employed, during any portion of the year, children within specific age limits. Like the tax on oleomargarine colored to look like butter, the tax on the income of persons or corporations employing child labor was intended to exert a prohibitive effect rather than to raise revenue. However, in *Bailey* v. *Drexel Furniture Company,*[31] Chief Justice Taft held for the majority that the child labor tax law was unconstitutional on the ground that the 10 per cent levy was a "penalty" on the doing of acts which Congress had no constitutional power to prohibit. As in the *Dagenhart* case, the majority opinion emphasized the dire consequences for the position of the states which would result from a contrary opinion. In Taft's opinion, a decision sustaining the law would "completely wipe out the sovereignty of the states."

It is true that the sustaining of the child labor tax law would have paved the way for federal regulation of a matter hitherto left to the states, but whether such a decision would have completely wiped out the "sovereignty of the states" is to be doubted. Certainly the *McCray* and *Doremus* cases upheld federal tax laws potentially as dangerous to traditional federalism even though the statutes sustained in those cases did not distinguish between wilful and accidental violations.

With the advent of the "penalty" doctrine, the Court had at its disposal two doctrines, that of the *McCray* case and the one discussed above. Possession of these doctrines enabled the Supreme Court to uphold or strike down at its discretion federal taxing legislation which smacked of regulation. In the period 1922 to 1930, the Court's attitude toward such legislation remained wholly unpredictable. In *Hill* v. *Wallace,*[32] for example, it applied the penalty doctrine to invalidate the Grain Futures Trading Act of 1921. Under the act, Congress had

31. 259 U.S. 20 (1922).
32. 259 U.S. 44 (1922); see *Trusler* v. *Crooks,* 269 U.S. 475 (1926).

levied a tax of twenty cents a bushel on all contracts for the sale of grain for future delivery and had included in the act detailed regulations of boards of trade.

The Court intimated in this case that while it would not uphold regulation of dealings in grain futures under the taxing power, it was prepared to uphold regulations of such dealings enacted under Congress' power over interstate commerce. This attempt at positive guidance of legislation by the Supreme Court was accepted by Congress. An act was immediately passed which provided for the regulation of transactions on grain futures exchanges to prevent obstructions and burdens on interstate commerce in grain. In the following year the Supreme Court upheld the new act in *Board of Trade* v. *Olsen*.[33] The suggestion made in *Hill* v. *Wallace* was apparently an indication that the Supreme Court was prepared to permit the use of the commerce power for broader regulatory purposes than the taxing power.[34]

By denying in *Alexander Theatre Ticket Office, Inc.* v. *United States*[35] a petition for a writ of certiorari, the White-Taft Court upheld a circuit court decision based squarely on the *McCray* rather than the *Bailey* doctrine. The federal circuit court had sustained a section of the Revenue Act of 1926 which levied a 5 per cent tax on the sale of theatre tickets away from box offices in excess of the price printed thereon where such excess did not exceed 50 cents, and a tax of 50 per cent where the amount of the excess was more than 50 cents above the printed price. By these graduations in the rates of the ticket excise taxes, Congress had sought to prevent ticket scalping.

In contrast, the Supreme Court, in *Tyson* v. *Banton*,[36] had held invalid a New York statute which prohibited the sale of theatre tickets at a greater advance than 50 cents over the price stamped on the ticket. Thus while a state was forbidden to regulate ticket scalping through exercise of its reserved police power, the Federal Government was able to regulate the same subject by graduations in the rates of excise taxes.[37]

The taxing power was a favored weapon of Congress in the regulation or virtual prohibition of narcotic drugs. Such use dates back to 1890. In that year Congress levied a tax of ten dollars a pound on opium manufactured in the United States for smoking purposes. This levy was not challenged in the courts. In 1914 Congress made its

33. 262 U.S. 1 (1923).

34. Carl B. Swisher, *American Constitutional Development*, pp. 830-31. Hereinafter cited as *Development*.

35. 279 U.S. 869 (1929).

36. 273 U.S. 418 (1927).

37. Reuschlein and Spector, "Taxing and Spending; the Loaded Dice of a Federal Economy," 23 *Cornell Law Quarterly* 32-33 (December, 1937).

prohibitive intent abundantly clear by raising the tax to three hundred dollars per pound.

In the Harrison Act, which was passed in the same year, Congress did not seek to prohibit the use of narcotic drugs by levying excessively high rates of taxation, but instead sought to insure that such drugs would be used for medical purposes only by setting up an elaborate scheme of regulations incidental to a single revenue raising provision. A tax of one dollar per year upon each person "who produces, imports, manufactures, compounds, deals in, dispenses, sells, distributes, or gives away any of the said drugs" was the only revenue feature in the entire act. On the basis of this single revenue provision, the White-Taft Court, in *Doremus* v. *United States,*[38] upheld the entire act as a constitutionally valid revenue measure.

The *Bailey* and *Hill* cases indicated a strong propensity on the part of the White-Taft Court to establish limits to the uses to which congressional taxing power could be put in the development of a broad federal police power. The *Hill* opinion actually sought to channel such developments toward the commerce clause. But the *Doremus* and *Alexander Theatre* decisions indicated that the area of police power control left to Congress under the taxing power was still quite broad. Apparently, the White-Taft Court felt that when an exercise of federal police power under the taxing clause regulated such matters as ticket scalping and the sale of narcotic drugs, it posed no threat to state powers and therefore was a tax "on its face." But when it touched upon the exploitation of child labor it encroached upon state power and therefore was a "penalty," not a tax.

The case of *Florida* v. *Mellon*[39] involved an attempt by the state of Florida to enjoin the Secretary of the Treasury and the Commissioner of Internal Revenue from collecting federal inheritance taxes in Florida. Because the Federal Estate Tax of 1926 contained a provision which granted to individuals paying state inheritance taxes a credit of 80 per cent toward their federal tax, Florida's counsel argued that the federal law was designed to coerce the state into passing an inheritance tax law of its own. Because of its peculiar position as a haven for retired persons, Florida had, by constitutional stipulation, prohibited the levying of such taxes.

Justice Sutherland's majority opinion retort was direct and unequivocal.

38. 249 U.S. 86 (1919); in a subsequent decision, however, the *Doremus* doctrine was narrowed considerably. See *Linder* v. *United States,* 268 U.S. 5 (1925); but in *Nigro* v. *United States,* 276 U.S. 332 (1928), its vitality was apparently restored.

39. 273 U.S. 12 (1927).

If the act interferes with the exercise by the state of its full powers of taxation or has the effect of removing property from its reach which otherwise would be within it, it is a contingency which affords no ground for judicial relief. The act is a law of the United States made in pursuance of the Constitution and, therefore, the supreme law of the land, the Constitution or laws of the states to the contrary notwithstanding.

Although Sutherland's opinion went on to sustain the federal tax, it must be admitted that he failed to face squarely the coercion issue. It could be assumed that the point was covered by implication in Sutherland's application of the principle of federal supremacy, but if this were true it would appear that so important a question in federal-state relations was dealt with in cavalier fashion. Actually the question whether or not a provision such as that included in the federal inheritance tax law coerced the states to conform with a national purpose was not answered conclusively by the Supreme Court until the late 1930's in the *Social Security* cases.

Another important problem in federal-state relations confronting the White-Taft Court was the question of the constitutionality of the use of federal spending power to foster federally-desired projects by means of the grant-in-aid method. Ever since the Morill Act of 1862, Congress has made use of the grant-in-aid technique to exercise some measure of control over affairs within the states. The federal government checks the projects for which the grants are made to be sure that the money is spent for the purposes designated in the particular act. The grants have generally been made on the condition that the states availing themselves of the grants match the federal funds with appropriations of their own. Since every state wishes to share in the distribution of funds raised through national taxation, such grants are seldom rejected.[40]

In 1921, Congress passed the Shepard-Towner Act which extended financial aid to states which would comply with provisions for reducing maternal and infant mortality and protecting the health of mothers and infants. The state of Massachusetts entered an original suit to enjoin enforcement of the act, urging that the grant-in-aid appropriations were for local rather than national purposes and constituted an effective means of inducing the states to yield a portion of their sovereign rights. In *Massachusetts* v. *Mellon,*[41] the Court countered with the answer that Massachusetts could avoid involvement simply by

40. Swisher, *Development*, p. 837; Jane Perry Clark, *The Rise of a New Federalism*, pp. 137-85.

41. 262 U.S. 447 (1923). In addition, Mrs. Frothingham, as a taxpayer, sought an injunction to enjoin enforcement of the act. The Supreme Court simply held that

refusing to accept the provisions of the act, and, invoking the doctrine of political questions, held that the state lacked sufficient interest in the matter to entitle it to bring suit. To the state's contention that it sought to protect the interests of its citizens the Court answered that such intervention was inconsistent with the nature of the federal system which permitted the federal government to deal directly with individuals.

It would appear that the effect of the *Mellon* decision for federal-state relations was that the federal government could exercise its spending power via the grant-in-aid method to persuade the states to undertake projects which the central government felt would be in the national interest. Such federal-state cooperation did not necessarily weaken state autonomy and could conceivably strengthen it by contributing to the economic or physical vitality of the people of the states concerned. In any case, the *Mellon* decision established that for most practical purposes there remained no way that federal grants-in-aid could be challenged by a state in the Supreme Court.

### THE TREATY-MAKING POWER

The case of *Missouri* v. *Holland*[42] is extremely interesting because of its bearing on the issue whether the treaty-making power of the federal government may be limited by the reserved rights of the states. In carrying out the provisions of a treaty between the United States and Canada, Congress adopted a migratory bird law similar to an earlier law which, enacted under the commerce power, had been declared unconstitutional in two lower federal court decisions.[43] The law based on the treaty power was challenged as an unconstitutional interference with the right of the state under the Tenth Amendment to control or protect its property, here wild fowl within its borders. The majority opinion, written by Justice Holmes, rejected forthrightly the suggestion that the existence of state powers limited the implementation by Congress of an otherwise valid treaty. The necessary and proper clause, which authorizes Congress to make laws not only necessary to the carrying out of its own powers, but also necessary to the implementation of "all other powers vested by this Constitution in

---

the interest of one citizen in the expenditures of Congress was too minute and indeterminable to entitle him to bring such a suit, and further, if one person could do so, so could every other and chaos would result; *Frothingham* v. *Mellon,* 262 U.S. 447 (1923).

42. 252 U.S. 416 (1920).

43. *United States* v. *Shauver,* 214 Fed. Rep. 154 (1914); *United States* v. *McCullough,* 221 Fed. Rep. 288 (1915).

the government of the United States, or in any department or officer thereof," was held by Holmes to be sufficient ground for sustaining the law. Pointing out that the majority did not wish to imply that there were no qualifications to the treaty-making power, Holmes observed that

> It is obvious that there may be matters of the sharpest exigency for the national well-being that an Act of Congress could not deal with but that a treaty followed by such an Act could, and it is not lightly to be assumed that, in matters requiring national action, "a power which must belong to and somewhere reside in every civilized government" is not to be found.

The statement of one writer of the states' rights school that the *Holland* decision subordinates "the sovereignty of the state" to the treaty-making power and the legislative power of Congress in the enforcement of a treaty[44] is, of course, true, but it might be noted that this principle had been recognized and applied by the Supreme Court ever since the early case of *Ware* v. *Hylton*.[45]

#### FEDERAL CONTROL OF PRIMARY ELECTIONS

While the idea that the Tenth Amendment curtailed an otherwise valid exercise of federal treaty-making power was decisively rejected in the *Holland* case, *Newberry* v. *United States*[46] brought a limited victory for Court supporters of dual federalism in another area. The basic constitutional issue in the case was whether Congress had power under Article I, section 4, of the Constitution to regulate primary elections for party candidates to the office of United States senator. Only eight justices passed on this question and they divided four to four.

The opinion of the four who opposed congressional control was written by Justice McReynolds, who reasoned that Congress lacked power to control primary elections because "the term 'elections' in Section 4 of Article I did not embrace a primary election since that procedure was unknown to the framers." He also contended that exercise of such power would invade the reserved powers of the states. Four other justices upheld congressional power to regulate primaries on the ground that because of the close relationship of primaries to general congressional elections, congressional control could be validly implied from the grant of power to regulate general elections. The *Newberry* case apparently persuaded Congress that it lacked authority to regulate primary elections, for the Federal Corrupt

44. L. L. Thompson, "State Sovereignty and the Treaty-Making Power," 2 *California Law Review* 242-58.

45. 3 Dallas 199 (1796).

46. 256 U.S. 232 (1921).

Practices Act of 1925 expressly stated that its provisions did not apply to such elections.

### STATE EQUALITY

Two important issues involving the principle of state equality were decided by the White-Taft Court. Subject only to the limitation set down in Article IV, section 3, Congress can impose virtually any condition it desires in admitting new states. In *Coyle* v. *Smith,*[47] the question was raised whether Congress, in exercising its constitutional power, could place a new state on "a plane of inequality" politically with its sister states. The majority of the White-Taft Court took the position that Congress' responsibility to guarantee each state a republican form of government did not constitute a grant of power to impose conditions for admission which would place the new state in an inferior position politically to the older states. And second, it concluded that both the past practices of Congress and the prior decisions of the Court sustained the view that the principle of state equality extended to new as well as old states. It therefore held that Congress lacked power to impose upon a new state a restriction on its reserved power to choose its own seat of government.

The Fuller Court had held in *Stearns* v. *Minnesota*[48] that where the political rights of a state were not involved but an agreement or compact concerning property rights was in question, the principle of state equality could not be invoked to prevent action toward fulfillment of the compact. The White-Taft Court, in *Ex Parte Webb,*[49] indicated that the principle of state equality was no bar to the exercise of a valid congressional power, here the power to control Indians within the state of Oklahoma.

### AMENDING CLAUSE

The adoption of the Woman Suffrage Amendment brought two curious challenges to the constituent or amending power based on states' rights. Among the multifarious questions raised concerning the constitutionality of the Nineteenth Amendment in *Leser* v. *Garnett,*[50] it was argued that the addition of all eligible adult voters to the electorate in each state so enlarged the body of voters as to destroy the political autonomy of the states. Counsel for Maryland also contended that "the right of the state's own electorate to vote . . . is

47. 221 U.S. 559 (1911).
48. 179 U.S. 223 (1900).
49. 225 U.S. 663 (1912); see *United States* v. *Sandoval,* 231 U.S. 28 (1913).
50. 258 U.S. 130 (1922).

. . . withheld from the . . . operation of the amending power altogether."

The White-Taft Court did not answer these contentions in any detail but simply pointed out that the Fifteenth Amendment was similar in character and phraseology and had been long recognized as valid. The challenges actually posed the larger issue whether there are any inherent limitations upon the amending power arising from the nature of the federal system. The Court's position is not very clear because it refrained from discussing the questions which were raised, but its decision may be said to intimate that there are no inherent limitations upon the amending power.

### INTERGOVERNMENTAL TAX IMMUNITY

In regard to intergovernmental tax immunity, the White-Taft Court did not enunciate any new doctrines of the scope and importance of *Collector* v. *Day* or *South Carolina* v. *United States,* but it did limit the scope of the former doctrine somewhat in the *Metcalf* case.[51] For here it held that a consulting engineer with the New York water system could not claim immunity from a federal income tax merely by showing that his income was received as a compensation for services rendered under a contract with the state. The decision turned on the fact that the engineer was not a state governmental employee.

However, in cases in which either the national or a state government was trustee or lessor, the White-Taft Court achieved some curious results. For example, a non-discriminatory Oklahoma income tax was held void when levied upon the income of a state citizen which was derived from oil and gas lands owned by an Indian ward of the national government and leased for him by that government in its capacity as guardian. The net effect of the White-Taft Court's intergovernmental tax determinations was to create uncertainty in both the state and national governments regarding the limits to which their taxing policies could extend. Both state and national taxing policies were hampered at times by extreme applications of old doctrines.[52]

### DISPUTES BETWEEN STATES

In the exercise of its power to decide controversies between two states, the White Court was called upon to determine whether the Supreme Court, in enforcing a decision made under this jurisdiction, could issue a decree ordering a state in its governmental capacity to

51. *Metcalf and Eddy* v. *Mitchell,* 269 U.S. 514 (1926).

52. *Gillespie* v. *Oklahoma,* 257 U.S. 501 (1922); cf. Benjamin F. Wright, *The Growth of American Constitutional Law*, pp. 128-35.

perform a particular act. The occasion was the last in the long series of litigations between Virginia and West Virginia concerning the latter's liability for a portion of Virginia's debt.[53] Although it might be noted that the Court, in a sense, inherited this power from the Confederation Congress, the White Court grounded its affirmative decision upon the jurisdictional grant in Article III in the Constitution and upon the doctrine that the power to issue such decrees was derived from the jurisdictional grant. Before the necessity for issuing such a decree arose, the two states settled their differences.

### SUMMARY AND CONCLUSION

Viewed upon a purely comparative basis, the White-Taft Court period was manifestly similar to the Fuller Court period in many respects. The broad supervisory powers over the states assumed under the due process and equal protection clauses of the Fourteenth Amendment by the Fuller Court were not only continued but expanded by the White-Taft Court. The doctrine of business affected with a public interest clearly became a more formidable restrictive weapon in the *Wolff Packing Company* case, while *Gitlow* v. *New York* embodied a new enlargement of the meaning of due process which brought within the protection of the Fourteenth Amendment freedom of speech and freedom of the press. A good deal of progressive state regulatory legislation was sustained by the White-Taft Court, but, like its predecessor, it frequently substituted its judgment concerning the necessity for or wisdom of state laws for that of the state legislatures. Criticism by the apostles of judicial self-restraint—Holmes, Brandeis and Stone—was concentrated, not on the Court's assumption of supervisory power under substantive due process doctrines, but rather upon the manner in which such broad power was used.

Regarding the White-Taft Court's attitude toward the expansion of federal police power, again there was a great deal of similarity with that of the Fuller Court. In general, the White-Taft Court sustained broad expansions of federal police power under the commerce and taxing clauses. But in the *Dagenhart* and the *Bailey* cases it not only construed federal commerce and taxing powers narrowly, but assumed that the Tenth Amendment endowed the reserved powers of the states with an inviolate, static character capable of blocking further expansion of federal police power. In the *Hill* case, the Court sought to channel further expansion of federal police power from the taxing to the commerce power. Furthermore, Court opposition to particular

53. *Virginia* v. *West Virginia*, 246 U.S. 565 (1918).

federal police power regulations did not always manifest itself in direct judicial nullification of congressional enactments, but, as in the *Standard Oil* case, revealed itself in the rendition of extremely narrow statutory interpretations by the Court.

No new doctrines were handed down by the White-Taft Court in its intergovernmental tax immunity cases, but both state and federal taxing power was hampered at times by rather extreme applications of older doctrines. *Missouri* v. *Holland* established that Congress' power to enforce a valid treaty by appropriate legislation was broader than its delegated commerce power. This decision, in addition, rejected decisively the idea that the Tenth Amendment imposes limitations on the national treaty-making power.

The *Dagenhart* and *Bailey* cases ostensibly indicate White-Taft Court awareness of the need to preserve state autonomy against federal encroachment. However, one suspects that the motivating factor in decisions such as these was anti-regulatory—not pro-states' rights. Taken in the aggregate, both the federal police power and the due process clause decisions of the White-Taft Court were perhaps far more destructive of state autonomy than decisions such as *Hammer* v. *Dagenhart* were protective. The criticisms made of the Fuller Court in these respects apply with equal force to the White-Taft Court.

It is, of course, inaccurate to discuss the activities of a single institution such as the Supreme Court in terms which overstate its influence upon so complex a social and political development as federal centralization. Fundamentally, such a development evolved almost inevitably from the changes taking place in American society in the period beginning after the Civil War. But it is perhaps fair to say that the White-Taft Court, like its predecessor, did a great deal to accelerate the process not only by sustaining broad expansions of federal police power, but by frequently hampering state legislative activity and discouraging state legislative initiative.

# CHAPTER IX

## *The Hughes Court, 1930-1941*

IN MANY RESPECTS, the answers given to constitutional questions by the Hughes Court before 1937 were basically different from those given after that year. With a few important exceptions, the decisions of the pre-1937 Hughes Court were simply continuations of the judicial policies of the Fuller, White, and Taft Courts. After 1937, however, came a tremendously important period of re-evaluation and sometimes of reversal of earlier doctrinal trends.

### CONSTITUTIONAL LIMITATIONS ON THE STATES

#### *Due Process Clause of the Fourteenth Amendment*

Two developments of significance in federal-state relations took place in the decisions of the Hughes Court dealing with the due process clause of the Fourteenth Amendment. Under this provision the Court narrowed considerably its substantive due process doctrines which were protective of economic rights, and vigorously extended its judicial protection to non-economic civil and personal rights.

The protection of non-economic rights by the federal judiciary began early in the Hughes Court period and then accelerated tremendously after 1937. The doctrine of the *Gitlow* case was applied in *Near* v. *Minnesota*.[1] According to a Minnesota statute, anyone who engaged in the publication of a "malicious, scandalous and defamatory" newspaper or periodical might have his publication abated as a nuisance by means of "padlocking" by a suit instituted in the name of the state. Proof of the truth of the published material plus proof that it was published "with good motives and for justifiable ends" was to be accepted as an adequate defense in such suits. Disobedience of an injunction was made punishable as contempt of court. The Hughes Court, in a 5 to 4 decision, declared the statute invalid as a prior restraint on freedom of the press. But it refrained from giving its

1. 283 U.S. 697 (1931).

reasons for including freedom of the press within the protection of the due process clause of the Fourteenth Amendment. Here it was content to observe that "it was impossible to conclude that this essential personal liberty of the citizen was left unprotected by the general guaranty of fundamental rights of person and property."

Prior to the *Palko* case a number of important cases[2] were decided under the *Gitlow* doctrine or enlargements of it without discussion of the reasons for the inclusion of certain freedoms within the meaning of due process. In 1937, however, the rationale for such inclusion was given by Justice Cardozo in the majority opinion in *Palko* v. *Connecticut.*[3] The Court evidently felt that because the fundamental liberties were essential to democracy itself, the inclusion of such liberties within the meaning of "liberty" as used in the due process clause of the Fourteenth Amendment was justified even though the inclusion had important implications for state autonomy. The Supreme Court, in effect, took upon itself the protection of liberties, the safeguarding of which had hitherto been the responsibility of the appropriate state organs.

During the closing years of the Hughes Court period, 1937-41, the full impact of the inclusion of the fundamental liberties within the meaning of the due process clause of the Fourteenth Amendment was felt within the states. In *Lovell* v. *Griffin,*[4] a municipal ordinance prohibiting the distribution of leaflets and handbooks without the permission of the city manager was held void as a deprivation of freedom of speech and press forbidden by the due process clause of the Fourteenth Amendment. *Cantwell* v. *Connecticut*[5] established that freedom of religion was protected via the Fourteenth Amendment from previous and absolute restraint. Here a city ordinance vesting discretionary authority to grant certificates permitting the bearers to solicit money for religious purposes was considered a previous restraint on religious freedom.

However, in the first flag salute case,[6] a majority of eight justices rejected an argument based on religious freedom to sustain a school board ruling requiring all children attending the public schools in its

2. Included within the meaning of due process and therefore protected by the federal judiciary against state infringement were freedom of speech in *Stromberg* v. *California,* 283 U.S. 359 (1931); speech and assembly in *DeJonge* v. *Oregon,* 299 U.S. 353 (1937); and press in *Grosjean* v. *American Press Company,* 297 U.S. 233 (1936).

3. 302 U.S. 319 (1937).

4. 303 U.S. 444 (1938); *Schneider* v. *Irvington,* 308 U.S. 147 (1939).

5. 310 U.S. 296 (1940).

6. *Minersville School District* v. *Gobitis,* 310 U.S. 586 (1940).

district to give the flag salute at the opening of each school day. The majority opinion, written by Justice Frankfurter, is particularly significant in that it reflected an increasing awareness on the part of the Court of the implications of the *Gitlow* doctrine for the states. After recognizing that the Court was called upon to reconcile the conflicting claims of liberty of conscience and the authority to safeguard the nation's unity by compulsory flag salute, Frankfurter made it plain that the Court felt that the latter consideration overrode the former. But he also based his decision upon the recognition that the determination of an issue of this kind by the court assumed power belonging to the states or their political subdivisions.

Justice Stone, in dissent, stated clearly the close relationship of the constitutional guarantee of civil liberty and the problem of majority versus minority rights. He pointed out that "by this law the state seeks to coerce these children to express a sentiment, which as they interpret it, they do not entertain, and which violates their deepest religious convictions." He also felt that the Supreme Court must step in and assume power to protect civil liberties if their protection is to be assured. Stone's argument for assumption of federal supervisory power was destined to become the majority view.

### *Attitude toward Economic Rights*

In sharp contrast to the Hughes Court's expansion of federal judicial supervisory authority in regard to non-economic civil liberties was its rapid contraction of such authority concerning economic rights. The fate of two constitutional engraftments, "business affected with a public interest" and "freedom of contract," well illustrates the latter development. Interestingly enough, repudiation of the former doctrine came before the judicial "change of heart" of 1937.

As in the Taft Court period, however, the earlier years of the Hughes Court were characterized by a process of inclusion and exclusion of categories of business into the concept "business affected with a public interest." In 1931 a New Jersey regulation of the rates of insurance companies was sustained in *O'Gorman* v. *Hartford Insurance Company*;[7] but while insurance companies were held within the category of businesses affected with a public interest, ice companies were not. Thus an Oklahoma legislative requirement that newcomers in the ice industry secure a certificate of convenience and necessity from a state commission was held a deprivation of due process in *New State Ice Company* v. *Liebman*.[8]

7. 282 U.S. 251 (1931).

8. 285 U.S. 262 (1932).

Whether because of the persuasiveness of dissenting attacks made first by Holmes and continued by Brandeis and Stone or because of the impact of the economic depression of the 1930's on the judicial attitudes, in *Nebbia* v. *New York*[9] a bare majority of the Hughes Court completely discarded the idea that price control need be justified constitutionally by virtue of the fact that the businesses so controlled are "affected by a public interest" in the traditional sense.

Just as the concept "business affected with a public interest" was relegated to interpretative limbo in the *Nebbia* case, so was another concept abandoned in *West Coast Hotel Company* v. *Parrish*.[10] Even as late as 1936 the *Lochner-Adkins* doctrine of liberty of contract was utilized to invalidate a New York minimum wage law.[11] Within a year, the Hughes Court, in a 5 to 4 decision, overruled the *Adkins* decision and sustained a Washington minimum wage law for women on the grounds that the parties entering into a labor contract were not in fact equals and, further, that the law was a valid and reasonable exercise of state police power. The doctrine of liberty of contract was abandoned. That the lessons of the great depression had not been lost upon the Hughes Court majority was further indicated in the statement that

> . . . The exploitation of a class of workers who are in an unequal position with respect to bargaining power and are thus relatively defenseless against the denial of a living wage is not only detrimental to their health and well being but casts a direct burden for their support upon the community.

Neither the *Nebbia* nor the *Parrish* decision repudiated the power of judicial review over the subject matter of state laws under the due process clause. Both rejected judicial concepts which in the hands of justices motivated by laissez faire economic principles had been utilized rigorously to restrict state social experimentation and economic regulation. However, while the doctrines of liberty of contract and business affected with a public interest were discarded,[12] the basic substantive due process test of reasonableness was retained. And furthermore no substantial movement developed within the Court to repudiate the latter.

The two decisions discussed above were, of course, indicative of

9. 291 U.S. 502 (1934); see *Olsen* v. *Nebraska*, 313 U.S. 236 (1941), which overruled *Ribnik* v. *McBride*.

10. 300 U.S. 379 (1937).

11. *Morehead* v. *New York ex rel Tipaldo*, 298 U.S. 587 (1936).

12. Conceivably, a state law dealing with the right to contract could still be held void as an arbitrary and unreasonable exercise of state power.

the general Hughes Court policy of narrowing almost to the vanishing point the previously dominant Supreme Court propensity to utilize substantive due process doctrines to safeguard economic rights against state regulation. *Thornhill* v. *Alabama*[13] might be cited as an exception, but here a labor-management dispute provoked Hughes Court intervention because a majority of the Court viewed peaceful picketing and the unrestrained discussion of the issues of a labor dispute as part of the freedoms of speech and assembly protected against state action by the Fourteenth Amendment.

Justice Black, who among the justices of the post-1937 Hughes Court was perhaps most strongly opposed to federal judicial supervision of state regulation of economic matters, proposed reversal of the Court's doctrine of more than a half century's standing that the word "person" in the Fourteenth Amendment includes corporate as well as natural persons.[14] Black's proposal was not accepted then or later by other members of the Hughes Court, but by and large the Court did withdraw itself from intervention in state economic affairs without repudiating its basic substantive due process assumption of power over such matters. In other words, the relative freedom of action in economic affairs the states enjoyed under the post-1937 Hughes Court (and its successors) was not enjoyed as a matter of unassailable right, but was in effect permitted by the Court, because that tribunal was willing to accept as reasonable many state legislative acts and policies which its predecessors would have rejected.

In the field of state legislative or administrative rate-making, the post-1937 Hughes Court similarly did not abandon its substantive due process powers, but simply adopted an interpretative policy much less rigorous than that of earlier courts. A majority statement in *Railroad Commission of Texas* v. *Rowan and Nichols Oil Company*[15] sums up its attitude on the subject of federal judicial control of state regulatory administration: ". . . it is clear that the Due Process Clause does not require the feel of the expert to be supplanted by an independent view of judges on the conflicting testimony and prophesies and impressions of expert witnesses."

Under the post-1937 Hughes Court, the states enjoyed far greater freedom in the field of economic experimentation and regulation than they had in nearly a half century. However, as has been noted previous-

13. 310 U.S. 88 (1940); but compare *Milk Drivers Union* v. *Meadowmoor Dairies, Inc.*, 312 U.S. 287 (1941).

14. *Connecticut General Life Insurance Company* v. *Johnson*, 303 U.S. 77 (1938).

15. 311 U.S. 570 (1941).

ly, they were subjected to stringent supervision regarding legislation or action concerning non-economic personal freedoms such as speech, religion, or press. This difference in policy evidently grew from a conviction shared by nearly all the members of the Court that the fundamental freedoms must be accorded preferential treatment because they were on a higher plane in the scheme of constitutional values.

*Procedural Due Process*

The due process clause in its procedural aspect was utilized in several important cases by the Hughes Court to enforce the rules of judicial fair treatment. Chief among these cases were *Powell* v. *Alabama* and *Brown* v. *Mississippi*. In *Powell* v. *Alabama*[16] deprivation of the opportunity to be heard by counsel in time to permit the preparation of an adequate defense in a capital case in certain unusual circumstances was held to constitute a denial of due process of law as guaranteed by the Fourteenth Amendment. And in *Brown* v. *Mississippi*[17] a conviction for murder based solely upon a confession wrung from the convicted by state officers through torture was also held a violation of that clause.

*Equal Protection Clause*

One of the most far-reaching developments in the interpretation of the equal protection clause during the Hughes Court period came in *Missouri ex rel Gaines* v. *Canada*.[18] Here the Hughes Court held void an action of the curators of the state university of Missouri denying to a Negro citizen of the state, who was educationally qualified, admission to the law school on the basis of race and color. A state-operated Negro university did not have a law school. And a Missouri statutory provision for legal education for Negroes outside the state was held insufficient to remedy the defect, since, according to the court, equal protection refers to equal opportunities afforded persons within their respective states. The obligation of a state under the constitutional provision must be performed within its jurisdiction. The *Missouri* decision did not, of course, modify the *Plessy* doctrine, which permitted state provision of separate, but equal facilities, but it did serve notice upon states having segregated educational systems that they must provide equal facilities for both races within their boundaries.

16. 287 U.S. 45 (1932); *Avery* v. *Alabama*, 308 U.S. 444 (1940).

17. 297 U.S. 278 (1936); see *Chambers* v. *Florida*, 309 U.S. 227 (1940); *Canty* v. *Alabama*, 309 U.S. 629 (1940); *White* v. *Texas*, 309 U.S. 631 (1940); *White* v. *Texas* (2nd), 310 U.S. 530 (1940).

18. 305 U.S. 337 (1938).

In *Nixon* v. *Condon*[19] the Hughes Court disallowed a second attempt by the Texas legislature to bar Negroes from participation in primary elections. Authorization by state law to the state executive committee of any political party to determine who shall vote in a party primary election was held to clothe such committees with state authority. Thus the action of a Democratic state executive committee barring Negroes was held to be state action taken in violation of the equal protection clause.

Undaunted by this rebuff, the Texas legislature adopted the expedient of leaving to the political parties the power to set the qualifications for voting in primary elections, without, however, expressly delegating such authority. In *Grovey* v. *Townsend*[20] the Hughes Court unanimously held that exclusion of Negroes by state party convention was private, not state, action and therefore was not prohibited by the equal protection clause.

*Contract Clause*

The multifarious problems of the Great Depression brought forth many attempts at solution at both the state and national levels of government. However, in the matter of the large number of property losses and transfers brought about by depression mortgage foreclosures, the contract clause represented a formidable obstacle to state action. Because of the seriousness of the foreclosure situation, particularly in the midwest, a number of states took legislative action to mitigate the effects of the depression. The Minnesota Mortgage Moratorium Act of 1933 was typical.

This act declared that the severe economic depression had created an emergency which demanded, as an exercise of state police power, the temporary extension of the time allowed under existing law for the redemption of real property from foreclosure and sale under existing mortgages. In more detail, the act provided that where the period of redemption has not already expired, the owner in possession might, by applying to a state court, obtain an extension for such time as the court may deem just and equitable, but not extending beyond May 1, 1935. Aside from the extension of time, all the other conditions of redemption were left unaltered—a rental had to be paid, the amount being determined by the court also.

In spite of an historically valid dissent by Justice Sutherland, in which he pointed out the similarity of the modern Minnesota law to

19. 286 U.S. 73 (1932). The *Herndon* case, decided in the Taft Court period, concerned the first.

20. 295 U.S. 45 (1935).

the eighteenth century "stay" laws feared by many of the framers, a five-man majority upheld the mortgage moratorium law as a valid exercise of state police power to protect the vital interests of the community during a period of economic emergency.[21] In effect, the contract clause was not an absolute and unqualified restriction on the powers of the states to preserve themselves and the societies they comprised. The majority spokesman also pointed out that the atomistic conception of society shared by the framers was no longer accepted, and that contract relationships affected society as well as the individuals who were party to them.

In the period between the *Blaisdell* decision and 1937, the doctrine of that case was construed narrowly.[22] However, even when interpreted strictly, the *Blaisdell* doctrine permitted the states temporarily to modify contract remedies in a period when such action was sorely needed.

### *The Commerce Clause as a Limitation on State Power*

Regarding the use of the commerce clause as a limitation on state police power, the Hughes Court was generally inclined to sustain rather than reject state regulations.[23] No new doctrines were adopted by the Hughes Court majority, but in a dissenting opinion in *McCarroll* v. *Dixie Greyhound Lines,*[24] three justices, Black, Douglas, and Frankfurter, took the position that since judicial control of state tax interference with interstate commerce was a "hit-or-miss method," the problem of state taxation and its relation to interstate commerce should be left to Congress. This advice was never acted upon by a Hughes Court majority, but served to indicate in some measure the greater feeling of deference to the legislative will shared by the post-1937 majority. This deference was also accorded, generally speaking, to the legislatures of the states.

## PRIVILEGES AND IMMUNITIES CLAUSE OF THE FOURTEENTH AMENDMENT

In *Colgate* v. *Harvey*[25] the Hughes Court resurrected the long devitalized privileges and immunities clause of the Fourteenth Amendment to invalidate a Vermont tax law exempting income derived from securities involving loans made within the state but denying exemption

21. *Home Building and Loan Association* v. *Blaisdell,* 290 U.S. 398 (1934).

22. See *W. B. Worthen Company* v. *Thomas,* 292 U.S. 426 (1934).

23. See *California* v. *Thompson,* 313 U.S. 109 (1941); *Maurer* v. *Hamilton,* 309 U.S. 598 (1940).

24. 309 U.S. 176 (1940).

25. 296 U.S. 404 (1935).

to similar loans made outside the state. The right lawfully to loan money outside one's home state was held to be a privilege of national citizenship. The *Harvey* doctrine was destined to survive only until 1940, for in that year it was overruled in *Madden* v. *Kentucky*.[26] The only significance of the *Madden* case for the Court's role as arbiter in federal-state relations lay in the Court's unwillingness to utilize or expand a constitutional clause which at best would enable the Court to invoke, at its pleasure, a substitute for the already adequate due process and equal protection clauses of the Fourteenth Amendment.

### TWENTY-FIRST AMENDMENT

The Twenty-first Amendment provides, in section 2, that "The transportation or importation into any state, . . . for delivery or use therein of intoxicating liquor in violation of the laws thereof is hereby prohibited." One unforeseen development arising out of the adoption of this amendment was that it permitted the states to engage in the very kind of interstate commercial warfare that the Constitution had originally sought to prohibit. Thus in *Mahoney* v. *Triner Company*[27] the Hughes Court admitted that a Minnesota tax discriminating against the alcoholic products of other states would, but for the Twenty-first Amendment, have been held unconstitutional under the equal protection clause. On the other hand, this amendment, indicated the Hughes Court, could not be utilized as a vehicle for state interference with purely federal matters. In this respect, *Collins* v. *Yosemite Park and Curry Company*[28] established that the Twenty-first Amendment did not grant to a state the authority to regulate the importation of intoxicating liquor into territory which it ceded to the United States.

### FEDERAL CONTROL OF PRIMARY ELECTIONS

In *United States* v. *Classic*[29] the Hughes Court held that where a primary election is by law an integral part of a general congressional election scheme or where victory in such a primary is tantamount to election in the general contest, the right of a qualified voter to participate in a primary election is a federal one guaranteed by the Constitution and consequently is a proper subject for congressional regulation under Article I, sections 2 and 4.

The *Classic* decision was extremely important in federal-state rela-

26. 309 U.S. 83 (1940).

27. 304 U.S. 401 (1938); see *Indianapolis Brewing Company* v. *Liquor Control Commission,* 305 U.S. 391 (1939).

28. 304 U.S. 518 (1938).

29. 313 U.S. 299 (1941).

tions for two reasons. First, it opened the way for full federal judicial intervention in situations which had been closed to such intervention by the *Grovey* doctrine. And further, it cleared up the uncertainty that had been created by the *Newberry* case regarding Congress' constitutional power to regulate congressional primaries.

### FEDERAL POLICE POWER

In the aggregate, the Hughes Court's due process and contract clause decisions lessened federal judicial supervisory pressures on state economic policies in a period crucial to the economic survival of both the states and the nation. However, before 1937 the Hughes Court majority set itself with determination against key portions of the "New Deal" legislative program.

#### *Judicial Attitudes Toward the New Deal*

By 1935 the Hughes Court began to hand down a series of decisions which produced a particularly serious clash between the political and judicial branches of the national government. Because of the almost complete inability of the impoverished state governments to meet the unprecedented demands created by the economic depression, the national government took positive action in a vast variety of projects to meet the depression problem. National governmental supervision and action encompassed many aspects of industrial and agricultural activity which even in the twentieth century had been considered squarely within the sphere of state police power regulation. As in the past, however, when the inability of the states to cope with problems of great magnitude became evident, the national government stepped in. And in this instance it did so decisively under the bold, imaginative leadership of President Franklin D. Roosevelt. Vast new projects were hurriedly set up to stimulate industrial and agricultural recovery.

As the *Blaisdell* decision indicated, the Hughes Court was not entirely unmoved by the depression experience. However, the four dissenters in that case, Justices McReynolds, Sutherland, Butler, and Van Devanter, resisted as a solid bloc most of the important New Deal legislation that was tested before the Supreme Court. Squarely opposed to the irreconcilables on most issues were Justices Brandeis, Stone, and Cardozo; and generally voting with this trio was the Chief Justice. The variable factor was Justice Roberts, who, in the period 1935-36, usually voted with the irreconcilables.

*Bankruptcy Power*

Because of the breadth and severity of the economic depression of the 1930's, Congress, after 1933, began to take action to mitigate its effects and to stimulate economic recovery. One such exercise of power was the Frazier-Lemke Act, which was based on Article I, section 8, of the Constitution, which provides that "Congress shall have Power . . . to establish . . . uniform laws on the subject of Bankruptcies throughout the United States." Its purpose was to preserve to farmers with mortgaged property the ownership and enjoyment of their property. At the time the act was passed there was grave danger that foreclosure of farms would become widespread. Congress felt that to permit such widespread foreclosure would transfer ownership to large corporations, transform the farm owners into tenants and thus tend to create a peasant class. Thus it was felt that the welfare of the nation demanded that farms be individually owned.

In *Louisville Joint Stock Bank* v. *Radford,*[30] the Hughes Court, in an opinion by Justice Brandeis, held that under the bankruptcy power Congress may discharge a debtor's personal obligation, because, unlike the states, it is not prohibited from impairing the obligation of contracts. However, Brandeis went on to point out that Congress' bankruptcy power was subject to the Fifth Amendment. Under the due process clause of that amendment, Congress is restrained from taking private property for even a wholly public use without providing for just compensation. Brandeis held that because of the lack of certain safeguards for the mortgage holder the Frazier-Lemke Act, as it operated in the case, took valuable rights in specific property from one person and gave them to another, and thus was repugnant to the Fifth Amendment. The congressional drafters of the new Frazier-Lemke Act had paid particular attention to the constitutional objections to the old act raised by Brandeis in the *Radford* case. Consequently, the new version was sustained by the Supreme Court in *Wright* v. *Vinton Branch of the Mountain Trust Bank of Roanoke.*[31] On the basis of the *Wright* decision, Congress, provided it keeps certain safeguards for mortgage holders, can exercise a federal police power under the bankruptcy clause to accomplish a result similar to an exercise of state police power such as in the Minnesota Moratorium Act of 1933.

*Delegation of Legislative Authority*

The earliest major clash between the judicial and political branches of the national government came in *Panama Refining Com-*

30. 295 U.S. 555 (1935).

31. 300 U.S. 440 (1937).

*pany* v. *Ryan*.[32] Here section 9c of the National Industrial Recovery Act, authorizing the President to prohibit transportation in interstate and foreign commerce of "hot oil,"[33] was held an unconstitutional delegation of legislative authority to the executive. According to the majority, "nowhere in the statute has Congress declared or indicated any policy or standard to guide or limit the President. . . ."

In the same term the entire complicated structure of the NRA was held void in *Schechter Poultry Corporation* v. *United States*[34] because authority to create and enforce codes of fair competition was given to the executive without a definition of fair competition or without standards to limit executive discretion. The fact that trade or industrial groups representative of an industry were to draw up such codes and that before approving them the President was required to find that these codes did not tend toward monopoly was held to be insufficient because an apparently boundless area for executive lawmaking remained.

After the "change-of-heart" of 1937, the Hughes Court modified its views appreciably on questions of delegation of legislative authority.[35] In *Opp Cotton Mills* v. *Administrator*,[36] provisions of the Fair Labor Standards Act were sustained against a charge that they delegated legislative authority to an administrator in the executive branch, despite the fact that they granted authority to the administrator to appoint industry advisory committees which were empowered to investigate working practices in certain industries, and upon the finding of conditions specified in the act to recommend higher minimum wage rates. The administrator was authorized to adopt these recommendations and enforce them. The Hughes Court upheld this portion of the act on the grounds that Congress had set a definite policy and that it would be impractical for Congress to attempt to set minimum wages for specific industries. The Court apparently accepted this congressional grant of broad discretionary authority because of two factors. First, executive

32. 293 U.S. 388 (1935). Only Justice Cardozo dissented in this case.

33. Oil produced or taken from storage in excess of the amount set by state law.

34. 295 U.S. 495 (1935).

35. Even before 1937, the Court made it clear that in congressional statutes dealing with foreign affairs, the scope of permissible "delegation" was much broader than in domestic affairs because national authority in external affairs was not carved from the powers of the states, but was devolved directly from Great Britain. Secondly, since the President as the sole organ of foreign affairs possesses broad powers of his own he may be accorded "a degree of discretion and freedom from statutory restriction which would not be admissible were domestic affairs alone involved." *United States* v. *Curtiss-Wright Export Corporation*, 299 U.S. 304 (1936).

36. 312 U.S. 126 (1941); see *Currin* v. *Wallace*, 306 U.S. 1 (1939); *United States* v. *Rock Royal Cooperative*, 307 U.S. 533 (1939).

administrators undoubtedly took greater care in the actual drafting of laws than they had in the halcyon days of NRA and the first AAA. And second, the Hughes Court unquestionably was willing to accept as constitutional much broader legislative grants of discretionary authority to the executive than it would have been before 1937.

The doctrine of the non-delegability of legislative authority had been invoked to safeguard the principle of the separation of powers. But since the doctrine was used frequently by the pre-1937 Hughes Court to disallow portions of the New Deal economic regulatory program, it did, of course, retard for a time the rather rapid process of federal centralization. After 1937, however, the doctrine of non-delegation of legislative authority no longer was a serious bar to the expansion of federal police power.

*Taxing and Spending Powers*

Before 1937, the doctrine of non-delegation of legislative authority of the *Ryan* case and the extremely narrow interpretation of the commerce clause of the *Carter* case, discussed below, had in themselves been severe restrictions on congressional efforts to cope with a depression which was national in scope. This problem was not susceptible to piecemeal solution by individual states which were generally unequal to the task. Nevertheless, the pre-1937 Hughes Court majority administered a serious setback to Congress in regard to the uses of its taxing and spending powers.

In 1933 Congress passed an Agricultural Adjustment Act in order to restore the level of farm prices and thus increase the purchasing power of farmers. This was to be accomplished by reducing production of certain basic agricultural commodities to restore pre-war market prices. Benefit payments were to be made to farmers who decreased production; the farmers were not compelled by law to reduce production, but were merely well paid if they complied. The Act provided for processing taxes on industries which prepared farm products for market, and the money collected through these levies was earmarked for the crop-reduction payments.

Justice Roberts, speaking for the majority in *United States* v. *Butler,*[37] held the processing taxes unconstitutional because the money raised from them was to be used to finance a system of federal regulation of agriculture which lay outside the delegated powers of Congress. This ruling was not an application of the penalty doctrine laid down in the *Bailey* case, but rather was a statement of the doctrine of dual

37. 297 U.S. 1 (1936).

federalism. The processing taxes actually were levied to raise money and were placed in the general treasury, but were earmarked for crop-reduction purposes. The use of the processing tax money for this purpose was held to be a purpose within the reserved powers of the states and thus violated the Tenth Amendment. By this doctrine the delegated powers of Congress were held to be impliedly limited by the existence of the reserved powers of the states. Roberts made the additional point that the agricultural adjustment program was coercive because the benefits offered to the farmer were so attractive that he could not afford to refuse them. Of great significance for subsequent spending power decisions was Roberts' *dicta* embodying the Hamiltonian view that while the phrase "provide for the general welfare" states the purpose for which money raised by federal taxation may be spent and is not a grant of power independent of taxation, the power is not to be interpreted narrowly as including only those objects falling squarely within the delegated powers of Congress. Thus Congress may tax in order to raise money to be used in promoting a broad public welfare which was general, not local, in scope. Within a year this doctrine was applied in the *Steward Machine Company* and *Helvering* cases to sustain broad programs of social reform.

The *Butler* decision did, of course, in its practical effect defeat an important exercise of federal police power in the agricultural field. But of far greater importance in federal-state relations was Justice Roberts' doctrine that the reserved powers of the states limit otherwise valid exercises of federal power. For as was noted in an earlier chapter this doctrine is in itself inconsistent with the cardinal principle of federal supremacy.

The over-all effect of decisions like those of the *Butler, Ryan,* and *Schechter* cases was the rather complete curtailment of federal police power regulations enacted to stabilize or protect the national economy. Through inability the states were powerless; and through judicial decision it seemed by 1937 that the national government was largely powerless also.

However, 1937 proved to be a decisive turning point for the Hughes Court. For, in a sense, *United States* v. *Butler* can be termed the swan-song of the laissez faire majority. After this decision the conflict between President Roosevelt and the conservative majority on the Supreme Court reached its climax. Although the President's proposal to increase the number of justices was rejected, within a few months of the *Butler* decision, there was an important change in judicial attitude without any corresponding change in the membership of the Court.

A few comparisons of cases in the years 1936 and 1937 are sufficient to point up the remarkable transformation. The Social Security Act, passed a few months before the *Butler* decision, had seemed in many respects to be as vulnerable to the doctrine of dual federalism as had been the Agricultural Adjustment Act. However, the Supreme Court did not invoke the *Butler* doctrine when the Social Security Act was considered in *Steward Machine Company* v. *Davis* and *Helvering* v. *Davis,*[38] but upheld it as a valid exercise of the spending power for the general welfare, and as a legitimate attempt at federal-state cooperation.

In *Helvering* v. *Davis,* the Court upheld the old-age pension provisions of the Social Security Act as an expenditure which was valid under Congress' power to lay and collect taxes to provide for the general welfare of the United States. Although these cases did not overrule the *Butler* doctrine, they were both based upon views of federal power fundamentally different from those expressed in the earlier case. For nowhere in the *Steward* and *Helvering* cases is there an intimation that a valid exercise of federal power is limited by the existence of any of the reserved powers of the states.

In *Carmichael* v. *Southern Coal and Coke Company,*[39] the "converted" Hughes Court upheld an Alabama unemployment compensation act which had been passed to permit the state to participate in the benefits set up under the National Social Security Act. The following passage from this opinion is indicative of the Hughes Court's attitude in the *Steward* and *Helvering* cases as well. In Justice Stone's words,

> Together the two statutes now before us [i.e., the National Social Security Law and the Alabama statute] embody a cooperative legislative effort by state and national government, for carrying out a public purpose common to both, which neither could fully achieve without the cooperation of the other. The Constitution does not prohibit such cooperation.

The *Steward* and *Helvering* cases marked a tremendously significant extension of the permissible scope of federal power under the spending and taxing clauses. Inherent in these decisions is the recognition that certain basic problems such as unemployment were really national in scope and required either national action or, if possible, national and state cooperation to cope with them. The latter aspect of these cases is of particular importance because, instead of superficially "defending" states' rights after the manner of the *Butler* decision, the Hughes Court, after 1937, viewed the nation and the states not as antagonists but as partners. Such a view is premised upon the idea

38. 301 U.S. 548 (1937); 301 U.S. 619 (1937).
39. 301 U.S. 495 (1937).

that both the nation and the states continue to have vital roles to play, economically, socially and politically. And such a view probably contributed a great deal more to the vitality of the states than did doctrines like that of the *Butler* case; for through cooperation of the nation and the states the rigors of the depression were lessened and both the nation and the states benefited thereby.

*Commerce Power*

One important portion of *Schechter Poultry* v. *United States*[40] had concerned the doctrine of non-delegation of legislative authority, but another aspect of this case was the question whether the NRA poultry marketing regulations could be sustained under the commerce power. One of the stated purposes of the enactment was the removal of obstructions to interstate and foreign commerce. And in section 3f penalties were established for violations of a code provision "in any transaction in or affecting interstate or foreign commerce." Concerning this section, the Hughes Court held that in regard to the company's operations, interstate commerce in poultry had ended, and the code sought to regulate matters which only indirectly affected interstate commerce. The majority opinion insisted that the distinction between direct and indirect effects had to be maintained to preserve the federal system.

Further attention was given to this distinction in a majority opinion written by Justice Sutherland in *Carter* v. *Carter Coal Company*,[41] in which the Bituminous Coal Conservation Act of 1935 was held unconstitutional on the ground that Congress had not regulated interstate commerce, but had invaded the reserved powers of the states. The difference between direct and indirect effect was held by Sutherland to be not one of degree, but of kind. The laissez faire majority made it clear in the *Carter* case that any attempt by the national government to regulate subjects deemed by the majority to be "local" under the pretext that such subjects "affected" interstate or foreign commerce would be rejected. This rigid viewpoint effectually blocked congressional regulation of labor conditions in the midst of a period of serious labor unrest and unemployment.

After the "change of heart" of 1937, however, a majority of five sustained, in *National Labor Relations Board* v. *Jones-Laughlin Steel Corporation*,[42] the National Labor Relations Act against the charge that

40. 295 U.S. 495 (1935).
41. 298 U.S. 238 (1936).
42. 301 U.S. 1 (1937); see *National Labor Relations Board* v. *Fruehauf Trailer Company*, 301 U.S. 49 (1937); *National Labor Relations Board* v. *Friedman-Harry Marks Clothing Company*, 301 U.S. 58 (1937); *Associated Press* v. *Labor Board*, 301 U.S.

it regulated matters outside the scope of congressional commerce power. The act prohibited unfair labor practices which affected interstate commerce and included among such practices employer attempts to prevent unionization of employees.

Although the court discussed the "flow of commerce" doctrine it preferred to base its decision on the doctrine that Congress can regulate labor relations in manufacturing because the unfair labor practices prohibited by the act substantially affect interstate and foreign commerce. The formalistic *Carter* doctrine respecting direct and indirect effect was, for all practical purposes, discarded. Henceforth, as the *Fruehauf, Harry Marks,* and *Santa Cruz* cases indicated, the substantial effect doctrine was applied to permit broad federal regulation of labor relations in such industries as truck and clothing manufacturing and fruit packing.

As was noted above in the section on the spending power, the doctrine of dual federalism enunciated in the *Butler* decision was not overruled in the *Social Security* cases, but was merely bypassed. However, in 1941 the issue was faced squarely in a case arising under the commerce clause. In that year the Hughes Court upheld the Fair Labor Standards Act in *United States* v. *Darby*.[43] The statute prohibited the shipment in interstate commerce of goods produced under substandard labor conditions and the employment of workers at wages or hours other than those prescribed by the act. The working conditions set by the act included a comprehensive wages and hours formula. This case represents a decisive return to the broad constructionist tradition of the Marshall Court. The act was sustained as a necessary and proper implementation of the commerce power. The doctrine of dual federalism was expressly rejected and the *Dagenhart* decision overruled.

The *Jones-Laughlin* and *Darby* decisions thoroughly disposed of the two most important doctrinal barriers to a broad expansion of federal police power under the commerce clause. As former Supreme Court Justice Owen Roberts has pointed out, the *Darby* decision has placed "the whole matter of wages and hours . . . with slight exceptions, under a single federal regulatory scheme, and in this way completely [superseded] state exercise of the police power in this field."[44]

Less controversial than the foregoing cases, but of importance as

103 (1937); *Santa Cruz Company* v. *Labor Board*, 303 U.S. 453 (1938); *Labor Board* v. *Fainblatt*, 306 U.S. 601 (1939).

43. 312 U.S. 100 (1941).

44. Owen J. Roberts, *The Court and the Constitution*, p. 56.

expansions of federal commerce power, were the Hughes Court decisions in *Arizona* v. *California* and *United States* v. *Appalachian Power Company*.[45] In the first case congressional power to construct Boulder Dam was sustained on the ground that congressional commerce power extended not only to streams which were presently navigable, but also to those which had been navigable in the past. The scope of congressional commerce authority was further broadened in the second case. Here the commerce power was held to extend to non-navigable streams which might be "reasonably" improved and made navigable.

By 1941 the Hughes Court, largely "reconstructed" through resignations and appointments since 1937, had disposed of most of the older doctrines restricting or construing narrowly the scope of the commerce power. This development was not, however, an unprecedented abandonment of all constitutional scruples on the part of the Court. Rather it was, as the Court itself pointed out in the *Darby* case, a return to the long overlooked broad constructionist principles laid down by Chief Justice John Marshall in *Gibbons* v. *Ogden*. Once again the commerce clause was construed broadly instead of narrowly. By 1941 the only real limits to a tremendous expansion of federal police power under this clause were the compunctions of congressmen.

### INTERGOVERNMENTAL TAX IMMUNITY

One fundamental difference in attitude displayed by the Hughes Court after the "court packing" scare of 1937 was its tendency to narrow down the effect of earlier doctrines which had carried the principle of intergovernmental tax immunity to some rather absurd extremes. In a dissent in the *Panhandle Oil Company* case of 1928, Justice Holmes had pointed up the dangers of placing too many restrictions on governmental taxing power particularly in situations where rather remote burdens, if any, were placed on the state or federal governments. In this dissent he had also challenged a constitutional shibboleth derived directly from Marshall's *McCulloch* decision. "The power to tax," said Holmes, "is not the power to destroy while this court sits."

In 1937 the Hughes Court raised the question of "revision or restriction" of earlier immunity doctrines in *James* v. *Dravo Contracting Company*.[46] Restriction was not long in coming. In *Helvering* v. *Gerhardt*[47] the Hughes Court held that tax immunity does not extend to the salaries of employees of a state instrumentality, the New York

45. 283 U.S. 423 (1931); 311 U.S. 377 (1940).
46. 302 U.S. 134 (1937); *Mason Company* v. *Tax Commission,* 302 U.S. 186 (1937).
47. 304 U.S. 405 (1938).

Port Authority. The Court did so on the ground that where the burden of a tax is so speculative and uncertain that application of the doctrine of governmental tax immunity restricted federal taxing power without affording to the state a corresponding, tangible protection, tax immunity was not necessary to safeguard the federal system. The claim for immunity had been brought by three employees of the New York Port Authority. Their salaries were held taxable under the new doctrine.

Another important change in judicial policy was made in the case of *Graves* v. *New York ex rel O'Keefe*[48] in 1939. Justice Stone held that the doctrine "that a tax on income is legally and economically a tax on its source is no longer tenable," thus overruling the nearly century old *Collector* and *Dobbins* decisions. He also noted that the distinction between "proprietary" and "governmental" functions laid down in the *South Carolina* case did not apply to federal agencies because the federal government is one of delegated powers, and, therefore, all its functions are governmental.

The *O'Keefe* and *Gerhardt* cases did not, of course, repudiate the entire concept of intergovernmental tax immunity. But they did open up new sources of tax revenue for both the state and national governments which had long been closed to them by essentially unrealistic doctrines. At the same time, the new doctrines did not weaken the positions of either the states or the nation and probably contributed to the economic stability of both by removing formalistic restrictions on their taxing powers.

### DIVERSE CITIZENSHIP JURISDICTION AND STATE AUTONOMY

The controversial doctrine of *Swift* v. *Tyson*[49] had been applied by the Supreme Court for nearly a century when the Hughes Court rejected it in *Erie Railroad Company* v. *Tompkins*[50] in 1938. Basing this decision on Charles Warren's discovery that the *Swift* case involved an erroneous interpretation of section 34 of the Judiciary Act of 1789,[51] as well as upon criticisms of the doctrine by Justices Field and Holmes and members of Congress, the Court held that

> There is no federal general common law. Congress has no power to declare substantive rules of common law applicable to a state whether they be local in their nature or federal, be they commercial law or a part of the

48. 306 U.S. 466 (1939).
49. 16 Peters 1 (1842).
50. 304 U.S. 64 (1938).
51. "New Light," 37 *Harvard Law Review* 49-88 (1923).

law of torts. And no clause in the Constitution purports to confer such a power upon the federal courts.

The *Swift* case interpretation of this section was held unconstitutional as invading "rights which . . . are reserved by the Constitution to the several States."

The *Tompkins* decision not only corrected a serious interpretative error, but restored to the states the measure of autonomy of which they had been deprived by the Taney Court's *Swift* decision. However, the *Tompkins* case has been characterized by Professor Corwin as "remarkable" on three grounds: first, because it reversed a ninety-six-year-old precedent which had not been challenged by counsel; second, because, for the first time, it held a ruling of the Supreme Court itself unconstitutional; the third, because it ignored the power of Congress under the commerce clause and Congress' power to prescribe rules of decision for the federal courts under Article III.[52] Of the three observations, the third is perhaps the only one of substantial importance to federal-state relations.

### SUMMARY AND CONCLUSION

When Chief Justice Hughes retired in July, 1941, only one justice, Harlan Fiske Stone, remained of the group that had comprised the Court when Hughes assumed the duties of Chief Justice.[53] During Hughes' eleven-year tenure, the Court had accomplished what constituted in effect a peaceful revolution. Yet fundamentally this doctrinal revolution was a conservative one if that adjective may be used to connote a return to principles long-established but temporarily discarded. For in regard to the Hughes Court's approval of hitherto unknown expansions of federal police power, such approval had as its basis the broad constructionist constitutional interpretations of Chief Justice John Marshall. And similarly, the Hughes Court's tendency

52. *Constitution*, pp. 605-6.

53. Chief Justice Taft was succeeded by Charles Evans Hughes in February, 1930; Justice Sanford died in March, 1930, and Owen J. Roberts succeeded him in June of the same year; Justice Holmes retired in January, 1932, and his successor was Benjamin N. Cardozo, appointed in February of the same year; Justice Van Devanter retired in June, 1937, and was succeeded by Hugo L. Black in August of the same year; Justice Sutherland retired in January, 1938, and was succeeded by Stanley Reed in the same month; Justice Cardozo died in July, 1938, and was succeeded by Felix Frankfurter in January, 1939; Justice Brandeis retired in February, 1939, and was succeeded by William O. Douglas; Justice Pierce Butler died in November, 1939, and was succeeded by Frank Murphy in January, 1940; Justice McReynolds retired in February, 1941, and was succeeded by James F. Byrnes in July, 1941; Chief Justice Hughes retired in July, 1941; Harlan Fiske Stone was promoted to the Chief Justiceship in the same month; and Robert H. Jackson filled the associate justiceship vacated by Stone in July, 1941.

to permit greater experimentation in matters social and economic by the state legislatures also finds its basis in the past. For federal judicial restraint in dealing with the legislation of the states is well within the tradition of the Court during the tenures of Roger B. Taney and Morrison R. Waite.

The Hughes Court period was one of doctrinal extremes. Before 1937 important federal regulatory enactments were opposed by every doctrinal device at the disposal of the laissez faire majority. The taxing and spending power was limited by the doctrine of dual federalism of the *Butler* case. Federal commerce power was construed narrowly in the *Schechter* and *Carter* cases. And congressional grants of regulatory authority to the President under the commerce power also, on occasion, were invalidated under the non-delegability doctrine, as the *Ryan* and *Schechter* cases well attest. So rigorous was the pre-1937 Hughes Court in these cases, that sorely needed federal depression regulation was virtually halted. Out of the ensuing crisis came first a sudden and definite change of heart on the part of the Court, and then a series of resignations by some of the more conservative of the justices. The best explanation of the change of heart was given, perhaps unwittingly, by former Justice Roberts when, in commenting on doctrinal trends in a lecture at Harvard, he noted that

> An insistence by the Court on holding federal power to what seemed its appropriate orbit when the Constitution was adopted might have resulted in even more radical changes in our dual structure than those which have been gradually accomplished. . . .[54]

After 1937, the doctrine of dual federalism was decisively rejected in the *Darby* case. The formalistic distinction between "direct" and "indirect" effect in commerce clause questions was, in effect, rejected in the *Jones-Laughlin* case. Federal taxing and spending power was construed broadly in the *Social Security* cases. The net effect of these broad constructionist decisions was a tremendous expansion of federal police power. Many subjects, such as certain aspects of labor relations, which had heretofore been considered well within the reserved powers of the states, fell under the congressional commerce power. The Supreme Court after nearly a half century of "selective" uncertainty viewed the economy of the nation for most purposes as a unified one.

The great expansion of federal police power that characterized the post-1937 Hughes Court period did, of course, bring about a commensurate narrowing of the scope of state police power although in

54. *Court over Constitution*, p. 52.

many areas the states had been unable to cope with the tremendous depression problems of unemployment and relief. But the Hughes Court's abandonment of a number of substantive due process doctrines probably more than compensated for such state losses of authority, for by discarding the doctrines of "liberty of contract" and "business affected with a public interest," the Hughes Court in large part withdrew itself from the sort of rigorous supervision of state economic legislation which had characterized the Fuller, White, and Taft Courts. State control of internal economy was further enhanced by the important contract clause determination of the *Blaisdell* case. State judicial autonomy was enhanced by the *Tompkins* decision. In addition, the taxing powers of both the states and the nation were strengthened by the *Gerhardt* and *O'Keefe* decisions.

On the other hand, the decisions of the Hughes Court which represented applications and expansions of the *Gitlow* doctrine did seriously curtail state authority in the area of the intellectual freedoms, an area which before 1925 had been left entirely to the states.

In conclusion, the Hughes Court, in the period after 1937, by adhering to the broad constructionist tradition of the Marshall Court in determining the constitutionality of federal legislation, and by assuming, in general, the self-restraint of the Taney Court in considering the constitutional limitations on the states, contributed substantially to the continued vitality of both the states and the nation. It would appear that the Hughes Court not only considered the Constitution a positive charter for action by the governments of the parts as well as by the government of the whole in the federal system, but also felt that this fundamental document contemplated federal-state cooperation rather than antagonism in the face of serious national problems.

One contemporary French observer of American constitutional developments, Roger Pinto, in discussing the partial redistribution of federal and state powers which took place during the Hughes Court period, characterized the resulting division of powers and the manifestations of federal-state cooperation as the "new" federalism.[55] But it may be pointed out that the new distribution of powers was based on the old broad constructionist doctrines of the Marshall Court, and that federal-state cooperation, in reality, represented a return to first principles. For not only had the framers envisaged such cooperation, as well as conflict, but in the early years of the republic, state officials frequently performed federal as well as state duties.

55. Roger Pinto, *La Crise de L'Etat aux Etats-Unis*, p. 7.

# CHAPTER X

## *The Court under Stone, Vinson, and Warren, 1941-1957*

AFTER THE MOMENTOUS events of 1937, the Hughes Court had busied itself with the task of finding constitutional justification for the great peaceful revolution in federal-state relations ushered in by the administration of Franklin D. Roosevelt. By 1941, the year of Chief Justice Hughes' retirement, this had, for the most part, been accomplished. However, it remained for the post-Hughes court to carry the Hughes Court's doctrines to their logical limits. And, in addition, the successor to the Hughes Court was called upon to face unforeseen problems arising out of the new federal relationships.[1]

### COMMERCE CLAUSE

One of the most effective weapons utilized by the Fuller, White, and Taft Courts against state taxing and regulatory power had been the commerce clause. So repugnant to the post-1937 justices had been the uses of this clause that in 1940 three of them went so far as to suggest that the Court abdicate its role as protector, judicially, of nationwide free trade and leave the problem to Congress.[2]

After the retirement of Chief Justice Hughes in 1941, the pendulum swung back somewhat. It became apparent that the Court did not seriously consider the abdication urged by the dissenters in 1940. In exercising its interpretative powers under the commerce clause, the post-

1. All the appointments made in the Stone-Vinson period were made by Democratic Presidents Roosevelt and Truman. Justice Byrnes resigned in 1942 and was succeeded in the following year by Wiley Rutledge. Justice Roberts resigned in 1945 and was replaced in the same year by Harold H. Burton. Chief Justice Stone died in 1946 and was succeeded in the same year by Fred M. Vinson. Justices Murphy and Rutledge died in 1949. They were succeeded by Tom C. Clark and Sherman Minton, respectively, in the same year. Chief Justice Vinson died in 1953 and was succeeded in the same year by Earl Warren. The latter was appointed by Republican President Eisenhower. John Marshall Harlan was appointed in 1955 following Justice Jackson's death. Justice William Brennan succeeded Sherman Minton in 1956 and Charles Evans Whittaker succeeded Stanley Reed in 1957.

2. See the dissenting opinion in *McCarroll* v. *Dixie Greyhound Lines,* 309 U.S. 176 (1940), supported by Justices Black, Douglas, and Frankfurter.

Hughes Court displayed two contradictory tendencies. It consistently refrained from attempting to employ the clause as a lever to enforce a particular economic philosophy upon the states. The greater part of its commerce clause decisions thus are characterized by a strong presumption in favor of state legislation.[3] When this Court did intervene to strike down state taxes or economic regulations as violations of the commerce clause, it generally did so to preserve interstate free trade,[4] although some state laws were voided simply because they conflicted with congressional enactments.[5]

However, in the few commerce clause cases involving racial discrimination issues, the Court unhesitatingly utilized the clause as a means of forcing states to conform to the social philosophy of the Court's majority. A Virginia law providing for racial segregation on both interstate and intrastate vehicles was held an unconstitutional burden on interstate commerce, while a Michigan civil rights act prohibiting racial discrimination on an excursion vessel technically in foreign commerce was sustained.[6] The utilization of particular constitutional clauses to force states to conform to a social philosophy or policy espoused by a majority of the Supreme Court is scarcely novel in American history. The social issues involved since 1940 do, however, pose an unusual dilemma for American liberalism, a subject which will be developed in the concluding chapter.

The *Darby* decision had laid to rest the questionable doctrine of dual federalism. The existence of state power in any particular field no longer could serve as a bar to the exercise of a granted federal power, or, what is more important, a necessary and proper extension of it. The necessary and proper clause has frequently been called the "elastic" clause, and the Supreme Court during the tenures of Chief Justices Stone, Vinson, and Warren was uninhibited in demonstrating how far it could be stretched.* Perhaps one of the most controversial broad constructionist doctrines handed down by this Court was that in *Wickard* v. *Filburn*[7] which sustained a rather substantial extension of federal regulatory authority.

3. See *Northwest Airlines* v. *Minnesota,* 322 U.S. 292 (1944).

4. See *Nippert* v. *Richmond,* 327 U.S. 416 (1946); *Freeman* v. *Hewitt,* 329 U.S. 249 (1946).

5. See *Bus Employees* v. *Wisconsin Labor Board,* 340 U.S. 383 (1951).

6. *Morgan* v. *Virginia,* 328 U.S. 373 (1946); *Bob-Lo Excursion Company* v. *Michigan,* 333 U.S. 28 (1948).

7. 317 U.S. 111 (1942).

* Unless some qualification is made, further comments about the Court or the Supreme Court in this chapter refer to the post-Hughes period under Chief Justices Stone, Vinson, and Warren.

A farmer named Filburn had raised several acres of wheat in excess of the crop quota set up under the authority of the Agricultural Adjustment Act of 1938. The Department of Agriculture imposed marketing penalties on Filburn's total crop in spite of the fact that the wheat grown in excess of the quota was solely for home consumption. The Department's action was sustained on the ground that since wheat grown for home consumption is a variable factor substantially affecting interstate commerce in wheat, its regulation was necessary to effective congressional control of the amount of wheat marketed in commerce among the states.

Similarly, because the sale of milk transported solely in intrastate commerce adversely affected the price structure of milk sold in interstate commerce, federal regulation of the intrastate product was sustained as necessary for the regulation of interstate milk in *United States* v. *Wrightwood Dairy Company*.[8]

In sum, federal regulatory legislation under the commerce clause was construed broadly by the Court, but after 1947 the expansion of such power was slowed, not because of judicial interference but largely because of congressional reluctance. As to the uses of the commerce clause as a limitation on state police and taxing powers, the Court tended toward application of the presumption of validity doctrine. In the few cases involving racial discrimination, however, the Court unhesitatingly utilized the commerce clause to enforce its social views upon the states.

### NON-DELEGABILITY OF LEGISLATIVE AUTHORITY

The chief connection of the doctrine of non-delegability of legislative authority with the Supreme Court's role as arbiter in federal-state relations is that in the hands of laissez faire justices it was used to prevent the expansion of federal regulatory power before 1937. Convincing proof that the doctrine of non-delegability of legislative authority was dormant, if not dead, in the post-Hughes Court period was given in *Yakus* v. *United States*[9] in 1944. The wartime Emergency Price Control Act of 1942 was attacked as an unconstitutional delegation of legislative power to an executive officer, the price administrator. One section of the act authorized the administrator to promulgate price-fixing regulations which "in his judgment will be generally fair and equitable and will effectuate the purposes" of the act, when

8. 315 U.S. 116 (1942). For other broad constructionist decisions see *Polish Alliance* v. *Labor Board*, 322 U.S. 643 (1944); *Martino* v. *Michigan Window Cleaning Company*, 327 U.S. 173 (1946).

9. 321 U.S. 414 (1944); see *Bowles* v. *Willingham*, 321 U.S. 503 (1944).

in his judgment, prices have risen so as to threaten the anti-inflationary purposes of the act. The criteria adopted by the Court in sustaining the act were sufficiently broad to provoke from Justice Roberts, in dissent, the charge that the decision meant that "the function of legislation may be surrendered to an autocrat whose 'judgment' will constitute the law."

The majority felt, on the other hand, that the principle of the separation of powers did not impose a strait-jacket on Congress in the matter of legislative delegation. In rationalizing its position, the Court left little doubt that the career of the delegation doctrine as an effective bar to the expansion of federal police power had come to an end, at least in the era of "New Deal" justices.

### FEDERAL REGULATORY POWER

In 1944 in *United States* v. *Southeastern Underwriters' Association,*[10] the Court overruled the long established doctrine of *Paul* v. *Virginia* that insurance business is not a part of interstate commerce. The Court held that insurance business transactions across state lines were interstate commerce and were, therefore, subject to regulation under the Sherman Anti-Trust Act. However, Congress, within a year, passed the McCarran Act, which expressly authorized, with certain exceptions, state taxation and regulation of insurance businesses. In *Prudential Insurance Company* v. *Benjamin*[11] the Court could merely recognize that such state action, here South Carolina's, taken after congressional authorization, was valid.

The Gamblers' Tax Act of 1951, which levied an occupational tax of 50 dollars a year and compulsory registration with the Collector of Internal Revenue upon all persons "engaged in the business of accepting wagers" was sustained in *United States* v. *Kahriger.*[12] This case involved an extension of congressional regulatory authority under the taxing clause, but aside from an important question about self-incrimination, it did not differ fundamentally from other congressional taxes on narcotics, oleomargarine, or firearms. In many respects the majority opinion is reminiscent of the broad language of the *Veazie Bank* case.

### TIDELANDS OIL

The first so-called *"Tidelands Oil"* case[13] concerned the question whether the national government or the state of California had juris-

10. 322 U.S. 533 (1944).
11. 328 U.S. 408 (1946).
12. 345 U.S. 22 (1953).
13. *United States* v. *California,* 332 U.S. 19 (1947).

diction over the submerged land off the coast of California between low water mark and the three mile limit. The Court's majority held that the national government's rights were paramount both from the point of view of that government's proprietary interest in the submerged lands, and also as an incident of its international sovereignty. In regard to the latter, the Court observed that the disputed lands might become a subject of international dispute. California had based its claim in part on the argument that it must have jurisdiction over the disputed submerged lands in order to maintain a status equal to that of the original thirteen states. The post-Hughes Court admitted that the original colonies had acquired sovereignty over lands beneath navigable streams through devolution from the English Crown. However, it pointed out that the three mile limit was "a nebulous suggestion" at the time of the adoption of the Constitution, and thus could not have been included within the jurisdiction of the original states.

The off-shore oil jurisdictional issue was raised again in 1950 by the states of Louisiana and Texas in *United States* v. *Louisiana* and *United States* v. *Texas*.[14] Both cases were decided on substantially the same grounds as the *California* case, although several new questions concerning jurisdiction beyond the three mile limit plus Texas' historic claim based on its earlier existence as a republic were discussed. The Texas claim was disallowed under the doctrine of state equality. In the *California* case, the Court had held that the original states did not own the submerged land between their low water mark and the three mile limit. Texas did own this tract as a republic, but necessarily surrendered it, maintained the Court, upon its admission as a state because the doctrine of state equality was held to limit Texas' ownership of submerged lands between low water mark and the three mile limit, the limit set for all other coastal states. Thus for the first time the doctrine of state equality was utilized by the Supreme Court as a limitation on state power.

As Professor Corwin has pointed out, the application of this new doctrine modified an earlier rule, stated in 1886 in *Brown* v. *Grant*,[15] that unless Congress indicated otherwise, title to all property owned by a territory (and presumably an independent state) becomes, after admission to the Union, the property of the new state.

Interestingly enough, Congress refused to follow the policy all but

14. *United States* v. *Louisiana*, 339 U.S. 699 (1950); *United States* v. *Texas*, 339 U.S. 707 (1950). The Texas and Louisiana claims for portions of the continental shelf beyond the three-mile limit were disallowed because of international considerations.

15. 116 U.S. 207 (1886); *cf. Constitution*, p. 700.

openly stated by the Court in the three decisions mentioned above. For in 1953 the national legislature, in its controversial "Tidelands" Oil Act, gave to the three states the disputed undersea tracts after the Supreme Court had established federal ownership of them. In March, 1954, the Supreme Court in a *per curiam* opinion[16] acknowledged that Congress had paramount authority regarding the disposal of United States property, and on this ground refused to take jurisdiction in a suit brought by the states of Rhode Island and Alabama against the three recipients of the "tidelands" oil, Texas, Louisiana, and California.

### THE GRANT-IN-AID PRINCIPLE AND STATE AUTONOMY

A cardinal rule governing the acceptance of federal grants-in-aid is that federal regulatory authority follows federal money. The case of *Oklahoma* v. *United States Civil Service Commission*[17] indicated clearly the implications of that rule for state autonomy in the federal system.

In this case, a federal Hatch Act prohibition[18] against political management was applied against a state highway commissioner whose principal employment was in an agency largely financed by federal loans and grants. The commissioner had served as chairman of the Democratic State Central Committee of Oklahoma. To the objection that this application of the Hatch Act violated the Tenth Amendment, the Court took the position that, while the federal government had no power to regulate the political activities of state officials, it did possess power to fix the terms upon which its grants to the states were to be disbursed.

Federal grants-in-aid have, on occasion, been rejected by the states. And the *Oklahoma* decision is consistent with the holding of the Court regarding the Tenth Amendment in the *Darby* case. The moral of the *Oklahoma* decision apparently is that if a state feels that the regulations which are incidental to a federal grant-in-aid appear to threaten its autonomy it can reject the grant. If the state refuses to comply with such regulations, the federal government can reduce the grant. However, for the more impoverished of the state governments this may not be either economically feasible or politically expedient.

16. *Alabama* v. *Texas, Louisiana, California and Humphrey, McKay, Anderson, and Priest*, 347 U.S. 272 (1954).

17. 330 U.S. 127 (1947).

18. Section 12 of the Hatch Act provides that the Civil Service Commission shall notify any state agency financed, in part, by federal grants-in-aid of any employees engaged in political activities forbidden by the act. If such employees are not removed within a given time, the Commission shall order the appropriate federal agency to withhold funds equaling the salaries paid in a two-year period to such employees.

Thus the grant-in-aid principle and its attendant federal regulation could conceivably reduce some of the weaker states to the status of administrative subdivisions rather than cooperative partners in the federal system.

### FEDERAL SUPREMACY

In the first few decades after the adoption of the Constitution, Congress frequently authorized state courts to administer federal laws.[19] However, in 1842 the Supreme Court in *Prigg* v. *Pennsylvania*[20] took the position that state officials could not be compelled to enforce federal laws, and it was not until the turn of the twentieth century that Congress resumed its earlier practice of vesting the enforcement of certain federal rights in state as well as federal courts.

In *Testa* v. *Katt*[21] the Court was faced with a state challenge to a congressional statutory provision permitting suits in state as well as federal courts for treble damages by persons who were overcharged for products in violation of the federal Emergency Price Control Act of 1942. The supreme court of Rhode Island had taken the position that state courts lacked jurisdiction in such cases because one sovereign cannot enforce the laws of another. The Court unanimously rejected this argument as in conflict with the supremacy clause and with the "fact that the States of the Union constitute a nation." In Justice Black's words, "State courts do not bear the same relation to the United States as they do to foreign countries."

The Supreme Court's decision in *Testa* v. *Katt* affected seriously state judicial autonomy. During the formative years of the nation, the Congress, many of whose members had attended the Philadelphia Convention, had often depended upon the cooperation of the states for the enforcement of its laws. Nevertheless, the *Testa* decision indicated that if state cooperation were not forthcoming, it actually could be compelled.

Perhaps the strongest contemporary assertions of the principle of federal supremacy have occurred in decisions concerned with internal security problems. In *Pennsylvania* v. *Nelson,*[22] the Supreme Court held that the complex of federal laws dealing with internal security, particularly the Smith Act of 1940 and the Internal Security Act of 1950, superseded the enforceability of a sedition law of the state of Pennsylvania. Chief Justice Warren discussed, in the majority opinion, the "tests of supersession." First, the scheme of federal regulation must

19. Corwin, *Constitution*, p. 635.
20. 16 Peters 539 (1842).
21. 330 U.S. 386 (1947).
22. 350 U.S. 497 (1956).

be so persuasive that it is "a reasonable inference" that Congress left no room for the states. The majority maintained that after looking at the federal acts of 1940 and 1950, the "conclusion is inescapable that Congress intended to occupy the field." Second, if a federal statute touches a field in which the federal interest is so dominant that the federal system assumes preclusion of state intervention, state legislation is similarly superseded. The Court majority found that such a dominant federal interest is present in the internal security field. And thirdly, if state enforcement of sedition laws presents a danger of conflict with the administration program, such state action is prohibited. Again, the majority found such danger present.

This decision produced the most violent states' rights reaction in recent years. Traditional states' righters in Congress were immediately joined by congressmen who were particularly interested in emphasizing the dangers of "subversion." The fact that forty-two states and the territories of Alaska and Hawaii had statutes similar to that of Pennsylvania contributed to the strength of the opposition to the decision. Two bills were introduced which were calculated to overturn the decision. One simply would restore to the states their ability to share with the federal government the power—and glory—of pursuing subversives. The second, if passed, would undoubtedly have more far-reaching consequences for the Supreme Court in its role as federal arbiter. In this bill, Congress took into consideration a blanket enactment establishing that unless Congress specifically assumes that its legislation in a particular field is an exercise of exclusive power, the states may enact legislation dealing with matters not excepted concurrently.[23]

One aspect of the *Ullman* decision,[24] which dealt with a congressional act extending immunity from prosecution to persons testifying before congressional committees, concerned the constitutionality of an extension of immunity by the federal government against state prosecution. Justice Frankfurter held that

> The Immunity Act is concerned with the national security. It reflects a congressional policy to increase the possibility of more complete and open disclosure by removal of fear of state prosecution. We cannot say that Congress' paramount authority in safeguarding national security does not justify the restriction it has placed on the exercise of state power for the more effective exercise of conceded federal power.

23. *The Economist* (London), June 30, 1956, pp. 1281-82.

24. *Ullman* v. *United States*, 350 U.S. 422 (1956).

CONSTITUTIONAL LIMITATIONS ON THE STATES

*Due Process Clause of the Fourteenth Amendment*

Since the time of the Fuller Court, the due process clause of the Fourteenth Amendment has been the greatest single doctrinal source for federal judicial invalidation of state economic and social legislation. This was also true during the Hughes Court and the post-Hughes Court periods, but there were some marked differences in emphasis. While the Hughes Court had not gone along with Justice Black's suggestion that the clause historically had not been drawn up to provide protection for corporations, it did quietly withdraw from the economic arena.

In the years immediately following the great reversal of attitude by the Hughes Court in 1937, it had appeared that the Court would make one exception in its general policy of refraining from judicial interference with state economic legislation.[25] In cases like *Thornhill* v. *Alabama* it appeared that the activities of labor unions would be afforded special protection from state regulation whenever such activities could conceivably be held as involving free speech and assembly. The high tide for this point of view in this period was the case of *Thomas* v. *Collins*,[26] decided in 1945. Here, in a 5 to 4 decision, the Court held void a Texas requirement that labor organizers soliciting union members register with the Secretary of State before delivering solicitation speeches. The ground for the decision was that the requirement was a prior restraint on free speech and assembly.

By the late 1940's it became apparent that "big unions," like "big business," needed regulation in the public interest. Many state legislatures began to face the problem, and in time union opposition to state action took the form of litigation which eventually reached the Supreme Court.[27] The retreat of the post-Hughes Court from protection of labor under free speech and assembly doctrines coincided with this movement in the state legislatures. The *Giboney* and *Lincoln Union* cases provide excellent examples of this development.

The Hughes Court's *Thornhill* doctrine was modified in *Giboney* v. *Empire Storage and Ice Company*.[28] Here a Missouri court decision enjoining peaceful picketing was sustained against a charge that it violated freedom of speech and press. The state court's order was in

25. Under the *Thornhill* doctrine, the legislation was viewed as only incidentally economic.

26. 323 U.S. 516 (1945).

27. Herman Pritchett, *The Roosevelt Court*, pp. 224-25.

28. 336 U.S. 490 (1949); see *Cole* v. *Arkansas*, 338 U.S. 345 (1949).

pursuance of a state law prohibiting combinations in restraint of trade. The picketing, held the Court, was engaged in solely to induce the violation of a valid state law. To fail to uphold the state court, observed the Court, would give the labor union rather than the state paramount power to regulate trade practices. In the following year, the Court stated, unequivocally, in *Teamsters' Union* v. *Hanke*,[29] that "while picketing has an ingredient of communication, it cannot dogmatically be equated with the constitutionally protected freedom of speech."

It is particularly interesting to note that labor unions, subjected to employer-created restrictions under such doctrines as "liberty of contract" in the period from 1890 to 1937, attempted to invoke similar doctrines to invalidate a "right-to-work" law and a constitutional amendment of North Carolina and Nebraska, respectively. These provisions were allegedly designed to safeguard employment rights of non-union workers. This attempt was decisively rejected in *Lincoln Union* v. *Northwestern Company*.[30]

These cases indicate rather clearly that matters, such as peaceful picketing, which the Court first viewed as largely involving free speech and assembly questions, have since the late 1940's been viewed as incidental to various other economic problems. In this period, the Court generally left the state legislatures the same freedom for experimentation in labor problems that it had consistently accorded them in non-labor economic matters.

### *The Due Process Clause: Broad Construction* v. *Judicial Self-Restraint*

After 1937, the Hughes Court had begun the process of abandoning its role as the protector of economic freedom through broad application of the due process clause of the Fourteenth Amendment, but had contributed to the development begun in the *Gitlow* case in 1925 whereby certain freedoms safeguarded against federal action by the "Bill of Rights" were protected against state action by absorption into the meaning of liberty protected under the due process clause of the Fourteenth Amendment. In the period 1941-57 this process was accelerated. As a consequence, non-economic civil liberties issues predominated in the due process clause decisions of the period. Indicative of the Court's aggressive defense of the fundamental freedoms against state action were *West Virginia State Board of Education* v.

29. 339 U.S. 470 (1950).

30. 335 U.S. 525 (1949); *American Federation of Labor* v. *American Sash Company*, 335 U.S. 538 (1949).

*Barnette* and *Burstyn* v. *Wilson.*[31] The former abandoned the *Gobitis* doctrine over Justice Frankfurter's dissenting admonition that "it must be remembered that legislatures are ultimate guardians of the liberties and welfare of the people in quite as great a degree as the courts." The latter decision included expression via the motion picture within the meaning of free speech and press. A New York movie censorship law providing, in part, that the commercial showing of a film might be banned on the ground that it is "sacrilegious" was held an unconstitutional prior restraint on freedom of speech and press. The standard set by the word "sacrilegious" was held to vest in the censors unlimited control over motion pictures.

Three major problems fraught with significance for federal-state relations were faced by the post-Hughes Court in connection with its due process clause determinations involving non-economic civil liberties. First, a sharp disagreement arose between justices supporting a nearly absolutist view of the fundamental freedoms and the protagonists of judicial self-restraint in favor of broad state discretion in such matters. Spokesmen for the former were Justices Black and Douglas, while Frankfurter, Jackson, and Stone generally were the leaders of the latter group. Second, supporters of the nearly absolutist view strongly urged that since the fundamental freedoms enjoyed a preferred status in the constitutional scheme of values, the usual presumption of validity attaching to state legislation should be reversed when such freedoms were curtailed unless state action was required to meet a clear and present danger of substantive evil. This was strongly opposed by Justice Frankfurter and his supporters. And third, it was urged by a minority of the Court that all of the provisions of the "Bill of Rights" or first eight amendments should be incorporated into the meaning of due process. Leadership in the opposition to this suggestion fell to Justice Frankfurter.

Regarding the first divisive issue, certain decisions of the Court went so far in protecting the freedoms of religion, speech, and press that zealous minorities were able to invade the right to privacy of others or create public disorder and agitation while intervention by state authorities was held unconstitutional. In cases like *Martin* v. *Struthers, Saia* v. *New York, Terminiello* v. *Chicago,* and *Kunz* v. *New York* the nearly absolutist conception of the fundamental freedoms was adopted in majority opinions. But later, the supporters of judicial

31. 319 U.S. 624 (1943); 343 U.S. 495 (1952); see *Butler* v. *Michigan,* 352 U.S. 380 (1957).

self-restraint gained the ascendancy in cases such as *Kovacs* v. *Cooper, Breard* v. *Alexandria,* and *Poulos* v. *New Hampshire.*

The right to privacy versus the freedom to knock on doors or ring doorbells to facilitate the distribution of religious handbills was resolved in favor of the latter as incidental to freedom of speech and press in *Martin* v. *Struthers.*[32] But Justice Jackson's key dissenting comment indicated that he felt that the Court had gone too far in protecting minority rights. In his words, "Civil government cannot let any group ride roughshod over others simply because their 'consciences' tell them to do so." Although it was not concerned with an issue of religious freedom, *Breard* v. *Alexandria*[33] indicated that a majority of the Court had abandoned the nearly absolutist conception of the fundamental freedoms where the right to distribute literature door-to-door conflicts with the right of privacy. In the *Breard* case, a so-called "Green River" ordinance forbidding entrance "in and upon" private residences for soliciting purposes except with the prior consent of the owners or occupants was sustained against the contention that it violated freedom of speech and press when applied to a magazine solicitor for a foreign corporation. The majority held that it "would be . . . a misuse of the great guarantees of free speech and free press to use those guarantees to force a community to admit solicitors of publications to the home premises of its residents."

Another persistent problem facing the Court was that of balancing the demands for contemplative privacy in the homes and in public parks against the insistent claims of vocal minorities for the right to utilize public address systems and sound amplifiers to broadcast in the streets and the parks. In *Saia* v. *New York,*[34] a minority claim for freedom of speech was made the basis for invalidation of a city ordinance vesting in the police chief complete discretion in granting or withholding permission to use such devices in public places. The ordinance was held to establish a previous restraint on free speech. However, in *Kovacs* v. *Cooper*[35] a majority sustained a Trenton, New Jersey, ordinance which forbade the use of a sound truck or other instrument emitting loud and raucous noises because of "the need for reasonable protection in the homes and business houses from the distracting noises of vehicles equipped with such" devices. The limitation of the scope of the ordinance to those sound trucks emitting "loud and raucous" noises was held to be a sufficient standard for enforcing officers.

32. 319 U.S. 141 (1943).
33. 341 U.S. 622 (1951).
34. 334 U.S. 558 (1948).
35. 336 U.S. 77 (1949).

A controversial decision in *Terminiello* v. *Chicago*[36] held unconstitutional a Chicago ordinance prohibiting any behavior which "stirs the public to anger, invites dispute, brings about a condition of unrest, or creates a disturbance" as a violation of freedom of speech. However, as was strongly pointed out by the four dissenters, the state courts had assumed that the only conduct punished and punishable under the ordinance was that which constituted "fighting words." Portions of Terminiello's speech reproduced in Jackson's dissent obviously fitted into that category.

In writing the majority opinion in the *Terminiello* case, Justice Douglas gave a striking statement of the nearly absolutist viewpoint. He wrote:

> . . . a function of free speech under our system of government is to invite dispute. It may indeed best serve its high purpose when it induces a condition of unrest, creates dissatisfaction with conditions as they are or even stirs people to anger. . . . That is why freedom of speech, though not absolute . . . is nevertheless protected against censorship or punishment, unless shown likely to produce a clear and present danger of serious substantive evil that rises far above public inconvenience, annoyance or unrest.

In *Kunz* v. *New York*,[37] a city ordinance vesting in the Police Commissioner authority to issue permits to persons wishing to hold religious meetings was held void as a prior restraint upon freedom of speech and religion because it left such issuance to the administrative discretion of the Commissioner. Justice Jackson's dissent indicated the position of the disciples of judicial self-restraint on such matters. He called upon the Court to re-evaluate its decisions touching upon the fundamental freedoms in the light of the practical experience of municipalities or states. Discussing various permit systems, Jackson asked:

> Is everybody out of step but this Court? . . . It seems hypercritical to strike down local laws on their faces for want of standards when we have no standards. . . . I think that where speech is outside of constitutional immunity the local community or the State is left a large measure of discretion as to the means for dealing with it.

At least in the short run it appears that Jackson's plea for judicial self-restraint has been heeded and the nearly absolutist concept rejected. For in *Poulos* v. *New Hampshire*[38] the Court sustained a carefully worded regulation which authorized the proper city officials to under-

36. 337 U.S. 1 (1949).
37. 340 U.S. 290 (1951).
38. 345 U.S. 395 (1953).

take "the adjustment of the unrestrained exercise of religions" for the reasonable comfort and convenience of the people of the city of Portsmouth.

Should the advocates of self-restraint maintain majority control, it would appear that municipalities and the states could regain in large part the discretionary authority they had traditionally enjoyed in keeping public order before the late 1930's. Whether this development would endanger religious freedom is open to question.

As Justice Douglas' statement in the *Terminiello* case indicated, the advocates of the nearly absolutist view of the fundamental freedoms not only supported an exceedingly broad view of the permissible scope of individual action, but also sought to curb state authority under the preferred status and reversal of presumption doctrines. Although the latter doctrine was first stated in the Hughes Court period in *United States* v. *Carolene Products Company,*[39] it received its clearest enunciation in *Thomas* v. *Collins*[40] in the post-Hughes period. In this case a majority of the Court took the position that in cases involving the fundamental freedoms the presumption of validity ordinarily accorded state enactments would be reversed except in situations where state restriction of such freedoms was found by the Court to be necessary because of the existence of a clear and present danger of substantive evil to the community.

The reversal of presumption of validity doctrine evidently had been adopted to insure that the fundamental freedoms be accorded a "preferred status" in the constitutional scheme of values. However, the use of the phrase "preferred status" was challenged by Justice Frankfurter[41] as having "uncritically crept into some recent opinions." Justice Jackson also objected to the phrase on the ground that "we cannot give some constitutional rights a preferred position without relegating others to a deferred position."[42]

A second line of attack was directed against the use of the clear and present danger test as a judicial formula for insuring a "preferred status" to the fundamental freedoms. Justice Frankfurter argued that this "test" was in reality a literary phrase taken out of context.[43]

The fates of the "preferred status," reversal of presumption of validity, and clear and present danger doctrines are at present un-

39. 304 U.S. 144 (1938).
40. 328 U.S. 516 (1945).
41. In *Kovacs* v. *Cooper*, 336 U.S. 77 (1949).
42. *Brinegar* v. *United States*, 338 U.S. 160 (1949).
43. See his dissent in *West Virginia State Board of Education* v. *Barnette*, 319 U.S. 624 (1943).

certain. Several decisions seem to indicate that opponents of the previous uses of the doctrines are the ascendancy on the Court. *Garner* v. *Los Angeles Board, Adler* v. *New York Board of Education,* and *Beauharnais* v. *Illinois* support this view. State enforced loyalty programs came into vogue particularly after 1947. The loyalty oath provisions of the Los Angeles City charter were tested constitutionally in *Garner* v. *Los Angeles Board.*[44] It had been contended that the oath requirement violated the due process clause by affecting adversely persons who had belonged to a proscribed organization but who were innocent "of its purposes." Here the majority sustained the charter on the ground that the Court assumed that the charter "will not be construed" to cover such persons. In *Adler* v. *New York Board of Education,*[45] a similar law, applied to teachers but omitting the oath provisions, was sustained.

A recent decision, however, may harbinger another swing of the pendulum of judicial attitudes, at least in cases dealing with subversion. For in *Slochower* v. *Board of Higher Education of the City of New York,*[46] a five-man majority held unconstitutional as a violation of due process a New York City charter provision requiring the dismissal, without notice or hearing, of a municipal employee (here a city college professor) for invoking the constitutional privilege against self-incrimination before a Senate investigating committee. The clear and present danger test did not, however, figure in the majority or dissenting opinions.

The Illinois "Group Libel" law of 1949 which made it a crime to exhibit any publication which "portrays depravity, criminality, unchastity, or lack of virtue of a class of citizens, of any race, color, creed or religion" exposing them "to contempt, derision, or obloquy" was sustained against the charge that it violated freedom of speech and press in *Beauharnais* v. *Illinois.*[47] Here the majority refused to apply the clear and present danger doctrine since in its view libelous utterances were not within the area of constitutionally protected free speech. In rendering the majority opinion, Justice Frankfurter clearly indicated that the ordinary substantive due process test of reasonableness and not the more rigorous clear and present danger test was applicable.

It would appear that generally speaking the advocates of judicial

44. 341 U.S. 716 (1951).

45. 342 U.S. 485 (1952).

46. 350 U.S. 551 (1956).

47. 343 U.S. 250 (1952). Although the case of *Dennis* v. *United States,* 341 U.S. 494 (1951), did not involve any issues relating to federalism, the Court here applied the clear and present danger doctrine in such a manner as to virtually remove the requirement of immediacy in the test.

self-restraint blunted effectively the efforts of the supporters of the reversal of presumption and clear and present danger doctrines after the 1940's. Cases like that of *Beauharnais* v. *Illinois* indicated at least a strong tendency on the part of a majority to treat issues involving state restriction of the fundamental freedoms on a par with other substantive due process issues. The concomitant re-establishment of the presumption of constitutionality doctrine in such matters left to the states and municipalities commensurate freedom.

The third issue dividing the post-Hughes Court was whether the entire "Bill of Rights" should be included within the meaning of due process. The decisive case in this regard was *Adamson* v. *California*,[48] decided in 1947. Here a majority of the Court turned down the argument by two dissenters, Justices Black and Douglas, that the due process clause of the Fourteenth Amendment was intended by its framers and accepted by its ratifiers as incorporating all the safeguards against the federal government included in the first eight amendments. Writing for the majority, Justice Frankfurter contended that adoption of the minority view would "tear up by the roots much of the fabric of the law in the several states." He pointed out that the due process clause of the Fifth Amendment had the same meaning as that in the Fourteenth but protected individual rights against federal rather than state action. He then argued that "Madison and his contemporaries . . . [could not] be charged with writing into [the Bill of Rights] a meaningless clause. . . ."

As pertinent as both of these arguments were to the refutation of the contentions of Black and Douglas, it should be noted that they apply with equal force against the *Gitlow* and *Palko* doctrines. Frankfurter and the majority in the *Adamson* case did not indicate any inclination to abdicate the position taken by the court in the *Palko* case but did acknowledge that "an important safeguard against . . . merely individual judgment [in the determination of due process issues involving the fundamental freedoms] is an alert deference to the judgment of the State court under review."

### *Establishment of Religion and State Autonomy*

It was not until 1947 in *Everson* v. *Board of Education*[49] that the Supreme Court held that the due process clause of the Fourteenth Amendment prohibits the making of a law respecting an establishment of religion by a state. The justices unanimously supported this holding. But they divided 5 to 4 on the issue of whether the provision of free

48. 332 U.S. 46 (1947).

49. 330 U.S. 1 (1947).

bus transportation to students attending Catholic parochial schools by the school board of Ewing Township, New Jersey, helped maintain church schools in violation of the establishment prohibition incorporated in the due process clause of the Fourteenth Amendment. The majority held that the free bus transportation benefited the school children and not the church and thus did not breach the "wall of separation" erected between church and state by the Constitution.

A more serious question which arose in 1948 involved the constitutionality of a "released time" arrangement adopted by the Board of Education of Champaign, Illinois. According to this plan the public schools in the Champaign School District had permitted religious instructors, Protestant, Catholic, or Jewish, to utilize certain classrooms during school hours to teach religion. Students were not forced to attend such classes and could attend religious classes only if their parents consented. In *McCollum* v. *Champaign Board of Education,*[50] an 8 to 1 majority of the Court held this arrangement an unconstitutional use of tax-supported property for religious instruction under the First Amendment as made applicable to the states via the due process clause of the Fourteenth Amendment. However, several years later, in *Zorach* v. *Clauson,*[51] the Court took the position that a New York City "dismissed time" school regulation permitting public school children to attend religious instruction classes during "public school time" but not on public property was constitutional.

### *Equal Protection Clause*

The development in the law of the equal protection clause of the Fourteenth Amendment which was most significant for federal-state relations was the expansion by the Court of the use of the clause as a protection against state-enforced racial discrimination. A number of state-enforced discriminatory devices which had heretofore been accepted as valid were declared void under new doctrines adopted by the Court in the period 1941-53.

Perhaps one of the most important of these doctrines was that in *Shelley* v. *Kraemer*[52] in 1948. For many years it had been believed that there was no federal constitutional prohibition against private restrictive covenants designed to prevent the ownership of real estate by certain races. And the *Shelley* decision in effect confirmed this belief. However, it also established that any attempt by a state court to enforce such a private agreement was state action in violation of the equal protection clause of the Fourteenth Amendment.

50. 333 U.S. 203 (1948).
51. 343 U.S. 306 (1952).
52. 334 U.S. 1 (1948).

Since the Fuller Court period, the Supreme Court had applied the doctrine that where facilities were provided which were "substantially" equal, racial segregation enforced by state law in such fields as education did not violate the equal protection clause. Frequently, the Court had seemed blind in its evaluation of what was substantially equal. However, in 1950 in the important case of *Sweatt* v. *Painter*[53] the Court looked beyond formal provisions to consider the practical effect of a Texas law. After so doing it held that the establishment of a separate law school for Negroes did not fulfill the requirements of the equal protection clause because in terms of physical and less tangible matters the Negro school was not substantially equal to the law school provided by the state for whites. In regard to the less tangible factors important to the acquisition of a legal education, Chief Justice Vinson pointed out that the white law school possessed "to a far greater degree those qualities which are incapable of objective measurement but which make for greatness in a law school. Such qualities . . . include reputation of the faculty, experience of the administration, position and influence of the alumni, standing in the community, traditions and prestige."

The *Sweatt* decision put the states on notice that the Court intended to scrutinize closely actual conditions wherever states adopted segregation policies under the separate but equal doctrine of the *Plessy* case. States could, of course, continue to separate races, but because the Court was prepared sternly to apply the requirement that "substantially equal" facilities be provided where segregation is state-enforced, the traditional segregating states faced severe financial tests in their attempts to meet this vitalized requirement. The question might have been raised whether segregation is feasible under the *Sweatt* doctrine. However, the necessity for raising this question never arose, for in 1954, in *Brown* v. *Board of Education,*[54] the Supreme Court rejected completely the "separate but equal" doctrine as applied to education. Chief Justice Earl Warren, writing for an unanimous court, held that separation in education on the basis of race is inherently unequal and as such is in violation of the equal protection clause of the Fourteenth Amendment. This decisive interpretation aroused a storm of protest from the more extreme Southern leaders such as Governor Talmadge of Georgia. Later, in 1956, most

53. 339 U.S. 629 (1950). In *McLaurin* v. *Oklahoma State Regents,* 339 U.S. 637 (1950), the Court held void an attempt by Oklahoma to segregate Negroes who had been admitted to the state university.

54. 349 U.S. 294 (1954).

Southern members of Congress signed a "Southern Manifesto" condemning the decision as "judicial usurpation," a substitution of "naked power for established law" and an "unwarranted exercise of power . . . contrary to the Constitution."[55]

In 1955, the Court in the second *Brown* case issued a mandate leaving to the discretion of lower federal courts the rate of speed of racial integration in elementary schools.[56] It made clear, however, in *Florida ex rel Hawkins* v. *Board of Control,*[57] that no delay in admission of qualified negroes to graduate schools was implied.

### *Fifteenth Amendment*

The Hughes Court's *Classic* decision had effectively cut the ground from under the *Grovey* v. *Townsend* decision by underscoring the fact that the general election machinery of a state was inexorably connected with the primary election mechanism where the latter was utilized. When the doctrine of the *Grovey* case, that denial of the voting privilege by a political party was not state action, came before the post-Hughes Court in *Smith* v. *Allwright*[58] in 1944, it was overruled on the ground that the recognition in the *Classic* case "of the place of a primary in the electoral scheme makes clear that state delegation to a party of the power to fix the qualifications of primary elections is delegation of a state function that may make the party's action the action of the state." Under this doctrine the refusal on the part of the Democratic party of Texas to permit Negro participation in congressional primaries was held unconstitutional as state action prohibited by the Fifteenth Amendment.

That the *Allwright* doctrine lost none of its vitality during the remainder of the post-Hughes Court period is well illustrated by the case of *Terry* v. *Adams*[59] in which a Democratic county pre-primary election arrangement to bar Negroes was held void.

### *Contract Clause*

The *Blaisdell* decision of the Hughes Court had broadened greatly the permissible scope of state power in regard to the modification of contract remedies in times of grave economic depression. However, the *Blaisdell* doctrine had made it clear that such modification was constitutionally acceptable only for the emergency period. In *East New York Savings Bank* v. *Hahn*[60] the Court went a step further and ruled

55. *Congressional Record,* 84th Congress, Second Session, Vol. 102, No. 43, p. 3948.
56. 349 U.S. 294 (1955). See footnote 62.
57. 350 U.S. 413 (1956).
58. 321 U.S. 649 (1944).
59. 343 U.S. 461 (1953); see *Rice* v. *Elmore,* 333 U.S. 875 (1948).
60. 326 U.S. 230 (1945).

that a 1944 extension of a New York mortgage moratorium law originally adopted in 1933 was not a violation of the contract clause. In writing the majority opinion, Justice Frankfurter pointed out that the New York legislature had been advised by financial experts studying the problem that "the sudden termination of the legislation which has dammed up normal liquidation of these mortgages for more than eight years might well result in an emergency more acute than that which the original legislation was intended to alleviate." Thus while the 1933 enactment had been justified under the *Blaisdell* doctrine as a valid action to mitigate the effects of the economic emergency, it would seem that the 1944 enactment was upheld as an effective means of preventing the recurrence of the economic crisis.

### INTERGOVERNMENTAL TAX IMMUNITY

Perhaps the chief significance of the case of *New York* v. *United States*[61] lay in the fact that it brought to the surface the fundamental difficulty facing the Court in its application of the old doctrinal distinction of the *South Carolina* case regarding "proprietory" and "governmental" functions of state governments. Under the *South Carolina* doctrine the "proprietory" functions of a state were held subject to federal taxation, while the "governmental" functions were not.

In a six to two decision, the Court held that a federal tax could be validly levied upon the sale of mineral waters from Saratoga Springs, a project owned and operated by the state of New York. Justice Frankfurter, supported by Justice Rutledge, came to this conclusion after agreeing that the Court could not find adequate standards for distinguishing between the "proprietory" and "governmental" functions of states. The distinction to be drawn, wrote Frankfurter, is between discriminatory and non-discriminatory taxation.

The Chief Justice, supported by Justices Reed, Murphy and Burton, felt that the test suggested by Frankfurter had serious shortcomings. Consequently, they upheld the federal tax levy on the grounds that it was within the traditional sphere of federal taxing power and that it did "not unduly impair the state's functions of government." Although Stone's language was guarded, it would appear that he and his supporters were not prepared to abandon completely the old *South Carolina* doctrine.

Interestingly enough, the two dissenters, Justices Douglas and Black, took a stand reminiscent of the attitude of the Chase Court in

61. 326 U.S. 572 (1946).

the *Day* case and of the supporters of "dual federalism" in the White, Taft, and early Hughes Courts.

### SUMMARY AND CONCLUSION

In retrospect, the post-Hughes Court contributed few new doctrines in fulfilling the Supreme Court's role as arbiter in federal-state relations. This stemmed not from a lack of the innovating spirit on the part of the justices, but simply from the fact that this Court was substantially in agreement with the doctrinal outlook of its predecessor.

Like the Hughes Court after 1937, the post-Hughes Court construed the various grants of national power broadly and rejected the idea that the Tenth Amendment limited otherwise valid exercises of such power. In *Wickard* v. *Filburn* the Court carried the broad constructionist view of the commerce clause to its logical limits. The Court's decision in the *Southeastern Underwriters' Association* case actually extended congressional regulatory authority into an area, regulation of insurance businesses, which Congress preferred to leave to the states. Within a year of the decision Congress, in the McCarran Act, in effect returned, with certain exceptions, authority to regulate insurance to the states. Similarly, the Court's affirmation of federal authority over the so-called "Tidelands Oil" lands in three decisions was in practical effect undone by congressional enactment in 1953.

That federal-state cooperation through the grant-in-aid principle entailed the enforcement of federal contingent regulations was forcefully brought home to the states in *Oklahoma* v. *United States Civil Service Commission*. Here the application of the federal Hatch Act's prohibition against political management to a state officer employed in a state agency largely financed by federal loans and grants was sustained over the objection that such an application infringed state autonomy. *Testa* v. *Katt* established that, under the supremacy clause and because the states constitute a nation, state courts cannot refuse to enforce federal laws when designated by Congress as an enforcement agency.

In its uses of the constitutional limitations on the states, the post-Hughes Court was, in general, disposed to leave to the states as much freedom as possible without abandoning its judicial supervisory role. This was particularly true in regard to the Court's due process clause determinations which involved economic issues. However, in its earlier years, the Court reversed the presumption of validity usually accorded state legislation where the fundamental freedoms, speech, press, assembly, and religion, were concerned. In later decisions, such as that of the *Beauharnais* case, the Court treated such issues as on a par with other due process clause issues.

At the very end of the period studied, decisions in the *Nelson* and *Slochower* cases indicated that the Court might intervene more actively to protect individual freedom against state action in internal security matters.

The equal protection clause of the Fourteenth Amendment and the Fifteenth Amendment were utilized by the Court to disallow racial discriminations of various kinds. In the *Sweatt* case state enforced segregation under the old *Plessy* doctrine was made more difficult, at least in the field of high education. Finally, in the first case of *Brown* v. *Board of Education,* the separate but equal doctrine was completely rejected as applied to schools.[62] *Shelley* v. *Kraemer* prohibited, under the equal protection clause, the enforcement of restrictive covenants in state courts. The Fifteenth Amendment was invoked in the *Allwright* case to void deprivation by political parties of the privilege of voting in congressional primaries on racial grounds. The parties' actions were held to constitute state action prohibited by the amendment.

In conclusion, the post-Hughes Court fulfilled its role as arbiter in federal-state relations with an awareness that it had not only a responsibility to maintain proper federal authority, but also a duty to safeguard state autonomy wherever possible. Like its immediate predecessor, the Stone-Vinson-Warren Court treated questions of federal competence within the broad constructionist tradition, while generally enforcing the constitutional limitations on the states in such a manner as to avoid the substitution of federal judicial for state legislative wisdom.

62. Although private resistance to the integration rulings of inferior federal courts presented difficulties, the most complex problem arising out of this judicial mandate was the use of the Arkansas National Guard by Governor Faubus to prevent the entrance of Negro students into Central High School in Little Rock on September 2, 1957. After a delay of three weeks, President Eisenhower ordered the Arkansas National Guard into Federal service and ordered portions of the 101st Airborne Division to enforce the integration order of the Federal District Court. Governor Faubus challenged the validity of the Presidential intervention in, first, the Federal District Court, and, second, the Federal Court of Appeals for the Eighth Circuit. Faubus' contentions were rejected in both courts and are now subject to consideration by the Supreme Court of the United States. Many students of constitutional history feel that they will be rejected under the doctrine of *Sterling* v. *Constantin,* 287 V.S. 378 (1932).

# CHAPTER XI

## *Conclusion*

THIS STUDY INVOLVED two major investigations of the Supreme Court's role as final arbiter in federal-state relations. The first dealt with the origins of the Court's power as federal umpire. The second was an analysis of the manner in which the Court fulfilled this role.

The study of the origins of the Supreme Court's power in federal-state relations revealed that the framers of the Constitution clearly intended that the Court should be the umpire of the federal system. They did not, of course, spell out this intention explicitly in the Constitution. But the events of the years 1780-89 indicate unmistakably not only that the judicial arbiter concept had been discussed and fully understood before this Convention, but also that within the Constitutional Convention at Philadelphia this concept was supported by both the Federalists and the anti-Federalists.

The Federalists had held the view that in a system characterized by a division of powers between a government of the whole and governments of the parts, the chief danger to the system lay not in the possibility that the general government would encroach upon and eventually usurp the powers of the particular governments, but in the divisive tendencies which the state would exhibit. The anti-Federalists had taken an opposite view. But both the Federalists and anti-Federalists agreed that some organ of the national government should impartially settle conflicts of authority between the central government and the states.

The Federalists believed that the congressional negative on state laws proposed in the Randolph Plan would provide the proper safeguard against the states. But proposals for the congressional negative were defeated a number of times in the Convention, and, ultimately, the Federalists had to accept the judicial arbiter instead.

The power to determine justiciable conflicts of federal and state authority was not granted to the Supreme Court in one distinct Convention action, but came about through a complex series of parliamentary developments. Chief among them were the repudiation of coercion of the states by force and adoption of coercion of individuals by law, the readiness of every major bloc in the Philadelphia Convention to set up a federal judiciary, the recurring demands for a Council of Revision, Federalist support for a complete system of inferior federal tribunals, the repudiation of the congressional negative proposal, and the substitution of a supremacy clause.

Adoption of the judicial arbiter concept was in the nature of a compromise. The Federalists did not oppose it, but felt that the Supreme Court's chances of maintaining the supremacy of the national government through the indirect method of deciding bona fide cases within a jurisdiction set forth in the Constitution were slim indeed. The anti-Federalists, on the other hand, not only did not oppose the compromise, but apparently had actually taken the lead in suggesting the concept to the Convention. Trusting that such judicial power would be exercised impartially—and weakly—they envisaged the role of the Supreme Court as protector of the rights both of states and, at least in Jefferson's case, of individuals, as well as those of the national government.

In the ratification conventions, violent attacks were made on the judicial powers, but while the Supreme Court was sometimes characterized as a sort of super "Star Chamber," concrete proposals for amendment of the judicial grants were aimed chiefly at preventing the establishment of inferior federal tribunals and insuring that states would not be held liable by federal courts to suits by individuals. The judicial arbiter concept was discussed frankly in most of the conventions and was also given wide publicity in Numbers XXXIX and LXXX of the *Federalist.*

Final implementation of the concept came in the first Congress. As was the case in the Federal Convention, the anti-Federalists did not seriously oppose the granting of final appellate jurisdiction to the Supreme Court in cases involving a federal question, although they did seek to prevent the establishment of inferior federal tribunals. Thus the historical evidence fails to bear out the contentions of those who, like Calhoun,[1] have charged that the Supreme Court usurped its power as arbiter in federal-state relations.

Although the historical record leaves little doubt that the framers of the Constitution and its implementers in the ratifying conventions

1. Richard Crallé (ed.), "Discourse on the Constitution and Government of the United States," *Works of John C. Calhoun,* I, 238.

and the first Congress chose the federal Supreme Court as arbiter in American federalism, this fact contributes little toward settling the question: is a *judicial* arbiter necessary in every federal system? For the framers had considered legislative and executive federal arbiters as well as the judicial model and had made a final determination largely on the basis of practical contemporary political considerations rather than pronounced philosophical or theoretical convictions.

The analysis of the manner in which the Supreme Court fulfilled its role as arbiter in federal-state relations involved consideration of the question whether the Court in any given period of its history was partial to either the federal government or the states.[2] This question was not susceptible to the sort of clear-cut historical examination that could be applied in the study of origins discussed above. For two factors—the nature of the judicial process and the nature of the written Constitution—make it possible for the federal justices to be partial to some extent without straining either the judicial or the constitutional proprieties.

Justice Benjamin Cardozo's analysis[3] of the nature of the judicial process is particularly valuable in the evaluation of any charges of federal judicial partiality; for he concluded that the process is not a mechanistic one, but rather one which, at least in certain circumstances, permits of choice between interpretative alternatives. He pointed out that in long-established legal systems judicial discretion was considerably narrowed by precedent and tradition. However, in changing situations demanding fresh evaluation, the judge faces alternative paths rather than a single well-marked highway. In choosing a particular alternative, he may be influenced by the desire to achieve logical symmetry in the legal system, by the desire to maintain continuity with the past, or by the desire to adapt the law to meet changing situations. The last alternative was called by Cardozo the method of sociology; by others it has been called the method of social engineering. In choosing between alternatives in decisions permitting judicial discretion, judges, like other men, are generally influenced by their personal predilections, whether consciously or subconsciously.

With few exceptions the provisions of the Constitution are couched in general terms and are susceptible to more than one interpretation. A choice of interpretative alternatives was thus readily available to the federal justices in each period of the Supreme Court's history. That

2. For charges of partiality see Oliver P. Field, "States versus Nation and the Supreme Court," 28 *American Political Science Review* 233ff. (April, 1934). For a view more sympathetic to the Court, see Swisher, *The Growth of Constitutional Power.*

3. Benjamin N. Cardozo, *The Nature of the Judicial Process.*

the justices would choose one alternative over another was necessary. However, at times the personal preferences of the justices extended to the adoption of doctrines which violated or strained constitutional proprieties. For example, the Hughes Court's espousal of the doctrine of "dual federalism" in the *Butler* case is subject to the charge that it was inconsistent with the cardinal principle of federal supremacy.

With respect to the original role envisaged by the framers, the Supreme Court was expected to decide peacefully issues which under the Randolph Plan were to be decided by Congress and enforced by the military forces of the nation wherever the states refused to comply. As the case involving Judge Peters indicated, the decisions of the Supreme Court which concerned federal-state issues could be enforced by the military might of the Union.

The accuracy of the view of the Federalists concerning the necessity for an arbiter in federal-state relations to maintain federal authority against the erosive effects of local policies is well attested by the numerous issues of this kind raised before the Court down to the present day. In this regard the historical record bears out Justice Holmes' statement that

> I do not think the United States would come to an end if we lost our power to declare an act of Congress void. I do think the Union would be imperiled if we could not make that declaration as to the laws of the several states. For one in my place sees how often a local policy prevails with those who are not trained to national views and how often action is taken that embodies what the Commerce Clause was meant to end.[4]

As was noted above, the granting of authority to the Supreme Court to act as arbiter in federal-state relations actually left to the justices a good deal of discretion as to how they would fulfill that role. Viewing the entire history of the Court, one is struck by the fact that the framers, whether Federalist or anti-Federalist, had been concerned largely with establishing an arbiter to settle peacefully federal-state conflicts of authority. However, with the possible exception of Hamilton, they failed to realize that by granting this authority to the justices, they had provided a means by which the Court could influence appreciably the economic and social development of both the nation and the states. In some periods, particularly those of the Fuller, White, Taft, and the pre-1937 Hughes Courts, the justices attempted to channel American social and economic development into patterns of their own choosing, and often succeeded. In practical effect, the

4. Oliver Wendell Holmes, *Collected Legal Papers*, p. 291.

justices sometimes usurped the powers of the federal or state legislatures by determining questions of social policy while allegedly determining only the constitutionality of national or state laws.

Litigation, ostensibly concerned with maintaining the boundaries of federalism, became the vehicle for raising practically every major political, economic, or sociological question which has been of importance in the United States since 1789. This has given American constitutional law an essential practicality sometimes lacking in other federal systems,[5] but has not prevented the development of mechanistic interpretative formulae which were totally unrelated to the basic issues before the Court. The "Alice-in-Wonderland" use of phrases such as "state sovereignty" to camouflage judicial determinations dealing with basic conflicts involving government regulation versus economic laissez faire well illustrates the tendency.

The crises and difficulties faced by the Supreme Court are quite understandable. If it had merely to exercise its function in accordance with universally recognized and accepted principles of natural law such as were contemplated by some of the earlier (and not so early) American jurists[6] or the French physiocrats,[7] the American system of judicial umpiring in federalism might have operated with relative smoothness. But despite the lip-service given to natural law, American politics, economics, sociology, and even philosophy have had a remarkably pragmatic orientation.

It is not surprising, therefore, to find that the history of the Supreme Court's arbitership has been punctuated with a succession of crises. The federal judicial umpire, by the very nature of its function, has within its grasp and has fully utilized a particular type of supervision of both the state and federal governments. The positive influence of this essentially negative function of judicial review can obviously be easily overestimated. Constitutional amendments such as those following the *Chisholm* and *Pollock* cases, and congressional laws upheld in decisions such as the *Wheeling Bridge, "Tidelands Oil,"* or *Prudential Insurance Company* cases underscore the prudence of this qualification. Furthermore, complete empirical evidence is lacking which conclusively demonstrates the real impact of judicial arbitership upon the American federal system. But the number and magnitude of the constitutional crises occasioned by judicial thwarting of legislative majorities—state or federal—and the general success of the Supreme Court in weathering

5. Paul A. Freund, "Review and Federalism," in Edmond Cahn, ed., *Supreme Court and Supreme Law*, pp. 87-88.

6. *Cf.* Benjamin F. Wright, Jr., *American Interpretations of National Law.*

7. *Cf.* Mario Einaudi, *The Physiocratic Doctrine of Judicial Control*, pp. 13-59.

such crises well attests to both its potentiality for engendering conflict and the tremendous influence of the judicial arbiter in shaping social policy in the name of American federalism.

Whether dramatized by the fury aroused by the recent decision in *Pennsylvania* v. *Nelson* or the ancient controversy over *McCulloch* v. *Maryland,* the root cause for such crises lay in the simple fact that because of the nature of the selection, tenure, and removal possibilities for members of the Supreme Court the Court has frequently been out of step with the times. The crisis of 1937 is probably most typical because it provides a good illustration of the Court rendering decisions which were behind the times. However, the recent crisis developing over the civil rights and state sedition cases indicates the frequently overlooked possibility that the Court, as judicial arbiter, may occasionally be in advance of the executive and legislative branches of the nation and the states in meeting problems that actually are fundamental to American society, but merely incidental to American federalism.

Historically, it was, and presently it still is, the propensity of some justices to substitute their own views concerning the wisdom of state and federal enactments for those of the legislators that raised the most serious problems concerning the operation of the Court as federal judicial arbiter. The greatest offenders were the Fuller, White, Taft, and pre-1937 Hughes Courts. As was noted above, the provisions of the Constitution permitted a great deal of discretion in judicial interpretation. But the intervention of the Court rigidly to enforce some particular social or economic philosophy which had been discarded or found unacceptable by a majority of the people of the nation or of a particular state not only has threatened the orderly functioning of the Court as federal umpire by projecting it into partisan controversies, but frequently has endangered the orderly evolution of the American federal system.

It has been persuasively argued that the American Supreme Court has fulfilled its role as federal arbiter best when it has intervened least, permitting both federal and state action to meet new problems, but challenging either the nation or the states if constitutional limitations were clearly violated. Under this view, the Taney, Waite, post-1937 Hughes, and Stone-Vinson-Warren Courts exemplify the judicial arbiter concept functioning at its best. However, the fact that the Court itself must determine the scope of constitutional limitations makes this a formula more easily stated than applied. Actually, the temptation to substitute judicial "statesmanship" for political "compromise" has occasionally overcome the most restrained of justices.

Furthermore, if judicial self-restraint were carried to its logical conclusion, the Supreme Court, in recognition of the ultimate, if not contemporary, wisdom of legislative majorities, would openly abdicate its role as arbiter in federalism. Since such abdication hardly seems likely after over a century and one half of evolutionary growth and acceptance of the judicial power, a realistic appraisal of the Supreme Court as federal umpire must take into account not only such things as its successes in maintaining the constitutional imperative of federal supremacy, but its other characteristics as well.

The Supreme Court in its role as arbiter in American federalism has not only constituted a force for continuity and stability in the political system, but by occasionally defeating the wills of popular legislative majorities in the nation or the states has also precipitated recurring crises which may properly be viewed as necessary consequences of this form of judicial control. A second major consequence of judicial arbitership of American federalism is the probable weakening of democratic participation in meeting major social, economic and political problems. This was especially marked in the discouragement of social experiments by the states during the period from 1890 through 1937. Further, it is especially marked in the contemporary period with respect to the maintenance of fundamental freedoms and civil rights. However desirable in terms of the goals of American liberalism the judicial support of basic freedoms and racial equality has been, the question remains whether these freedoms and elements of equality are firmly established. Particularly pertinent to this portion of the analysis of judicial umpiring of American federalism is James Bradley Thayer's admonition that

> . . . it should be remembered that the exercise of [the power of judicial review], even when unavoidable, is always attended with serious evil, namely, that the correction of legislative mistakes comes from the outside, and the people thus lose the political experience, and the moral education and stimulus that come from fighting the question out in the ordinary way, and correcting their own errors.[8]

It should be pointed out that while judicial self-restraint[9] may provide a realistic and workable solution to the problem of recurring crises, it does not completely meet the dilemma posed by Thayer.

In conclusion, a comment should be made about the viewpoint of

8. As quoted in Justice Frankfurter's dissenting opinion in *West Virginia Board of Education* v. *Barnette,* 319 U.S. 624 (1943).

9. Which is not examined here, but which obviously takes many forms; see John P. Roche, "Judicial Self-Restraint," 49 *American Political Science Review* 762-72.

President Eisenhower's Commission on Intergovernmental Relations regarding the judicial arbiter. It was strongly suggested that in recent years the Supreme Court had abandoned its role as arbiter of the American federal system and that "the policy making authorities of the National Government are for most purposes the arbiters of the federal system."[10] This view mistakenly identifies dormancy with abandonment. It overlooks both the pulsating historical cycles of judicial activism and restraint which have characterized the Court's judicial arbitership and the recent and contemporary evidence of renewed judicial activism. And further, the very period cited by the analysts as indicative of abandonment, was one of *selective* rather than *complete* judicial self-restraint.

The very core to understanding of the recurring and often contrasting patterns of judicial activity and restraint lies in the fact that when the political branches in the national government consistently, through temporizing or compromise, fail to meet issues which are considered by the people to be fundamental, these issues are usually raised in bona fide cases before the courts. The Supreme Court may give subtle encouragement to the raising of these issues judicially in *dicta* or by means of a suggestive series of decisions such as those dealing with segregation in education prior to *Brown* v. *Board of Education*. Despite the limitations inherent in such activity, the Court may often jockey the elected branches into positions where political action is necessary. An additional point overlooked by the Commission Report relates to the very examples given to buttress the abandonment thesis. The tendency of the Court to uphold legislative enactments expansive of national power probably reflected judicial acquiescence in these policies rather than retirement from the umpire's role. In sum, the Supreme Court's policy of selective self-restraint, which has been so much in evidence since 1937, ought not be mistaken for abandonment of its determinative role as federal arbiter. For rather than an indication of abdication, such a policy is a manifestation of the Supreme Court's continued exercise of its power as guardian of American federalism.

10. Meyer Kestnbaum, *Commission on Intergovernmental Relations: A Report to the President for Transmittal to Congress*, pp. 59-60.

# *Table of Cases* *

Ableman v. Booth, 21 Howard 506 (1858).
Adair v. United States, 208 U.S. 161 (1908).
Adams v. Tanner, 244 U.S. 590 (1917).
Adamson v. California, 332 U.S. 46 (1947).
Addyston Pipe and Steel Company v. United States, 175 U.S. 211 (1899).
Adkins v. Children's Hospital, 261 U.S. 525 (1923).
Adler v. New York Board of Education, 342 U.S. 485 (1952).
Aikens v. Wisconsin, 195 U.S. 194 (1904).
Alabama v. Georgia, 23 Howard 505 (1859).
Alabama v. Texas *et al.*, 347 U.S. 272 (1954).
Alexander Theatre Ticket Office v. United States, 279 U.S. 869 (1929).
Allgeyer v. Louisiana, 165 U.S. 578 (1897).
American Federation of Labor v. American Sash Company, 335 U.S. 538 (1949).
American Insurance Company v. Canter, 1 Peters 511 (1828).
Arizona v. California, 283 U.S. 423 (1931).
Armstrong v. Athens County, 16 Peters 281 (1842).
Associated Press v. Labor Board, 301 U.S. 103 (1937).
Athanasaw v. United States, 227 U.S. 326 (1913).
Avery v. Alabama, 308 U.S. 444 (1940).

Bacon v. Walker, 204 U.S. 311 (1907).
Bailey v. Drexel Furniture Company, 259 U.S. 20 (1922).
Ballard v. Hunter, 204 U.S. 241 (1907).
Baltimore and Susquehanna R.R. v. Nesbit, 10 Howard 395 (1850).
Bank of Augusta v. Earle, 13 Peters 519 (1839).
Bank of Commerce v. Commissioners of Taxes and Assessments, 2 Black 620 (1863).
Bank of the United States v. Deveraux, 5 Cranch 61 (1809).
Bank of the United States v. Halstead, 10 Wheaton 51 (1825).
Bank of the United States v. January, 10 Wheaton 66 (1825).

* A number of the cases cited in this table have been reported only in the works of legal historians such as Charles Warren or William Meigs.

Bank of the United States v. Planters' Bank of Georgia, 9 Wheaton 904 (1824).
Banks, The, v. Mayor of New York, 7 Wallace 16 (1868).
Bank Tax Case, The, 2 Wallace 573 (1864).
Barrington v. Missouri, 205 U.S. 483 (1907).
Barron v. Baltimore, 7 Peters 243 (1833).
Bartemeyer v. Iowa, 18 Wallace 129 (1873).
Beaty v. Lessee of Knowles, 4 Peters 152 (1830).
Beauharnais v. Illinois, 343 U.S. 250 (1952).
Beer Company v. Massachusetts, 97 U.S. 25 (1877).
Beers v. Haughton, 9 Peters 329 (1835).
Bennett v. United States, 227 U.S. 333 (1913).
Bethlehem Motors Corporation v. Flynt, 256 U.S. 421 (1921).
Binghamton Bridge, The, 3 Wallace 51 (1865).
Board of Liquidation v. McComb, 92 U.S. 531 (1876).
Board of Trade v. Olsen, 262 U.S. 1 (1923).
Bob-Lo Excursion Company v. Michigan, 333 U.S. 28 (1948).
Bolen v. Nebraska, 176 U.S. 83 (1900).
Booth v. Illinois, 184 U.S. 425 (1902).
Boston Chamber of Commerce v. Boston, 217 U.S. 189 (1910).
Bowles v. Willingham, 321 U.S. 503 (1944).
Bowman v. Chicago and Northwestern Ry., 125 U.S. 465 (1887).
Boyd v. Alabama, 94 U.S. 645 (1877).
Bradley v. The People, 4 Wallace 459 (1866).
Bradwell v. Illinois, 16 Wallace 130 (1872).
Brass v. Stosser, 153 U.S. 391 (1894).
Breard v. Alexandria, 341 U.S. 622 (1951).
Brennan v. Titusville, 153 U.S. 289 (1893).
Bridge Proprietors v. Hoboken Company, 1 Wallace 116 (1864).
Brimmer v. Rebman, 138 U.S. 78 (1890).
Brinegar v. United States, 338 U.S. 160 (1949).
Briscoe v. The Bank of Kentucky, 11 Peters 257 (1837).
Bronson v. Kinzie, 1 Howard 311 (1843).
Brooks v. United States, 267 U.S. 432 (1925).
Brown v. Board of Education, 349 U.S. 294 (1954).
Brown v. Board of Education (2nd), 349 U.S. 294 (1955).
Brown v. Grant, 116 U.S. 207 (1886).
Brown v. Maryland, 12 Wheaton 419 (1827).
Brown v. Mississippi, 297 U.S. 278 (1936).
Brown v. Walker, 161 U.S. 591 (1896).
Brown v. Walling, 204 U.S. 320 (1907).
Budd v. New York, 143 U.S. 517 (1892).
Bunting v. Oregon, 243 U.S. 426 (1917).
Burgess v. Seligman, 107 U.S. 20 (1882).

Burns Baking Company v. Bryan, 264 U.S. 504 (1924).
Burstyn v. Wilson, 343 U.S. 495 (1952).
Burton's Lessee v. Williams, 3 Wheaton 529 (1818).
Bus Employees v. Wisconsin Labor Board, 340 U.S. 383 (1951).
Butchers' Union Company v. Crescent City Company, 111 U.S. 746 (1883).
Butler v. Michigan, 352 U.S. 380 (1957).
Butler v. Pennsylvania, 10 Howard 402 (1850).
Butz v. Muscatine, 8 Wallace 575 (1869).

Calder v. Bull, 3 Dallas 386 (1798).
California v. Thompson, 313 U.S. 109 (1941).
Caminette v. United States, 242 U.S. 470 (1917).
Campion and Dickason v. Casey, Charles Warren, *The Supreme Court in United States History,* I, 66 (1792).
Canfield v. United States, 167 U.S. 518 (1897).
Cantwell v. Connecticut, 310 U.S. 296 (1940).
Canty v. Alabama, 309 U.S. 629 (1940).
Cardwell v. American Bridge Company, 113 U.S. 205 (1884).
Carmichael v. Southern Coal and Coke Company, 301 U.S. 495 (1937).
Carrol v. Greenwich Insurance Company, 199 U.S. 401 (1909).
Carter v. Carter Coal Company, 298 U.S. 238 (1936).
Carver v. Jackson, 4 Peters 1 (1830).
Chadwick v. Kelley, 187 U.S. 540 (1903).
Chambers v. Florida, 309 U.S. 227 (1940).
Champion v. Ames, 188 U.S. 321 (1903).
Charles River Bridge v. Warren Bridge, 11 Peters 420 (1837).
Charlotte, Columbia and Augusta R.R. v. Gibbs, 142 U.S. 386 (1891).
Cherokee Nation v. Georgia, 5 Peters 2 (1831).
C. & O. R.R. v. Miller, 114 U.S. 176 (1884).
Chicago, Burlington and Quincy R.R. v. Chicago, 166 U.S. 226 (1897).
Chicago, Burlington and Quincy R.R. v. Iowa, 94 U.S. 155 (1877).
Chicago, I. & L. R.R. v. United States, 219 U.S. 486 (1911).
Chicago, Milwaukee and St. Paul R.R. v. Ackley, 94 U.S. 179 (1877).
Chicago, Milwaukee and St. Paul R.R. v. Minnesota, 134 U.S. 418 (1890).
Chirac v. Chirac, 2 Wheaton 259 (1817).
Chisholm v. Georgia, 2 Dallas 419 (1793).
Christ Church Hospital v. County of Philadelphia, 24 Howard 300 (1860).
Chy Lung v. Freeman, 92 U.S. 275 (1875).
Cincinnati, New Orleans and Texas Pacific Ry. v. Interstate Commerce Commission, 162 U.S. 184 (1896).
City of New York v. Miln, 11 Peters 102 (1837).
Civil Rights Cases, The, 109 U.S. 3 (1883).
Clark Distilling Company v. Western Maryland R.R., 242 U.S. 311 (1917).
Clerke v. Harwood, 3 Dallas 342 (1797).
Clyatt v. United States, 197 U.S. 207 (1905).

Coe v. Errol, 116 U.S. 517 (1885).
Coffey v. Harlan County, 204 U.S. 659 (1907).
Cohens v. Virginia, 6 Wheaton 264 (1821).
Cole v. Arkansas, 338 U.S. 345 (1949).
Cole v. LaGrange, 113 U.S. 1 (1884).
Colgate v. Harvey, 296 U.S. 404 (1935).
Collector v. Day, 11 Wallace 113 (1870).
Collet v. Collet, 2 Dallas 294 (1793).
Collins v. Yosemite Park and Curry Company, 304 U.S. 518 (1938).
Connecticut General Life Insurance Company v. Johnson, 303 U.S. 77 (1938).
Cooley v. Board of Port Wardens, 12 Howard 299 (1851).
Cooper Manufacturing Company v. Ferguson, 113 U.S. 727 (1884).
Coppage v. Kansas, 236 U.S. 1 (1915).
Cotling v. Kansas City Stockyards Company, 183 U.S. 79 (1901).
Counselman v. Hitchcock, 142 U.S. 547 (1892).
County of Mobile v. Kimball, 102 U.S. 691 (1880).
Covington and Cincinnati Bridge Company v. Kentucky, 154 U.S. 204 (1894).
Coyle v. Smith, 221 U.S. 559 (1911).
Craig v. Missouri, 4 Peters 410 (1830).
Crandall v. Nevada, 6 Wallace 35 (1867).
Crossman v. Turman, 192 U.S. 189 (1904).
Crowell v. McFadden, 8 Cranch 94 (1814).
Cumming v. Richmond Board of Education, 175 U.S. 528 (1899).
Curran v. Arkansas, 15 Howard 304 (1853).
Currin v. Wallace, 306 U.S. 1 (1939).

Daniel Ball, The, 10 Wallace 557 (1870).
Darrington v. Bank of Alabama, 13 Howard 12 (1851).
Dartmouth College v. Woodward, 4 Wheaton 518 (1819).
Davidson v. New Orleans, 96 U.S. 97 (1878).
Davis v. Gray, 16 Wallace 203 (1872).
Dayton-Goose Creek Ry. v. United States, 263 U.S. 456 (1924).
DeJonge v. Oregon, 299 U.S. 353 (1937).
Dennis v. United States, 341 U.S. 494 (1951).
Dewey v. Des Moines, 173 U.S. 193 (1899).
Dillingham v. McLaughlin, 264 U.S. 370 (1924).
Dobbins v. Commissioners of Erie County, 16 Peters 435 (1842).
Dodge v. Woolsey, 18 Howard 331 (1855).
Dorchy v. Kansas, 264 U.S. 286 (1924).
Doremus v. United States, 249 U.S. 86 (1919).
Dow v. Beidelman, 125 U.S. 680 (1888).
Dred Scott v. Sanford, 19 Howard 393 (1856).
Ducat v. Chicago, 10 Wallace 410 (1870).

Eakin v. Raub, 12 Sergeant and Rowle 330 (1825).
East Hartford v. Hartford Bridge Company, 10 Howard 511 (1850).
East New York Savings Bank v. Hahn, 326 U.S. 230 (1945).
Edwards v. California, 314 U.S. 160 (1941).
Edwards v. Kearzery, 96 U.S. 595 (1877).
Elkinson v. Deliesseline, Federal Cases No. 4366 (1823).
Employer's Liability Cases, The, 207 U.S. 463 (1908).
Erie R.R. v. Pennsylvania, 21 Wallace 492 (1874).
Erie R.R. v. Tompkins, 304 U.S. 64 (1938).
Everson v. Board of Education, 330 U.S. 1 (1947).
Ex Parte Ayers, 123 U.S. 443 (1887).
Ex Parte Clarke, 100 U.S. 399 (1879).
Ex Parte Jackson, 96 U.S. 727 (1878).
Ex Parte McCardle, 6 Wallace 318 (1867).
Ex Parte Siebold, 100 U.S. 371 (1879).
Ex Parte Virginia, 100 U.S. 339 (1879).
Ex Parte Webb, 225 U.S. 663 (1912).
Ex Parte Yarbrough, 110 U.S. 651 (1885).
Ex Parte Young, 209 U.S. 123 (1908).

Fairfax's Devisee v. Hunter's Lessee, 7 Cranch 603 (1813).
Fairmont Creamery Company v. Minnesota, 274 U.S. 1 (1927).
Fanning v. Georgoire, 16 Howard 524 (1853).
Farmers' and Mechanics' Bank of Pennsylvania v. Smith, 6 Wheaton 131 (1821).
Farrington v. Tennessee, 95 U.S. 679 (1877).
Feinch and Company v. McKittrick, 305 U.S. 395 (1939).
Felsenheld v. United States, 186 U.S. 126 (1902).
Felts v. Murphy, 201 U.S. 123 (1906).
Fertilizing Company v. Hyde Park, 97 U.S. 659 (1878).
Field v. Barber Asphalt Company, 194 U.S. 618 (1904).
Finlay v. California, 222 U.S. 28 (1911).
Fiske v. Kansas, 278 U.S. 380 (1927).
Fletcher v. Peck, 6 Cranch 87 (1810).
Florida v. Georgia, 17 Howard 478 (1854).
Florida v. Mellon, 273 U.S. 12 (1927).
Florida ex rel Hawkins v. Board of Control, 350 U.S. 413 (1956).
Fox v. Ohio, 5 Howard 410 (1847).
Freeman v. Hewitt, 329 U.S. 249 (1946).
Fretz v. Bull, 12 Howard 466 (1851).
Frothingham v. Mellon, 262 U.S. 447 (1923).

Garner v. Los Angeles Board, 341 U.S. 716 (1951).
Gelpcke v. Dubuque, 1 Wallace 175 (1863).
Gelston v. Hoyt, 3 Wheaton 246 (1818).

Genesee Chief, The, 12 Howard 443 (1851).
Georgia v. Brailsford, 3 Dallas 1 (1794).
Georgia v. Stanton, 6 Wallace 50 (1867).
Georgia Railroad and Banking Company v. Smith, 128 U.S. 174 (1888).
Gibbons v. Ogden, 9 Wheaton 1 (1824).
Gibbs v. Burke, 337 U.S. 773 (1949).
Giboney v. Empire Storage and Ice Company, 336 U.S. 490 (1949).
Gibson v. Chouteau, 13 Wallace 92 (1871).
Gillespie v. Oklahoma, 257 U.S. 501 (1922).
Gilman v. Philadelphia, 3 Wallace 713 (1865).
Gitlow v. New York, 268 U.S. 652 (1925).
Glass v. Sloop Betsy, 3 Dallas 6 (1794).
Gloucester Ferry Company v. Pennsylvania, 114 U.S. 196 (1884).
Gordon v. Appeal Tax Court, 3 Howard 133 (1845).
Gordon v. Caldclouch, 3 Cranch 268 (1807).
Gordon v. Longest, 16 Peters 97 (1842).
Governor of Georgia v. Madrazo, 1 Peters 110 (1828).
Gozler v. Georgetown, 6 Wheaton 593 (1821).
Graves v. New York ex rel O'Keefe, 306 U.S. 466 (1939).
Green v. Biddle, 8 Wheaton 1 (1823).
Grenada Lumber Company v. Mississippi, 217 U.S. 433 (1910).
Grosjean v. American Press Company, 297 U.S. 233 (1936).
Groves v. Slaughter, 15 Peters 449 (1841).
Grovey v. Townsend, 295 U.S. 45 (1935).
Guinn v. United States, 238 U.S. 347 (1915).
Gulf, Colorado and Santa Fe Ry. v. Ellis, 165 U.S. 150 (1897).
Gunn v. Barry, 15 Wallace 610 (1872).
Guy v. Baltimore, 100 U.S. 434 (1879).

Hall v. Decuir, 95 U.S. 485 (1877).
Hall v. Geiger-Jones Company, 242 U.S. 539 (1917).
Hallett v. Jenks, 3 Cranch 210 (1807).
Halter v. Nebraska, 205 U.S. 34 (1907).
Hamilton Company v. Massachusetts, 6 Wallace 632 (1867).
Hammer v. Dagenhart, 247 U.S. 251 (1918).
Hammond Packing Company v. Arkansas, 212 U.S. 322 (1909).
Hampton v. McConnell, 3 Wheaton 234 (1818).
Harman v. Chicago, 147 U.S. 396 (1893).
Harris v. United States, 227 U.S. 340 (1913).
Havenmeyer v. Iowa County, 3 Wallace 294 (1866).
Hawkins v. Barney's Lessee, 5 Peters 457 (1831).
Hawthorne v. Calef, 2 Wallace 10 (1864).
Heath and Milligan Manufacturing Company v. Worst, 207 U.S. 338 (1907).
Helvering v. Davis, 301 U.S. 619 (1937).

Helvering v. Gerhardt, 304 U.S. 405 (1938).
Henderson v. Mayor of New York, 92 U.S. 259 (1875).
Hibbon v. Smith, 191 U.S. 310 (1903).
Higginson v. Greenwood, Charles Warren, ***The Supreme Court in United States History,*** I, 65 (1793).
Hill v. Wallace, 259 U.S. 44 (1922).
Hinson v. Lott, 8 Wallace 148 (1868).
Hipolite Egg Company v. United States, 220 U.S. 45 (1911).
Hoke v. United States, 227 U.S. 308 (1913).
Holden v. Hardy, 169 U.S. 366 (1898).
Holmes v. Jennison, 14 Peters 540 (1840).
Home Building and Loan Association v. Blaisdell, 290 U.S. 398 (1934).
Home Insurance Company v. Augusta, 93 U.S. 116 (1876).
Home of the Friendless v. Rouse, 8 Wallace 430 (1869).
Hopkins v. Bell, 3 Cranch 454 (1807).
Houston, East and West Texas Ry. v. United States, 234 U.S. 342 (1914).
Howard v. Bugbee, 24 Howard 461 (1860).
Howard v. Kentucky, 200 U.S. 164 (1906).
Huidekoper's Lessees v. Douglass, 3 Cranch 1 (1807).
Hunter v. Fairfax's Devisees, 3 Dallas 305 (1796).
Hunter v. Martin, 4 Mumford 8-9 (1814).
Hunter v. Pittsburgh, 207 U.S. 161 (1907).
Hurtado v. California, 110 U.S. 516 (1884).
Huse v. Glover, 119 U.S. 543 (1886).

Illinois Central R.R. v. Illinois, 163 U.S. 142 (1895).
Illinois Central R.R. v. McKendree, 203 U.S. 514 (1906).
Indianapolis Brewing Company v. Liquor Control Commission, 305 U.S. 391 (1939).
In Re Debs, 158 U.S. 564 (1894).
In Re Neagle, 135 U.S. 1 (1889).
In Re Rahrer, 140 U.S. 545 (1891).
In Re Rapier, 143 U.S. 110 (1891).
Interstate Commerce Commission v. Brimson, 154 U.S. 447 (1894).

Jack v. Kansas, 199 U.S. 372 (1905).
Jackson v. Lamphire, 3 Peters 289 (1830).
Jackson v. The Steamboat Magnolia, 20 Howard 296 (1857).
James v. Dravo Contracting Company, 302 U.S. 134 (1937).
Jefferson Branch Bank v. Skelly, 1 Black 436 (1862).

Kansas v. Colorado, 206 U.S. 46 (1907).
Kenosha v. Lamson, 9 Wallace 477 (1870).
Kentucky v. Denison, 24 Howard 66 (1860).
Kirtland v. Hotchkiss, 100 U.S. 491 (1879).
Kovacs v. Cooper, 336 U.S. 77 (1949).

Kunz v. New York, 340 U.S. 290 (1951).

Labor Board v. Fainblatt, 306 U.S. 601 (1939).
Lake Shore and Michigan Southern Ry. v. Smith, 173 U.S. 684 (1899).
Lane v. Vick, 3 Howard 464 (1845).
Larned v. Burlington, 4 Wallace 275 (1867).
Lee County v. Rogers, 7 Wallace 181 (1868).
Leisy v. Hardin, 135 U.S. 100 (1890).
Leloup v. Mobile, 127 U.S. 640 (1888).
Lemieux v. Young, 211 U.S. 489 (1909).
Leser v. Garnett, 258 U.S. 130 (1922).
Lessee of Livingston v. Moore, 7 Peters 469 (1833).
L'Hote v. New Orleans, 177 U.S. 587 (1900).
License Cases, The, 5 Howard 504 (1847).
Lincoln Union v. Northwestern Company, 335 U.S. 525 (1949).
Linder v. United States, 268 U.S. 5 (1925).
Lloyd v. Dollison, 194 U.S. 445 (1904).
Loan Association v. Topeka, 20 Wallace 655 (1874).
Lochner v. New York, 195 U.S. 45 (1905).
Loewe v. Lawlor, 208 U.S. 274 (1908).
Louisiana v. Jumel, 107 U.S. 711 (1882).
Louisville, Cincinnati, and Charleston R.R. v. Letson, 2 Howard 497 (1844).
Louisville Joint Stock Bank v. Radford, 295 U.S. 555 (1935).
Lovell v. Griffin, 303 U.S. 444 (1938).
Luther v. Borden, 7 Howard 1 (1849).
Lying v. Michigan, 135 U.S. 161 (1889).

Madden v. Kentucky, 309 U.S. 83 (1940).
Mahoney v. Triner Company, 304 U.S. 401 (1938).
Marbury v. Madison, 1 Cranch 137 (1803).
Martin v. Hunter's Lessee, 1 Wheaton 304 (1816).
Martin v. Mott, 12 Wheaton 19 (1827).
Martin v. Pittsburgh and Lake Erie R.R., 203 U.S. 284 (1906).
Martin v. Struthers, 319 U.S. 141 (1943).
Martino v. Michigan Window Cleaning Company, 327 U.S. 173 (1946).
Maryland v. Baltimore and Ohio R.R., 3 Howard 534 (1845).
Mason v. Haile, 12 Wheaton 370 (1827).
Mason Company v. Tax Commission, 302 U.S. 186 (1937).
Massachusetts v. Mellon, 262 U.S. 447 (1923).
Massachusetts v. New York, *Journal of the Confederation Congress,* IX, 221 (1787).
Mathews v. Zane, 4 Cranch 382 (1808).
Maurer v. Hamilton, 309 U.S. 598 (1940).
Maxwell v. Dow, 176 U.S. 581 (1900).
McCall v. California, 136 U.S. 104 (1889).

McCarroll v. Dixie Greyhound Lines, 309 U.S. 176 (1940).
McClung v. Silliman, 6 Wheaton 598 (1821).
McCollum v. Champaign Board of Education, 333 U.S. 203 (1948).
McCracken v. Haywood, 2 Howard 608 (1844).
McCray v. United States, 195 U.S. 27 (1903).
McCready v. Virginia, 94 U.S. 319 (1876).
McCulloch v. Maryland, 4 Wheaton 316 (1819).
McDermott v. Wisconsin, 228 U.S. 115 (1913).
McElmoyle v. Cohen, 13 Peters 312 (1839).
McGee v. Mathis, 4 Wallace 143 (1866).
McGoon v. Scales, 9 Wallace 23 (1869).
McKim v. Voorhis, 7 Cranch 279 (1812).
McLaurin v. Oklahoma State Regents, 339 U.S. 637 (1950).
McLean v. Arkansas, 211 U.S. 539 (1909).
McMillan v. McNeil, 4 Wheaton 209 (1819).
McNutt v. Bland, 2 Howard 9 (1844).
McPherson v. Blacker, 146 U.S. 1 (1892).
Mechanics' and Traders' Bank v. Debolt, 18 Howard 380 (1856).
Memphis Gas Company v. Taxing District of Shelby County, 109 U.S. 398 (1883).
Metcalf and Eddy v. Mitchell, 269 U.S. 514 (1926).
Meyer v. Muscatine, 1 Wallace 384 (1863).
Milk Drivers Union v. Meadowmoor Dairies, Inc., 312 U.S. 287 (1941).
Miller v. New York, 15 Wallace 478 (1873).
Miller v. Nicholls, 4 Yeates 251 (1805).
Mills v. St. Clair County, 8 Howard 569 (1850).
Minersville School District v. Gobitis, 310 U.S. 586 (1940).
Minneapolis Eastern R.R. v. Minnesota, 134 U.S. 467 (1890).
Minnesota v. Barber, 136 U.S. 313 (1889).
Minnesota Iron Company v. Kline, 199 U.S. 593 (1905).
Minor v. Happersett, 21 Wallace 162 (1874).
Mississippi v. Johnson, 4 Wallace 475 (1866).
Missouri v. Holland, 252 U.S. 416 (1920).
Missouri v. Iowa, 10 Howard 1 (1850).
Missouri ex rel Gaines v. Canada, 305 U.S. 337 (1938).
Missouri, K. & T. Ry. v. May, 194 U.S. 267 (1904).
Missouri, Pacific R.R. v. Humes, 115 U.S. 512 (1885).
Mitchell v. Burlington, 4 Wallace 270 (1867).
Montello, The, 11 Wallace 411 (1870).
Moore v. Dempsey, 261 U.S. 86 (1923).
Morehead v. New York ex rel Tipaldo, 298 U.S. 587 (1936).
Morgan v. Virginia, 328 U.S. 373 (1946).
Morgan's Steamship Company v. Louisiana Board of Health, 118 U.S. 455 (1885).

Mugler v. Kansas, 123 U.S. 623 (1887).
Muller v. Oregon, 208 U.S. 412 (1908).
Mumma v. Potomac Company, 8 Peters 281 (1834).
Munn v. Illinois, 94 U.S. 113 (1877).
Myers v. Anderson, 238 U.S. 368 (1915).

National Bank v. Kentucky, 9 Wallace 353 (1869).
National Cotton Oil Company v. Texas, 197 U.S. 115 (1905).
National Labor Relations Board v. Friedman-Harry Marks Clothing Company, 301 U.S. 58 (1937).
National Labor Relations Board v. Fruehauf Trailer Company, 301 U.S. 49 (1937).
National Labor Relations Board v. Jones-Laughlin Steel Corporation, 301 U.S. 1 (1937).
Neal v. Delaware, 103 U.S. 370 (1880).
Near v. Minnesota, 283 U.S. 697 (1931).
Nebbia v. New York, 291 U.S. 502 (1934).
Neil, Moore and Company v. Ohio, 3 Howard 720 (1845).
Nelson v. St. Martin's Parish, 111 U.S. 716 (1883).
Newberry v. United States, 256 U.S. 232 (1921).
New Jersey v. New York, 5 Peters 284 (1831).
New Jersey v. Wilson, 7 Cranch 164 (1812).
New Orleans Gas Company v. Louisiana Company, 115 U.S. 650 (1885).
New Orleans Waterworks Company v. Rivers, 115 U.S. 674 (1885).
New State Ice Company v. Liebman, 285 U.S. 262 (1932).
New York v. Connecticut, 4 Dallas 1 (1799).
New York v. Squire, 145 U.S. 175 (1891).
New York v. United States, 326 U.S. 572 (1946).
Nigro v. United States, 276 U.S. 332 (1928).
Nippert v. Richmond, 327 U.S. 416 (1946).
Nixon v. Condon, 286 U.S. 73 (1932).
Nixon v. Herndon, 273 U.S. 536 (1927).
Norfolk and Western R.R. v. Pennsylvania, 136 U.S. 114 (1889).
Northern Securities Company v. United States, 193 U.S. 197 (1904).
Northwest Airlines v. Minnesota, 322 U.S. 292 (1944).
Northwestern Life Insurance Company v. Riggs, 203 U.S. 243 (1906).
Norwood v. Baker, 172 U.S. 267 (1898).

Ogden v. Saunders, 12 Wheaton 213 (1827).
O'Gorman v. Hartford Insurance Company, 282 U.S. 251 (1931).
Ohio Insurance Company v. Debolt, 16 Howard 416 (1853).
Ohio Oil Company v. Indiana (No. 1), 177 U.S. 190 (1900).
Oklahoma v. United States Civil Service Commission, 330 U.S. 127 (1947).
Olcott v. Supervisors of Fond du Lac County, 16 Wallace 678 (1873).
Olney v. Arnold, 3 Dallas 308 (1796).

Olsen v. Nebraska, 313 U.S. 236 (1941).
Opp Cotton Mills v. Administrator, 312 U.S. 126 (1941).
Orient Insurance Company v. Daggs, 172 U.S. 557 (1899).
Osborn v. Bank of the United States, 9 Wheaton 738 (1824).
Osborne v. Mobile, 16 Wallace 479 (1872).
Oswald v. New York, 2 Dallas 401 (1793).
Otis v. Bacon, 7 Cranch 589 (1812).
Otis v. Watkins, 9 Cranch 339 (1815).
Owings v. Norwood, 5 Cranch 344 (1809).

Palko v. Connecticut, 302 U.S. 319 (1937).
Palmer v. Allen, 7 Cranch 550 (1812).
Panama Refining Company v. Ryan, 293 U.S. 388 (1935).
Passenger Cases, The, 7 Howard 283 (1849).
Patterson v. Colorado, 205 U.S. 454 (1907).
Paul v. Virginia, 8 Wallace 168 (1868).
Pease v. Peck, 18 Howard 595 (1855).
Peik v. Chicago and Northwestern R.R., 94 U.S. 164 (1877).
Penhallow v. Doane's Administrators, 3 Dallas 54 (1795).
Pennoyer v. McConnaughy, 140 U.S. 1 (1891).
Pennoyer v. Neff, 95 U.S. 714 (1878).
Pennsylvania College Cases, 13 Wallace 190 (1872).
Pennsylvania v. Connecticut, *Journal of the Confederation Congress,* VIII, 44 (1788).
Pennsylvania v. Nelson, 350 U.S. 497 (1956).
Pensacola Telegraph Company v. Western Union Telegraph Company, 96 U.S. 1 (1877).
People v. Board of Supervisors, 7 Wallace 26 (1868).
People v. Compagnie Generale Transatlantique, 107 U.S. 59 (1882).
Phalen v. Virginia, 8 Howard 163 (1850).
Philadelphia and Reading R.R. v. Pennsylvania, 15 Wallace 284 (1872).
Philadelphia and Wilmington Railroad Company v. Maryland, 10 Howard 376 (1850).
Pine Grove Township v. Talcott, 19 Wallace 666 (1873).
Piqua Branch Bank v. Knoop, 16 Howard 369 (1853).
Planters' Bank of Mississippi v. Sharp, 6 Howard 301 (1848).
Plessy v. Ferguson, 163 U.S. 537 (1895).
Polish Alliance v. Labor Board, 322 U.S. 643 (1944).
Pollard's Lessee v. Hagan, 3 Howard 212 (1845).
Pollock v. Farmers Loan and Trust Company, 157 U.S. 429 (1895).
Poulos v. New Hampshire, 345 U.S. 395 (1953).
Powell v. Alabama, 287 U.S. 45 (1932).
Powell v. Pennsylvania, 127 U.S. 678 (1888).
Presser v. Illinois, 116 U.S. 252 (1886).
Price v. Illinois, 238 U.S. 446 (1915).

Prigg v. Pennsylvania, 16 Peters 539 (1842).
Prince v. Bartlett, 8 Cranch 432 (1814).
Providence Bank v. Billings, 4 Peters 514 (1830).
Provident Institution v. Massachusetts, 6 Wallace 611 (1867).
Prudential Insurance Company v. Benjamin, 328 U.S. 408 (1946).
Prudential Insurance Company v. Cheek, 259 U.S. 530 (1922).
Public Clearing House v. Coyne, 194 U.S. 497 (1904).
Public Service Company v. St. Cloud, 265 U.S. 352 (1924).
Pullman Company v. Kansas, 216 U.S. 59 (1910).

Quachita Packet Company v. Aiken, 121 U.S. 444 (1886).
Quaker City Cab Company v. Pennsylvania, 277 U.S. 389 (1928).

Railroad Commission of Texas v. Rowan and Nichols Oil Company, 311 U.S. 570 (1941).
Railroad Company v. Fuller, 17 Wallace 560 (1872).
Railroad Company v. Hecht, 95 U.S. 168 (1877).
Railroad Company v. Husen, 95 U.S. 465 (1877).
Railroad Company v. Maryland, 21 Wallace 456 (1874).
Ratterman v. Western Union Telegraph Company, 127 U.S. 411 (1887).
Rawlins v. Georgia, 201 U.S. 638 (1906).
Reagan v. Farmer's Loan and Trust Company, 154 U.S. 362 (1893).
Reid v. Colorado, 187 U.S. 137 (1902).
Respublica v. Cobbett, 3 Dallas 473 (1798).
Rhode Island v. Massachusetts, 12 Peters 657 (1838).
Rhode Island v. Massachusetts (2nd), 4 Howard 591 (1846).
Rhodes v. Iowa, 170 U.S. 412 (1898).
Ribnik v. McBride, 277 U.S. 350 (1928).
Rice v. Elmore, 333 U.S. 875 (1948).
Richmond, Fredericksburg and Petersburg R.R. v. Richmond, 96 U.S. 521 (1878).
Richmond, Fredericksburg, and Potomac R.R. v. Louisa R.R., 13 Howard 71 (1851).
Rogers v. Peck, 199 U.S. 425 (1905).
Rosenthal v. New York, 226 U.S. 260 (1912).
Royster Guano Company v. Virginia, 253 U.S. 412 (1920).
Rutgers v. Waddington, William M. Meigs, *The Relation of the Judiciary to the Constitution,* p. 83 (1786).

Saia v. New York, 334 U.S. 558 (1948).
St. Tammany Waterworks v. New Orleans Waterworks, 120 U.S. 64 (1886).
Salt Company v. East Saginaw, 13 Wallace 373 (1872).
Samuel Brailsford v. James Spaulding, Charles Warren, *The Supreme Court in United States History,* I, 65 (1792).
San Bernardino County v. Southern Pacific R.R., 118 U.S. 417 (1885).

San Mateo County v. Southern Pacific R.R., 116 U.S. 138 (1885).
Sands v. Knox, 3 Cranch 499 (1807).
Sands v. Manistee River Improvement Company, 123 U.S. 288 (1887).
Santa Clara County v. Southern Pacific R.R., 118 U.S. 394 (1886).
Santa Cruz Company v. Labor Board, 303 U.S. 453 (1938).
Satterlee v. Matthewson, 2 Peters 380 (1829).
Schaefer v. Werling, 187 U.S. 616 (1908).
Schechter Poultry Corporation v. United States, 295 U.S. 495 (1935).
Schick v. United States, 195 U.S. 65 (1904).
Schneider v. Irvington, 308 U.S. 147 (1939).
Schollenberger v. Pennsylvania, 171 U.S. 1 (1898).
Searight v. Stokes, 3 Howard 151 (1845).
Seattle v. Kelleher, 195 U.S. 351 (1904).
Seré and Laralde v. Pitot, 6 Cranch 332 (1810).
Seven Cases of Eckman's Alternative v. United States, 239 U.S. 510 (1915).
Shelley v. Kraemer, 334 U.S. 1 (1948).
Shepard v. Burrow, 194 U.S. 553 (1904).
Silver v. Silver, 280 U.S. 117 (1929).
Sinnot v. Davenport, 22 Howard 227 (1859).
Slaughterhouse Cases, The, 16 Wallace 36 (1872).
Slochower v. Board of Higher Education of the City of New York, 350 U.S. 551 (1956).
Slocum v. Mayberry, 2 Wheaton 1 (1817).
Sloop Active, The, *Journal of the Confederation Congress,* II, 46 (1786).
Smiley v. Kansas, 196 U.S. 447 (1905).
Smith v. Alabama, 124 U.S. 465 (1887).
Smith v. Allwright, 321 U.S. 649 (1944).
Smith v. Maryland, 6 Cranch 286 (1810).
Smith v. Maryland, 18 Howard 71 (1855).
Smyth v. Ames, 169 U.S. 466 (1898).
Society for Savings v. Coite, 6 Wallace 594 (1867).
Society for the Propagation of the Gospel v. New Haven, 8 Wheaton 464 (1823).
South Carolina v. Georgia, *Journal of the Confederation Congress,* XI, 157 (1786).
South Carolina v. United States, 199 U.S. 437 (1905).
Southern Cotton Oil Company v. Texas, 197 U.S. 134 (1905).
Southern Ry. v. Reid, 222 U.S. 424 (1912).
Southern Ry. v. United States, 222 U.S. 20 (1911).
Spring Valley Waterworks v. Schottler, 110 U.S. 347 (1883).
Stafford v. Wallace, 258 U.S. 495 (1922).
Standard Oil Company v. United States, 221 U.S. 1 (1911).
State Freight Tax Cases, The, 15 Wallace 232 (1872).
Steamboat New World v. King, 16 Howard 469 (1853).

Stearns v. Minnesota, 179 U.S. 223 (1900).
Steward Machine Company v. Davis, 301 U.S. 548 (1937).
Stone v. Farmer's Loan and Trust Company, 116 U.S. 307 (1886).
Stone v. Mississippi, 101 U.S. 814 (1880).
Stone v. Wisconsin, 94 U.S. 181 (1877).
Strader v. Graham, 10 Howard 82 (1850).
Strauder v. West Virginia, 100 U.S. 303 (1879).
Stromberg v. California, 283 U.S. 359 (1931).
Sturges and Burn v. Beauchamp, 231 U.S. 320 (1913).
Sturges v. Crowninshield, 4 Wheaton 122 (1819).
Sweatt v. Painter, 339 U.S. 629 (1950).
Swift and Company v. United States, 196 U.S. 375 (1905).
Swift v. Tyson, 16 Peters 1 (1842).

Talbot v. Jensen, 3 Dallas 133 (1798).
Tarble's Case, 13 Wallace 397 (1871).
Teamsters' Union v. Hanke, 339 U.S. 470 (1950).
Tennessee v. Davis, 100 U.S. 257 (1879).
Terminiello v. Chicago, 337 U.S. 1 (1949).
Terrett v. Taylor, 9 Cranch 43 (1815).
Terry v. Adams, 343 U.S. 461 (1953).
Testa v. Katt, 330 U.S. 386 (1947).
Texas v. White, 7 Wallace 700 (1869).
Thomas v. Collins, 323 U.S. 516 (1945).
Thomas Jefferson, The, 10 Wheaton 428 (1825).
Thompson v. Lee County, 3 Wallace 327 (1866).
Thomson v. Union Pacific R.R., 9 Wallace 579 (1870).
Thornhill v. Alabama, 310 U.S. 88 (1940).
Tierman v. Rinker, 102 U.S. 123 (1880).
Town of Pawlet v. Clark, 9 Cranch 292 (1815).
Trade Mark Cases, The, 100 U.S. 434 (1879).
Transportation Company v. Wheeling, 99 U.S. 273 (1878).
Traux v. Corrigan, 257 U.S. 312 (1921).
Trevett v. Weeden, William M. Meigs, *The Relation of the Judiciary to the Constitution,* p. 70 (1787).
Trusler v. Crooks, 269 U.S. 475 (1926).
Turner v. Maryland, 107 U.S. 38 (1883).
Turnpike Company v. Illinois, 96 U.S. 63 (1877).
Turpin v. Burgess, 117 U.S. 504 (1885).
Twining v. New Jersey, 211 U.S. 78 (1908).
Tyson and Brothers v. Banton, 273 U.S. 418 (1927).

Ullman v. United States, 350 U.S. 422 (1956).
Union Pacific R.R. v. Penison, 18 Wallace 5 (1873).
United States v. American Tobacco Company, 221 U.S. 106 (1911).

United States v. Appalachian Power Company, 311 U.S. 377 (1940).
United States v. Arredondo, 6 Peters 691 (1832).
United States v. Baltimore and Ohio Railroad Company, 17 Wallace 322 (1872).
United States v. Butler, 297 U.S. 1 (1936).
United States v. California, 332 U.S. 19 (1947).
United States v. Carolene Products Company, 304 U.S. 144 (1938).
United States v. Chicago, 7 Howard 185 (1849).
United States v. Classic, 313 U.S. 299 (1941).
United States v. Coolidge, 1 Wheaton 415 (1816).
United States v. Coombs, 12 Peters 72 (1838).
United States v. Cruikshank, 92 U.S. 542 (1875).
United States v. Curtiss-Wright Export Corporation, 299 U.S. 304 (1936).
United States v. Darby, 312 U.S. 100 (1941).
United States v. Deveaux, 5 Cranch 61 (1809).
United States v. Dewitt, 9 Wallace 41 (1869).
United States v. E. C. Knight Company, 156 U.S. 1 (1894).
United States v. Ferger, 250 U.S. 199 (1919).
United States v. Fisher, 2 Cranch 358 (1805).
United States v. Gale, 109 U.S. 65 (1883).
United States v. Gratiot, 14 Peters 526 (1840).
United States v. Hill, 248 U.S. 420 (1919).
United States v. Hudson and Goodwin, 7 Cranch 32 (1812).
United States v. Judge Peters, 5 Cranch 115 (1809).
United States v. Kahriger, 345 U.S. 22 (1953).
United States v. La Vengeance, 3 Dallas 297 (1798).
United States v. Louisiana, 339 U.S. 699 (1950).
United States v. Marigold, 9 Howard 560 (1850).
United States v. McCullough, 221 Fed. Rep. 288 (1915).
United States v. Reese, 92 U.S. 214 (1875).
United States v. Rock Royal Cooperative, 307 U.S. 533 (1939).
United States v. Sandoval, 231 U.S. 28 (1913).
United States v. Shauver, 214 Fed. Rep. 154 (1914).
United States v. Southeastern Underwriters' Association, 322 U.S. 533 (1944).
United States v. Texas, 339 U.S. 707 (1950).
United States v. Worrall, 2 Dallas 384 (1798).
United States v. Wrightwood Dairy Company, 315 U.S. 116 (1942).
University v. People, 99 U.S. 309 (1878).

Van Allen v. The Assessors, 3 Wallace 584 (1865).
Van Horne's Lessee v. Dorrance, 2 Dallas 304 (1795).
Veazie v. Moore, 14 Howard 568 (1852).
Veazie Bank v. Fenno, 8 Wallace 533 (1869).
Village of Euclid v. Ambler Realty Company, 272 U.S. 365 (1926).

# *Bibliography*

## *Books*


Adams, Henry. *History of the United States of America during the First Administration of Thomas Jefferson.* New York: Charles Scribner's Sons, 1889.

——— (ed.). *Documents Relating to New England Federalism, 1800-1815.* Boston: Little, Brown and Company, 1877.

Ames, Herman V. (ed.). *State Documents on Federal Relations.* 3 vols. Philadelphia: University of Pennsylvania, 1900.

Bancroft, George. *History of the Formation of the Constitution of the United States of America.* New York: D. Appleton and Company, 1903.

Beard, Charles A. *Economic Origins of Jeffersonian Democracy.* New York: Macmillian Company, 1912.

Beard, Charles and Mary. *The Rise of American Civilization.* New York: Macmillan Company, 1927.

Benson, George C. S. *The New Centralization.* New York: Farrar and Rinehart, Inc., 1941.

Beveridge, Albert. *The Life of John Marshall.* 4 vols. New York: Houghton Mifflin Company, 1916.

Brant, Irving. *James Madison, Father of the Constitution.* 3 vols. Indianapolis: Bobbs-Merrill Company, Inc., 1950.

Buck, Solon J. *The Agrarian Crusade.* New Haven: Yale University Press, 1920.

Burgess, John William. *Political Science and Constitutional Law.* 2 vols. Boston: Ginn and Company, 1896.

Cahn, Edmond (ed.). *Supreme Court and Supreme Law.* Bloomington: Indiana University Press, 1954.

Cardozo, Benjamin N. *The Nature of the Judicial Process.* New Haven: Yale University Press, 1921.

Carson, Hampton L. *The History of the Supreme Court of the United States.* Philadelphia: P. W. Ziegler Company, 1891.

Clark, Jane Perry. *The Rise of a New Federalism.* New York: Columbia University Press, 1938.

Corwin, Edward Samuel. *The Twilight of the Supreme Court.* New Haven: Yale University Press, 1934.

———. *Court over Constitution.* Princeton: Princeton University Press, 1938.

———. *The President, Office and Powers.* New York: New York University Press, 1940.

——— (ed.). *The Constitution of the United States: Analysis and Interpretation.* Washington: Government Printing Office, 1953.

———, Cushman, Robert E., *et al. Selected Essays on Constitutional Law.* 3 vols. Chicago: Foundation Press, 1938.

Crallé, Richard K. (ed.). *The Works of John C. Calhoun.* 6 vols. Columbia: General Assembly of South Carolina, 1851.

Crosskey, William Winslow. *Politics and the Constitution.* 2 vols. Chicago: University of Chicago Press, 1953.

Dickerson, Oliver M. *American Colonial Government, 1695-1765.* Cleveland: Arthur M. Clark Company, 1912.

Dunning, William Archibald. *Essays on the Civil War and Reconstruction.* New York: Macmillan Company, 1898.

Einaudi, Mario. *The Physiocratic Doctrine of Judicial Control.* Cambridge: Harvard University Press, 1938.

Elliot, Jonathan. *Debates on the Adoption of the Federal Constitution.* 5 vols. Philadelphia: J. B. Lippincott, 1901.

Fairman, Charles. *Mr. Justice Miller and the Supreme Court, 1862-1890.* Cambridge: Harvard University Press, 1939.

Farrand, Max (ed.). *The Records of the Federal Convention.* 3 vols. New Haven: Yale University Press, 1911.

Ford, Paul Leicester. *The Writings of Thomas Jefferson.* New York: G. P. Putnam's Sons, 1898.

Frankfurter, Felix. *The Public and Its Government.* New Haven: Yale University Press, 1930.

———. *The Commerce Clause under Marshall, Taney, and Waite.* Chapel Hill: University of North Carolina Press, 1937.

Freund, Ernst. *The Police Power, Public Policy, and Constitutional Rights.* Chicago: Callaghan and Company, 1904.

Goodnow, Frank Johnson. *Social Reform and the Constitution.* New York: Macmillan Company, 1911.

Haines, Charles Grove. *The Role of the Supreme Court in American Government and Politics, 1789-1835.* Los Angeles: University of California Press, 1944.

Henderson, Gerard Carl. *The Position of Foreign Corporations in American Constitutional Law.* Cambridge: Harvard University Press, 1918.

Hockett, Homer. *The Constitutional History of the United States.* 2 vols. New York: Macmillan Company, 1939.

Holmes, Oliver Wendell. *Collected Legal Papers.* New York: Harcourt, Brace, and Horne, 1920.

Jameson, John Franklin. *Essays in the Constitutional History of the United States in the Formative Period, 1775-1789.* New York: Houghton, Mifflin Company, 1889.

Jensen, Merrill. *The New Nation: A History of the United States During the Confederation, 1781-1789.* New York: Alfred A. Knopf, Inc., 1951.

Johnson, Allen (ed.). *Readings in American Constitutional History, 1776-1876.* Boston: Houghton, Mifflin Company, 1912.

Kestnbaum, Meyer. *Commission on Intergovernmental Relations: A Report to the President for Transmittal to Congress.* Washington: Governmental Affairs Institute, 1955.

Lodge, Henry Cabot (ed.). *The Federalist.* New York: S. P. Putnam's Sons, 1904.

McFarland, Carl. *Judicial Control of the Federal Trade Commission and the Interstate Commerce Commission.* Cambridge: Harvard University Press, 1933.

McRee, Griffith J. (ed.). *Life and Correspondence of James Iredell.* New York: Peter Smith, 1949.

Meigs, William Montgomery. *The Relation of the Judiciary to the Constitution.* New York: Neale Publishing Company, 1919.

Pinto, Roger. *La Crise de L'Etat aux Etats-Unis.* Paris: Librairie Generale de Droit et de Jurisprudence, 1951.

Pritchett, C. Herman. *The Roosevelt Court, 1937-1947.* New York: Macmillan Company, 1948.

Randall, J. G. *The Civil War and Reconstruction.* New York: D. C. Heath and Company, 1937.

Roberts, Owen J. *The Court and the Constitution.* Cambridge: Harvard University Press, 1951.

Rogers, Henry Wade (ed.). *Constitutional History of the United States as Seen in the Development of American Law.* New York: G. P. Putnam's Sons, 1890.

Schlesinger, Arthur Meier. *Political and Social Growth of the American People, 1865-1940.* New York: Macmillan Company, 1941.

Swisher, Carl Brent. *American Constitutional Development.* New York: Houghton, Mifflin Company, 1943.

———. *The Growth of Constitutional Power.* Chicago: University of Chicago Press, 1946.

———. *Roger B. Taney.* New York: Macmillan Company, 1935.

Tocqueville, Alexis de. *Democracy in America.* London: Longman, Green, Longman, and Roberts, 1862.

Warren, Charles. *The Making of the Constitution.* Boston: Little, Brown and Company, 1929.

———. *The Supreme Court in United States History.* 2 vols. Boston: Little, Brown and Company, 1937.

Wharton, Francis. *State Trials.* Philadelphia: Carey and Company, 1849.

Willoughby, Westel Woodbury. *The Constitutional Law of the United States* (2nd ed.). 2 vols. New York: Baker, Voorhis and Company, 1929.

Wilson, Woodrow. *Constitutional Government in the United States.* New York: Columbia University Press, 1908.

Wright, Benjamin F., Jr. *American Interpretations of Natural Law.* Cambridge: Harvard University Press, 1931.

———. *The Contract Clause of the Constitution.* Cambridge: Harvard University Press, 1938.

———. *The Growth of American Constitutional Law.* New York: Reynal and Hitchcock, 1942.

*Articles*

Anderson, Frank Malory. "The Enforcement of the Alien and Sedition Laws," *Annual Report of the American Historical Association, 1912.* Washington: American Historical Association, 1914, pp. 113-126.

*Annals,* 9th Congress, 2nd Session, December, 1806, pp. 131-138.

Carpenter, William S. "Repeal of the Judiciary Act of 1801," *9 American Political Science Review,* August, 1915, pp. 519-528.

Chamberlain, Daniel H. "Osborn v. the Bank of the United States," *1 Harvard Law Review,* December, 1887, pp. 223-225.

*Congressional Record,* 84th Congress, 2nd Session, Vol. 102, Number 43, p. 3948.

Corwin, Edward S. "Due Process Before the Civil War," *24 Harvard Law Review,* 1911, pp. 366-385, 460-479.

Davis, Horace A. "Annulment of Legislation by the Supreme Court," 7 *American Political Science Review,* November, 1913, pp. 541-587.

Dodd, William E. "Chief Justice Marshall and Virginia, 1813-1821," *12 American Historical Review,* July, 1907, pp. 776-787.

*The Economist,* June 30, 1956, pp. 1281-1282.

Farrand, Max. "The Judiciary Act of 1801," *5 American Historical Review,* July, 1900, pp. 682-686.

Field, Oliver P. "States versus Nation and the Supreme Court," *28 American Political Science Review,* April, 1934, pp. 233-245.

McLaughlin, Andrew. "The Background of American Federalism," *12 American Political Science Review,* May, 1918, pp. 215-240.

Phillips, Ulrich Bonnell. "Georgia and States Rights," *Annual Report of the American Historical Association,* vol. II, 1901, pp. 15-224.

Reuschlein and Spector. "Taxing and Spending; the Loaded Dice of a Federal Economy," *23 Cornell Law Quarterly,* December, 1937, pp. 1-38.

Rezneck, Samuel. "The Depression of 1819-1822, a Social History," *39 American Historical Review,* October, 1933, pp. 28-47.

Roche, John P. "Judicial Self-Restraint," 49 *American Political Science Review,* September, 1955, pp. 762-772.

Thompson, L. L. "State Sovereignty and the Treaty-Making Power," 2 *California Law Review,* 1922-1923, pp. 242-258.

Warren, Charles. "Legislative and Judicial Attacks on the Supreme Court of the United States—a History of the Twenty-fifth Section of the Judiciary Act," 47 *American Law Review,* January-February, 1913, pp. 1-34.

———. "New Light on the History of the Federal Judiciary Act of 1789," 37 *Harvard Law Review,* 1923-1924, pp. 49-132.

———. "The First Decade of the Supreme Court," 7 *University of Chicago Law Review,* June, 1940, pp. 631-654.

Wickersham, George W. "Federal Control of Interstate Commerce," 23 *Harvard Law Review,* February, 1910, pp. 241-259.

# *Index*